BANISHED

BANISHED

Surviving My Years in the
Westboro Baptist Church

Lauren Drain
with Lisa Pulitzer

GRAND CENTRAL
PUBLISHING

NEW YORK   BOSTON

Scripture quotations are taken from the King James Version of the Bible.

In the text that follows, the names of individuals identified as Will, Brian, and Scott have been changed.

Copyright © 2013 by Lauren Drain

Grand Central Publishing
Hachette Book Group
237 Park Avenue
New York, NY 10017

www.HachetteBookGroup.com

Printed in the United States of America

RRD-C

First Edition: March 2013
10 9 8 7 6 5 4 3 2

Grand Central Publishing is a division of Hachette Book Group, Inc.
The Grand Central Publishing name and logo is a trademark of Hachette Book Group, Inc.

The Hachette Speakers Bureau provides a wide range of authors for speaking events. To find out more, go to www.hachettespeakersbureau.com or call (866) 376-6591.

The publisher is not responsible for websites (or their content) that are not owned by the publisher.

LCCN: 2012041784
ISBN 978-1-4555-1242-3

This book is dedicated to:

Taylor Simone Drain
Boaz Abel Drain
Faith Marie Drain

BANISHED

PROLOGUE

January 20, 2005

A particularly large crowd was packing the National Mall in Washington, D.C., on the third Thursday in January for the second inauguration of President George W. Bush. This big day for our country was a perfect opportunity for us to spread the Word of God, and I was proud to be a part of it. At only nineteen years old, I was going to be sharing my beliefs with the world, showing the sin-loving masses a better, righteous way. Anticipating huge crowds, my fellow church members and I had gotten there especially early that winter morning.

The energy around the capital was unlike anything I had ever experienced, and my adrenaline was pumping. The intermittent freezing rain had not deterred hundreds of thousands of people from swarming into the city. Even though the inauguration didn't begin until noon, the streets around the Mall were already jammed five hours before. There were twenty of us in our group, which made it one of our larger assemblies of picketers. Shirley Phelps-Roper, the daughter of our pastor, Fred Phelps, was in charge of the protest. She had set the minimum age at sixteen, so my best friends and I were eligible. She

1

had contacted the National Park Service, the authority for the event, months earlier, enough in advance to secure the church a high-visibility position right by one of the Mall entrances. With the pastor getting older, Shirley and her sister Margie had become two of the church's bigwigs, and they were both along for this picket.

I was happy to be with my three closest friends, Megan, Rebekah, and Jael, who were a few of the pastor's many grandchildren and the only girls around my age in our community. We had all packed what we called our "picketing clothes"—apparel that was practical and warm. Since we were accustomed to hours in the freezing cold, these outfits included many layers to protect us from the elements, like Columbia ski jackets, plenty of gloves, glove liners, hats, scarves, and thin thermal underwear.

We had flown into Washington from Topeka the night before, concealing our signs in our carry-on bags. We were scattered throughout the plane, and our fellow passengers had no idea we were associated with the group many of them had seen on TV. I had been saving up for the $400 airplane ticket for a few weeks, working part-time as a front-desk receptionist at St. Francis Hospital in Topeka and as an assistant in the church office. It was an expensive ticket for a twenty-four-hour trip, but the opportunity to represent my family and my church on the national stage made it worth the cost. All of us who had been selected were thrilled.

We had spent the night at a local Super 8, our hotel chain of choice. They were reliable, clean, and inexpensive. Shirley had booked the rooms early enough to guarantee all of us a bed. We still didn't get much sleep, because we were up before dawn to get dressed and organized. By 7 a.m., five hours before the event was scheduled to start, we were at the Mall.

We made our way to the protester registration area, where huge numbers of people had gathered to voice their objections to any number of issues. We knew from watching the news that the event was going to be drawing plenty of Bush detractors, and sure enough, the counterinaugural groups were there in force. Most of the opposition was angry over the Iraq War—one such group carried one thousand coffins representing dead soldiers. Turn Your Back on Bush was a group encouraging everybody to turn his back when the president's motorcade came down the street, and Not One Damn Dime Day protesters urged people not to spend any money on Inauguration Day. Others were the mouthpieces for civil rights, abortion rights, environmental issues, health care, voting rights, and the evils of corporate influence.

Because this was the first inauguration since the terrorist events of September 11, 2001, the level of security was unprecedented. None of the registered groups was threatening violence, only civil disobedience, but the event organizers weren't taking any chances. Every protester from every group had to go through airport-type scanners before they could enter the protest area. Despite our early arrival, we still had to wait more than two hours to get through the checkpoint. We had no intention of trying to get anywhere near Bush. We only wanted our message to be seen by the thousands of people walking by and by the media, who with any luck might put us on national television.

We kept our signs, shirts, and caps hidden from view so that we wouldn't be harassed as we made our way through thousands of heavily armed security and military agents to our assigned protest site. Finally, almost in position, some of us started announcing our message. "God Hates You!" I declared, as we pushed forward. The high we got from picketing took over.

"You are going to hell! You are all fag enablers!" we hollered over one another. "We are the only true patriots," I added. "If you people were really patriotic and religious, you would be standing with us holding signs." I told them that God mocked their calamities, and good Christians were supposed to warn nations against sin. "Thank God for September 11!" I yelled, the strongest insult to the sinners and the one most certain to get a rise out of the people within earshot.

I looked at Megan, Shirley's oldest daughter. She had the same fiendishly excited look on her face that I did. All of us were brimming with passion. We quickly became the center of attention, and we reveled in it. Our objective was to stir up as much controversy and animosity as we could in the four hours our permit allowed us. We were succeeding before we even reached our positions. Finally, when we were at our site, we pulled off our sweatshirts and jackets to expose our godhatesfags.com T-shirts. We held our picket signs high in the cold air; mine was a big poster with the words GOD HATES FAG ENABLERS printed in bold, straight lettering.

Our picket spot was only a hundred yards from the entrance to the arena in which the inauguration would be held. We wanted to get people riled up and angry as they came in, all the while remaining calm and controlled ourselves. That way the people scoffing and cursing at us would come off as the hostile ones. I tried to think of powerful and jarring things to yell, hoping to connect with someone in the crowd and engage him in a match he couldn't win. I desperately wanted to share my beliefs and insights from my four years with the Westboro Baptist Church with a hell-bound, ignorant sinner. Finding the right words to express our dogma to an outsider was one of the most fulfilling parts of being so faithful and obedient. Of course, my insecurity was also at work. I was equally eager to assert myself

4

at pickets for the praise, and maybe even a little respect, from church leaders. My family was one of the only ones not related to the Phelpses by blood or marriage, so it was important for me to show that I was worthy.

Since my family's move to Topeka, the Westboro Baptist Church's hometown, I had worked hard to learn the Bible stories and the church's interpretations of them. Now I was trying to reinforce that I was a faithful follower. The pastor judged us by our fervency and knowledge of the scripture, and a weak or unenthusiastic performance would be reported back to him. On our return to Kansas, we'd be admonished in church to the point of embarrassment. I knew it was my duty and obligation to let the sinners at the inauguration know what God thought of them, and I was more than up to the task.

The Washington crowd that day reacted strongly to us, which reinforced our sense of success. The more enraged they became, the more we felt we were making our message known. If they had thought we were just a bunch of crazies, they would have simply ignored us, but their heated interest in us obviously meant that our words were making an impact. We were delivering the message of the Holy Ghost, making us superior and perhaps even omniscient. In a sea of heathens, we were the messengers.

I was in a very supernatural and spiritual community, guided by the Holy Spirit. A member would feel the Holy Ghost upon him, and then we would know how to act. The Holy Ghost would come over us to picket one place rather than another, or send us to be a guest on a program such as *The Tyra Banks Show*. The Holy Ghost would come over us to bring someone into the church. That was how my family got in. God put it into the Phelpses' hearts to invite us in. The Holy Ghost was the real source of the power.

At first, people walked past without stopping, but as the morning wore on, a group began to form in front of our picket. People were hovering and trying to intimidate us by yelling angry taunts. It began to get heated and dangerous when about a hundred inauguration-goers started to close in on us. One man was screaming at each of us individually, challenging our picket signs. Usually, we would answer back, but with a crowd this big Shirley and Margie decided to silence him by leading us in song. "O Wicked Land of Sodomites," they cued us, before we all enthusiastically joined in the parody of "America the Beautiful." We relied on a repertoire of mockeries of patriotic songs and popular music, many of them written by my father. Twenty of us singing in unison was loud enough to drown out the angry mob yelling at us. The wall of sound it created was our favorite tactic when we needed to counterintimidate our detractors.

Despite our audience's sense that we were nothing but hate-mongers, our real objective was to enlighten sinners before Judgment Day. We were telling them that they needed to obey God if they wanted to save their souls, even though we didn't really believe their souls were salvageable. We were the chosen ones, and we were going to heaven to live in the presence of God. From our heavenly perch, we'd be able to mock the sinners burning in the Lake of Fire below us in their place of eternal punishment and torture.

I had never seen so many people get as violent toward us as they did that day. Our signs were sturdily constructed and designed to endure weather and abuse at our hundreds of annual pickets, but as people in the crowd started grabbing them, stomping on them, and ripping them, they couldn't hold up. Others were yelling and cursing at us. The Christian types were telling us God loved everybody—a retort we'd heard plenty of times before. The more politically minded people were telling us God was reasonable. The others, who seemed especially offended by our September 11 comments, told us we shouldn't be in this country and should all be locked up.

The physical attacks caught me by surprise. Some of the people were so worked up that they tried to push and punch us. Others got up into our faces to yell, and some even spat at us. There was a small crowd pushing toward our police barricade, so we moved back a couple of feet to keep people from stampeding and crushing us.

Police nearby tried to defuse the venom being aimed at us. "They're not worth it. Move along," they'd say over and over to the protesters around us. The cops knew we had a constitutional right to be there, so even though they most likely didn't agree with us, they were obligated to protect us. However, hearing ourselves called "not worth it" made me feel disrespected.

As much as we loved the anger, in this case we were worried about the mob mentality. People were becoming so aggressive that we had to stand on overturned trash cans behind the barricades to protect ourselves. These perches also gave us more visibility, and kept our remaining signs from being seized. Still, the crowd kept pushing forward. It was always such a strange experience to see grown men and women, seemingly intelligent and well-mannered, shouting, cursing, spitting, giving us the finger, and throwing drinks at us as they walked by. As seasoned a picketer as I was, I still felt overwhelming fear and intimidation. For the most part, I didn't even wait for the end of an insult before I reacted with a response I knew by heart.

The threats rattled me, but I believed that God would protect us in all circumstances, as long as we obeyed His Word and held up our signs. I was taught that it was a good test to endure affliction for His sake and rise above it; it was my demonstration of God's love. This deep belief kept me extremely calm despite

7

the danger of the situation, and I could even invite threats and assaults with a Christian heart.

My friend Rebekah once told me, her eyes welling up with tears as she spoke, that she hoped she would be able to die for God one day. I considered myself to be a martyr as I shouted and taunted my audience with the true message from God. The bravery of staring down evil in the name of God was inspirational, fanaticism was just, martyrdom was worthy, and God was on our side. The passion was truly empowering.

Our allotted picket time ended before the actual start time of the inauguration. With such a hostile crowd around us, Shirley advised us to pack up our signs and cover up our T-shirts. She wanted us to be stealthy and quick, so that as soon as we started to move, no one would recognize us in the crowd. One or two people cheered our exit, yelling at us, "Yeah, go home!"

The rental minivan was parked a good ten blocks away, but with most of the people already at the Mall, the crowd around it was thinning. We had never intended to stay for the swearing-in. Our mission had been to incite the guests in attendance, and everyone agreed we had been highly successful. When we reached the van, I climbed in next to Rebekah and Megan. We all pulled out our cell phones and started calling home to Kansas to report back on the protest. Dad answered the phone at my house. He was always so proud of me for representing the Drains at an important event, and no event had been more important than this one. I told him I had never been in the middle of so many angry people, but I had delivered God's Word and been a respectable Christian martyr.

"I love you," he told me. "You are my little prophetess."

CHAPTER ONE

Lo, children are a heritage of the Lord: and the
fruit of the womb is his reward.

—Psalm 127:3

I was five years old when I was uprooted for the first time. I was just beginning school, but having skipped kindergarten, I was already in first grade. My parents had taught me how to read and write at home, and they knew I was capable, even though I was one of the youngest in the class. My mother had recently given birth to my baby sister, Taylor, so I was also getting used to sharing my parents with her when my father suddenly announced that we were moving from our home near Tampa, Florida, to Kansas. He had been accepted into the master's program in philosophy at the University of Kansas in Lawrence. Not only that, he was going to be paid to teach a course in Western Civilization while he pursued his degree.

I could tell Mom didn't want to go to Kansas at all, but Dad was insistent that this was best for us. She told me she hated the idea of leaving her family, who lived near us, but she tended to be more passive and was willing to do things just to please my father. Dad was very dominant, and he didn't like her family very much, which may have played a role in his decision to move us out of state and out from under their influence. Even at the time, I had the vague impression that my father wanted to control my mother by isolating her from the people who supported her.

I was in the middle of the school year when we packed up and moved to Olathe, a small city about thirty miles east of Lawrence, where Mom found a dental hygienist job, and Dad went to class, studied at home, and worked as a teaching assistant at the university. Taylor went to a university-sponsored day care, where I joined her when I was done with my school day. Sometimes one of Dad's students would pitch in and babysit. Our first week there, Dad took me on a bike ride around the campus and showed me the different buildings that meant something to him—the humanities building where he taught, the film school, the law school, and the building that housed his office. I thought it was so cool, seeing all the students walking and biking around the campus. I quickly became an avid KU fan, and Dad encouraged my interest by taking me to all of the home basketball games. When we were at the sports hall, we'd see the players, who were like celebrities to me, working out or doing physical therapy. Even Dad got kind of giddy when we saw them. He embraced our new life, and I think he wanted me to be as excited about Kansas as he was. He loved it when we expanded our horizons and our minds, especially on his terms.

From my earliest memories, everything I did, from dance recitals to fishing trips, was with my parents. The two, Steve and Luci Drain, had been together for what seemed like forever. They met in junior high school in Florida when they were both thirteen, and dated through all of high school. My mother, a beautiful and slender blue-eyed blonde, loved my father, and as a good Catholic she married him so she wouldn't have to feel guilty about having sex out of wedlock. They tied the knot on May 5, 1983, as soon as they both turned eighteen.

My father rarely spoke about his early childhood with me, and when he did, he sounded quite bitter about his parents. Based on this and his strained relationships with his family, I guessed that it must have been a very unhappy childhood. He had been born in Tampa, Florida, in 1965, and named after his father, Steven Sr. His mother, Joy, was an aspiring actress who had appeared in several small roles in feature films and television commercials. She was dramatic, flamboyant, and a bit of a narcissist. From what I understood, she paid very little attention to my dad because she was obsessively focused on her acting career. She had already been married several times and had given birth to two daughters before she married my grandfather, and she remained married to him for only a short time. I had no idea how old my father was when his parents divorced or what their reasons were, but he told me he had been very angry when his parents split, and he blamed it on his mother. He said he would never forgive her. Whether or not this was true, it was clear to me that he deeply resented her.

Both of Dad's parents eventually remarried. My father lived with his mother, his two half sisters, and his stepfather, whom he called Popper. His two half sisters had different fathers, so nobody in his household had the same set of parents. It seemed like my father had had a love/hate relationship with his sisters. He was the youngest and the only boy, which made him a natural target for their sisterly teasing. The two girls played mean-spirited pranks on him all the time, which of course made him angry. He told me he was also bullied at school. He had been considered a runt until he was in sixth grade, when he shot up to six foot two. After his growth spurt, the bullying stopped.

Dad's biological father remarried a woman my father didn't particularly like. She also brought children into the marriage, so he had stepbrothers and stepsisters on that side as well. He really distanced himself from all of them and everybody else from his childhood. We didn't have any photos of his family around the house. I got the sense that being around them made him sad, but he never talked about it, and I never asked. I had two sets of grandparents on my father's side alone, and there were so many half- and stepsiblings that when I'd see them at a rare Drain family event, I didn't even know how anyone was related to whom, if they were steps, or halves, or in-laws.

My father didn't make much of an effort to stay in touch with any of them. Because he didn't care for his stepmother, he took me to visit his real dad, whom I called Pop, only on occasion. Pop died of a stroke when I was nine or ten and we were living in Kansas. Dad had to fly back to Florida for the funeral. When he returned, he was very upset. I was surprised by this, because they had never seemed close. Typical of my father, he didn't describe any of his feelings of sadness. But he had a way of acting arrogantly and as though things were okay to mask his vulnerabilities.

All of his family relationships seemed really dysfunctional. Dad himself told me his mother hadn't cared when he dropped out of high school at his first opportunity, which he had done not because he wasn't smart but because he had a problem with rules and authority figures. She also paid little attention to his bad behavior, marijuana smoking, or drinking. Most teens would have been delighted to do as they pleased, but my dad was really hurt that his mother didn't even seem to notice. She told him to pursue whatever he wanted; it was fine with her. I think what he really would have liked was for her to take an interest in him and offer him guidance, but that never happened.

To me, Grandma Joy didn't seem self-absorbed. She was really fun and a big personality. She and Popper lived in West

Palm Beach, and Dad and I would drive the four hours from the Gulf Coast to visit them. Their house was warm and welcoming with a big, flowery jungle of a backyard, a kids' swing set, a hot tub, and a basketball court. We didn't visit that often, and when we did, it wasn't for a religious holiday. Grandma Joy was not a religious person. She was Presbyterian in name only, because she never went to church. She was the kind of person who celebrated Christmas not for Jesus, just for Santa.

In contrast to my father's family, my mother's parents, Frank and Madelyn Stout, were Catholic and quite devout. Their home was ornamented with crucifixes, pictures of Jesus, and statues of the Virgin Mary. At Christmastime, they built a nativity scene on their front lawn. They also hosted all the holidays at their house, which were great fun.

Mom had been born in October 1965, and she grew up in Tampa as the youngest of Frank and Madelyn's five children. The oldest was Lisa, followed by Sam, Amy, Stacy, and Mom. My aunt Lisa had a very sad story. She had gotten involved in drugs at a very young age and led a very promiscuous lifestyle. By the time she was halfway through her twenties, she already had two children with different men. She was a total hippie, always on the road. We never knew if she was in Florida, Texas, Arizona, or New Mexico. Being the youngest, and with my grandmother always preoccupied with Lisa and all her problems, my mother didn't get much of her parents' time or attention. I think my mother thought of herself as the lost child, although she was close to her sister Stacy, who was four years her senior.

I loved being with my grandparents, but there was a heavy, unspoken undertone of friction between my father and them. I assumed it was because they had wanted Mom to marry a Catholic, and Dad didn't believe in God. In my earliest memories, Dad always described himself as an atheist, before I even knew what the word meant. He loudly made fun of organized religion, God, and the fact that my mother's family attended church, not keeping his disdain to himself. Mom's parents didn't like him any more than he liked them. They thought he was pushy and controlling, and that he'd lead her away from her faith. They also felt he had nothing going for him. According to my mother's family, my father was a bit of a wild child in those days and very defiant. He smoked cigarettes and supposedly smoked marijuana. He did have a few redeeming qualities. He always had some kind of part-time work, and he loved tinkering with cars and motorcycles, even rebuilding an old Camaro, but he was still a high school dropout, an on-again, off-again drug user, a bigmouth, and a control freak.

Despite his shortcomings, my mother was swept up by him, seeing him as a smart, charismatic, motorcycle-riding rebel. He was tall and handsome, with red hair, blue eyes, and a baby face. She liked that he had opinions he was willing to go out on a limb for—and she was a meek follower type, so they balanced each other out. And she did almost everything he told her, except with regard to church. Despite his antireligious stance, Mom continued to go to Catholic Mass on holidays and on an occasional Sunday, far less often than the mandatory weekly Mass of her youth, but still enough to demonstrate her faith.

My parents had been married for a little more than two years when I was born on New Year's Eve, December 31, 1985. They were both only twenty years old at the time. My father still wanted to do cool, young things, which he could do in the daytime because he was a night shift manager for a trucking company. My mother was going to school to be a dental hygienist when I was born. My father had wanted to let her go to vocational school first, so when she finished she could get a job and he could go back to school. While she worked in a dental office and supported our family, he earned his GED and then went for an undergraduate degree at the University of South Florida in Tampa.

My mother's parents still lived in the same house where she had been raised, and while we lived in Florida our house was in the same neighborhood, so I would see them all the time. Since my mother had so many siblings, there were always plenty of cousins around in my early life, and I always had someone to play with. I didn't let the simmering feelings between my dad and my grandparents affect my relationship with them.

Once we were in Kansas, my life was very lonely without my grandparents and cousins around the corner. I loved the activities I did with Dad, but I still missed my relatives. Less than a year after we'd been there, we got the devastating news that Taylor had been diagnosed with a rare form of kidney cancer called Wilms' tumor. She had to have one of her kidneys removed, and then spent a whole year living in the hospital. For my sake, my parents made sure to stay optimistic and tried to make visiting her in the hospital fun for me. I don't remember being sad that often, almost certainly because of the way Mom and Dad handled it.

When Taylor was well enough, doctors put a catheter in her belly so that my parents could administer her chemotherapy treatments at home—a task they sometimes let me help with. She had to have three years of chemo, as well as weekly CAT scans to see if the tumor was shrinking. She was always very tired. She didn't have any hair until she was three or four years old. Finally, when her treatments stopped, she grew her first mop of dirty blonde hair.

I was really happy that Taylor was finally home from the hospital, and that I could see her every day. She had gotten a whole bunch of toys for her first birthday that she had never been able to play with. I had given her a corn-popper push toy that she could play with outside, and I was delighted when she took such a liking to it that she ran to it first thing every morning. And for our first snow (a big novelty for us, being from southern Florida), we stayed outside for hours building snowmen and making snow angels until Mom called us in. On warmer days, she loved having me push her on the swing in our backyard.

Slowly, Taylor got stronger and stronger. My parents bought a trampoline for the backyard, and I taught my sister how to jump on it, although we had to be mindful not to dislodge the catheter, which was taped safely to her stomach. I admired Taylor's bravery. Even though she was often worn out and weak, she had such a happy disposition and was always smiling. Mom, Dad, and I had all banded together to help her get better, and we all rejoiced together when the doctors let us know her prognosis was excellent for a full remission and a long life.

Throughout Taylor's illness, Dad had been working on his master's. Shuttling back and forth between Olathe and Lawrence was hard, so as soon as Taylor was better, we moved to a house closer to campus. We hadn't lived there long when a missionary-type preacher came to the door proselytizing. Dad invited him in, wanting to challenge him to an intellectual debate he felt sure he would win.

My father loved arguing with people. He was pompous and wanted to discredit the visitor with reason and logic. The preacher gave him answers that he hadn't expected, though, ones that were intriguing and intelligent. It wasn't long before he and Dad began meeting once or twice a week in our dining room to study the Bible together. My mother was wary of the relationship at first, but she trusted my father to know what he was getting into. I thought it was weird, because my father

16

didn't really like zealots, but I guessed that maybe it had to do with Taylor's brush with death, and that Dad was searching for the meaning of life or the promise of ultimate salvation.

Throughout all this, though, Dad remained adamant that his interest was intellectual, not theological or spiritual. My father still had an extreme opposition to going to any church, saying nobody learned anything there, but he was interested in studying privately, one-on-one, so he could ask questions and get answers.

I noticed we made a lot of changes that year. Mom started studying the Bible again, too. She really loved that Dad was including religion in his life in a serious way for the first time. Of course, everything Dad did was always obsessive and compulsive—he put 100 percent into anything he took on. In no time, he had us dressing according to what he had learned in his readings. He got rid of all his hats at a garage sale; according to Corinthians, every man who prays or prophesies with his head covered dishonors his head, so hats and caps had to go. Mom sewed a bunch of long skirts for herself, because modesty was part of being submissive to God and your husband. She didn't force Taylor and me to change our style of dress, but I wanted to, because Mom was doing it and I liked to be just like her. I swapped my short skirts for new ones Mom sewed for me that fell below the knee.

Dad started inviting all kinds of weird people to have meals with us. He explained that they were less fortunate than us, and that charity was our obligation as Christians. We even opened our home to university-affiliated people who couldn't afford to live on campus. Taylor moved into my room so there would be a vacant room for the boarders who usually stayed with us for a month or two at a stretch. I was happy to have her as a roommate. After the year she had spent in the hospital, I loved having her close to me. She slept on a little toddler bed right next to mine. We'd stay up talking until one of us fell asleep. On some nights, I'd even get out of my bed and slide in next to her.

That fall, one woman who looked Middle Eastern and her three-month-old baby moved into Taylor's room. She was one of Dad's students and had been living in an apartment on campus until she couldn't afford it anymore. From the state of her clothes, she seemed to be very poor. She always wore long dresses and kept her head covered with a scarf. The baby's father didn't appear to be in her life. She was soft-spoken, humble, and thankful to be living with us. She was very nice and babysat for Taylor and me a couple of times.

We skipped Halloween that year—it was a pagan celebration, and my father said it honored the Devil. We didn't plan to celebrate Christmas, either, much to my unspoken disappointment. My father told us that December 25 was not the true date when Christ was born, and even if it had been, the Bible did not say it was a cause for celebration. My father also thought that Christmas was too commercialized, and he didn't want to celebrate it in that fashion.

By mid-December, though, almost a year into their relationship, Dad and his mentor had a falling-out. Dad later related the conversation to me. It had something to do with the six millennia following God's creation of Adam and Eve. He told me that the preacher said that if you studied the Bible correctly, believed in God, and did the right things, you would live on earth forever. The preacher said that God's chosen people never die a physical death. Moses and Elijah were still on earth and had been for almost six thousand years. I didn't know what that meant. What would you look like if you were six thousand years old? I agreed with Dad that it was absurd.

We never saw the missionary preacher again, and we stopped taking in free boarders. We celebrated Christmas after all, which made me very happy. After that, Mom and Dad tried studying the Bible on their own, but Mom also went back to wearing less conservative clothes and attending a Catholic Mass from time to time. She'd look in the newspaper to see where a service was and then go to listen, sometimes bringing me. All I knew about church was that it was early in the morning on Sunday, you wore a dress, and you listened to someone talk on and on. I liked the pageantry, but even more I loved having my mother all to myself.

The next year, my father moved away from religion, saying that it tended to go to extremes. He said the preacher's theory that some people lived on the earth forever was a perfect example. Instead of the faithful Bible student he'd been, he embraced his hippie rocker side and became the coolest dad in the world. He never missed a single one of my peewee softball games, and he was always on the sidelines cheering me on. Everybody liked him. He was so sociable and still in his twenties then; he was like a big kid. All of my friends adored him, too.

Dad filled the void left by the preacher's departure with a lot of wilder friends. He even started his own band called Boneyard. There always seemed to be a ton of people in the house drinking, smoking, and playing instruments in the basement. My mother had a few acquaintances from work, but they weren't really the kind of friends that came into their social life; those came from Dad. Mom would chat with them, but she really wasn't into the same kind of scene that Dad was. For one, she didn't like drinking. She might have a wine cooler here and there, but that was it. While Dad was playing rock and roll in the basement, Mom preferred being with Taylor and me in the backyard, watching us play on the trampoline, or making us treats in the kitchen. The one thing my parents liked to do together was play softball. They were on a coed University of Kansas club team, the Yahoos. Mom played catcher, second base, or shortstop, and Dad was either a pitcher or a catcher. Taylor and I would wear the green team colors and cheer them on from the bleachers.

Just as in our first weeks in Kansas, whenever I showed an interest in any of Dad's passions, he would be right there to help me foster it. When he saw that I liked softball, he started taking me to the batting cages at the university's sports complex to practice our swings. When I was eleven and took up guitar, he helped me start my first-ever all-girl band. The band was in the elementary school talent show, and I was the guitarist and lead singer. The performance was the great highlight of my seventh grade—in fact, of that whole stint in Kansas.

By the time Taylor was healthy, Mom liked living in Kansas, but I could tell she still missed her family. We were only in Lawrence a short time when we learned that her sister Lisa's lifeless body had been found on a beach in Myrtle Beach, South Carolina. Police believed she had been stabbed during some kind of drug deal gone wrong. Mom flew home to Tampa for the funeral. She was still upset when she came back a few days later, but with Lisa living a dangerous lifestyle there wasn't much shock and surprise that she had died young.

Dad took to life in Kansas a lot easier than Mom had. He was a perpetual student. I don't know if he had a clue what he wanted to do, but he told me he was seeking some type of truth. He took some philosophy, some civilization, and some religion courses—all of the subjects he chose had a spiritual or metaphysical bent. He changed his major so many times it took him seven years to graduate. KU paid for only two years of graduate school, so his ongoing searching for a major was a real financial burden on our family. Mom was still working hard, but what was supposed to be two years and a free ride had turned into seven years with huge student loans.

The debt caused a lot of arguments about money. Not only were the student loans growing, but Mom felt that Dad wasn't being fiscally responsible in everyday life, either. Whenever they had money, he'd want to upgrade his camera equipment rather than pay down the debt. My mother, meanwhile, wanted to make sure we weren't getting in over our heads. She was a very easygoing person and eager to please, but sometimes at night, I'd hear her fighting with my father, complaining about his frivolous money habits and his long hours away from the house, specifically the amount of time he was spending with some of his female students. "You're away too much," she would protest. "What is going on with these girls?" He would insist they were all just "friends."

One of Dad's undergraduate students particularly bothered my mother. She was supposedly in business with him, buying fixer-uppers and paying Dad to help with the renovations. My mother was uncomfortable with that arrangement, insisting it was inappropriate for a student to hire her professor. But it went further than that. My mother sensed that there was more to the relationship, but he denied it. Still, Mom wasn't convinced.

I could feel the tension around the house when my mother was in a confrontational mood. Short of leaving Dad, however, which he knew she would never do, my mother didn't have a lot of options. So she never took the arguments beyond the point of her suspicions, and Dad had no reason to take her seriously and change. Even in Florida, there had been hints that he had been unfaithful, but he knew she would never want to break up the family.

At long last, Dad graduated with a Master of Fine Arts in

film in 1997. Mom had no objection when he announced that summer that he wanted to go back to Tampa to start a film production company. I was twelve and Taylor was seven when we started packing up everything we were taking for the move. My best friend, a Pakistani girl named Anna, accepted the invitation to fly with us and to stay in Tampa for a week, which meant any sadness I had about leaving Kansas was delayed. Taylor, as usual, went with the flow. She was upset when she said good-bye to her best friend, Anna's little sister Parendi, but she was too young to understand we weren't coming back. Trying to emulate Taylor's optimistic disposition, I suppressed my deep anxiety about starting over and having to enter middle school with no friends.

CHAPTER TWO

Among whom also we all had our conversation
in times past in the lusts of our flesh, fulfilling the
desires of the flesh and of the mind; and were by
nature the children of wrath, even as others.

—Ephesians 2:3

Mom and Dad found us a house to rent in Bradenton, about twenty miles south of Tampa. It was a three-bedroom ranch in a gated community filled with families. Mom was in great spirits, thrilled to be back near her own family. She was back in a routine with her sister Stacy in no time, and it didn't take her long to find another job as a dental hygienist at an office not far from our house. Taylor and I spent the two weeks before school started riding our bikes around the neighborhood in search of new friends.

My father used his master's degree to get a job at the Home Shopping Network (HSN). He was really excited about his position as a creative director with a small staff under him. Even though he wouldn't be behind the camera, he was in the production department and learning a lot. When he'd take me to the office, I noticed everybody around him wanted to hear his ideas. If he had a concept for a song or a commercial, his coworkers always listened enthusiastically. He had a way about him that was so charismatic and magnetic that people were immediately drawn to him.

I loved being with my father. Now that we were back in Florida and he was happily employed in a career he loved, our time together was more fun than ever. He liked to take me to the HSN studio and impress me with all the production equipment. But I didn't care where we were or what we were doing—I was just content to be in his company.

His creative talents, combined with his business savvy, resulted in hugely successful projects for HSN. Taylor and I were even cast in a commercial he was producing for Ty, the maker of Beanie Babies. We were supposed to play with the stuffed animals and recite a line or two. I had never acted before, but thought I would be really good at it. I also wanted to make my father proud of me, but I kept screwing up my lines, and Dad grew increasingly annoyed. In front of everybody, he pointed out that I was the oldest kid in the commercial. He said that the younger kids, even Taylor, were getting their parts right, so why couldn't I? He didn't seem to realize how embarrassed I was to be singled out. Despite my struggle with the lines, the commercial was a big success, which brought him recognition and assignments to produce other important segments for jewelry and cooking shows.

My own transition back to Florida was not quite so easy. I entered the eighth grade without any friends. I tried to settle into a new version of my old life in Bradenton, but the friends I had known in my childhood weren't that interested in reconnecting with me. I stayed in touch with my friend Anna via e-mail, and over the next couple of years, she flew from Kansas to stay with me during winter vacations. One December break, she effectively ended our friendship when she developed a crush on my cousin and wanted to spend more time with him than me.

I still played the guitar, and Dad was keeping my interest alive by taking me with him to see two of his favorite artists, the

Red Hot Chili Peppers and Lenny Kravitz, when they played in the Tampa area. I wanted to perform in the school talent show, but I wasn't in a band, and I didn't have the confidence to do a solo act. My father came up with a solution—he volunteered to play bass, and my cousin Brennen offered to be the drummer. We performed Lenny Kravitz's "American Woman." I played lead guitar and sang. We were the very last act of the evening, and everyone was clapping and dancing. It was the coolest thing.

I could always count on my father to be cheering me on. Just like in Kansas, he was my greatest supporter in my extracurriculars. He coached my weekend softball team and was front row and center at all my school games. He had star status with my new girlfriends, a group of eight or ten really nice girls who'd accepted me by late fall. We all lived in the same neighborhood. We played on the same teams, had sleepovers, and, on weekends when the weather was nice, went to the beach. Their fathers were all older than Dad. They would tell me how cool my dad was and how they wished theirs were more like mine. I felt really lucky to have him.

I started the ninth grade at Lakewood Ranch High School. It was a brand-new campus located a couple of miles from my house. The school had amazing specialty clubs and teams, from horseback riding to scuba diving. I tried out for the dance team, a very elite group. Almost every girl at the school wanted to be a member, but it was highly selective. I spent hours after school practicing and memorizing the routines. When the JV tryout finally came, I nailed it. I was so proud when I learned I had made the team I couldn't wait for my parents to get home to tell them. The minute Dad walked in the door, I blurted it out.

"That's nice," he said flatly, "but you're not doing it."

I was speechless. "What are you talking about?" I finally asked.

He said being on the dance team was "too slutty." I was shocked. Mom had been on her high school dance team for four years, and the whole time they were dating, I reminded him.

Dad argued that they were dancers, not sex objects, back then. Mom was impressed and proud that I had made the team, so I held out hope that she would convince Dad it was innocent. But much to my disappointment, he wouldn't budge, and I had to give my spot to somebody else.

My father wasn't a hard driver when it came to grades, but I set a very high standard for myself and took my schoolwork seriously. My grades from junior high were good enough to meet the requirements for the honors classes in high school, and I filled my schedule with as many as I thought I could handle. At Lakewood, being an honor student was considered cool, and I wanted to be popular. Another route to popularity was playing a team sport, so since the dance team hadn't worked out, I tried out for the JV softball team and made the cut. Because I felt like a runt, this was a particular triumph for me. I started high school at only four foot eleven, and I was a year younger than my classmates, having skipped kindergarten. Under the best of circumstances, making the team was really hard, so when I saw my name on the list of players posted outside the gym door, I jumped for joy.

I played shortstop and second base, but being on a team was more than an athletic achievement. It also had social benefits. The football team would watch our team and vice versa, so we got to hang out with the guys during sanctioned activities. I was becoming self-conscious, so I did everything I could to make myself look more attractive. When I was thirteen, I started dyeing my mousy brown hair a golden blonde to fit in with my Florida girlfriends. I had a crazy overbite and had to wear braces. But I was okay with them, because all the cool kids had them.

During my freshman year, my father started talking more seriously about making a documentary. He liked working at the Home Shopping Network and was clearly doing well there, but wanted to do something more creative and on his own terms. He'd been thinking about a subject for the two years we'd been in Florida, and was looking for a controversial topic that hadn't yet received much exposure. The Westboro Baptist Church in Topeka, Kansas, came to his mind. He already knew a fair amount about the church from our seven years in Kansas, and he'd seen some of its outrageous protest activities right on campus and at the Lawrence City Hall. The group was known nationally as well as locally, often getting press for picketing large-scale gay pride events. Dad had been superoffended by the group's stance against homosexuals, objecting not only in principle but also because he had friends in his film classes who were gay. My father thought the church's leader and pastor, Fred Phelps, and his followers were full of crap. He hoped an exposé of their bizarre subculture and extremist beliefs and tactics would get people talking and get his own name out there as a provocative filmmaker. Dad even had a title for his documentary: *Hatemongers*. Once it was completed, he planned to enter it into the major film festivals, like the prestigious Telluride Film Festival in Colorado. He had volunteered there in the summers when he was a film major at KU, helping to set up booths and pitching in wherever anyone needed him. He had made lots of great contacts with independent filmmakers, so he was sure *Hatemongers* would get a serious consideration and probably a screening.

On April 29, 2000, Dad traveled to Washington, D.C., where

a number of gay pride organizations were holding the Millennium March in the nation's capital. My father knew the church would be there to protest the event, and he wanted to capture it on film. The largest gathering would be for the Equality Rocks concert at RFK Stadium, featuring Garth Brooks, George Michael, Melissa Etheridge, k.d. lang, and the Pet Shop Boys.

When Dad returned from D.C., he was really charged up about what he had learned. He was really mesmerized with the church, and no longer angry or highly critical when describing them. Instead, he was highly critical of the homosexuals who had been in the gay parade. Dad was certainly excited, but I didn't think much about it because he was always extremely animated whenever he had a new interest. He began explaining everything he had learned about the church to us, and telling us about its mission. He described the group as small, and comprised almost exclusively of members of the family of the pastor, Fred Phelps. Nine of his thirteen children and their children made up the majority of the congregation, which was about sixty or seventy people altogether. Above all else, the group wanted to warn sinners of God's anger, Dad said almost empathetically.

My father showed us the video he had taken of the protesters standing near the entrance to the stadium waving signs that said GOD HATES FAGS and MATT IN HELL. The "Matt" they were referring to was Matthew Shepard, who Dad said was an openly gay man who had been brutally tortured and murdered in 1998 by two men he had met in a bar in Laramie, Wyoming. They had promised him a ride home, but instead took him to a remote area near Laramie, pistol-whipped him, and tied him to a fence, where they left him to die. I learned that Matt's death had inspired hate crime legislation across the nation. But the church thought he had deserved to die.

My father was thrilled by his footage. I really liked when he was happy like this, because he tended to be moody when he wasn't fully immersed in something new. He wanted to take the project to the next level by speaking directly with church members, so he contacted their office in Kansas, where he reached the pastor's daughter Shirley Phelps-Roper. My father was pleasantly surprised when she invited him to come up to Topeka to interview its members, including Fred. "We're always willing to talk to anyone," she told him warmly. She assumed my father was another nosy documentarian whose work would be shown in some college classroom, which was fine with her. If my father's project went into a wider release, that would be even better. Exposure was the objective. The WBC wasn't like the Fundamentalist Church of Jesus Christ of Latter-day Saints or the Jehovah's Witnesses, who denied outsiders access to their inner circle and excommunicated anyone who exposed their secrets. In fact, the WBC thought that being open to media exposure would help them spread their message even further.

That June, Dad packed up his camera and equipment and headed to Kansas to conduct interviews for his documentary, still tentatively titled *Hatemongers*. When he invited my fifteen-year-old cousin, Brennen, to assist him on his film instead of me, I was disappointed. School was out for the summer, so I was free and eager to travel with him. It's possible that my father wanted to protect me from the group's hard-line ideology, but whatever the reason, I felt rejected and overlooked. My dad and Brennen were in Topeka for exactly one month, although to me it felt a lot longer. He called home a few times a week, always sounding pleased with his progress.

When he returned home a couple of weeks before school started, his attitude was completely different. He seemed really sad and cried about the littlest things. Though he'd had his ups and downs, I'd never seen him this moody and depressed before. He would spend hours looking at the footage and listening to the interviews from Kansas, then he would start criticizing himself for what seemed to be moral reasons. One afternoon, I watched the movie *Requiem for a Dream* with him. The movie was about four addicts whose lives were spiraling out of control, and at the time I had no idea how inappropriate it was for someone my age. I wasn't seriously watching it, though. I tended to be really hyper and easily distracted, so I was going in and out of the room to make myself snacks and only paying partial attention. As it was ending, I saw my father on the couch crying, so I started focusing on the movie, trying to figure out what had triggered such extreme sadness in him. I knew the film had a lot of depressing and even scary scenes, but I hadn't noticed which one had set Dad off. We'd watched plenty of sad movies together in the past, but I had never seen him cry.

"What's wrong, Dad?" I asked gently.

"I've done a lot of bad things in my life. I have got to fix my life," he sobbed.

I wished I knew what in the film had cut him so hard.

I knew my father had a reputation. I had heard some things from my mother's family over the years. I'd seen the scar on his nose from a barroom brawl that happened before I was born. More than once, he had told me the story of how he had gotten it. He said he had been in a fight when he was a teenager and had been pistol-whipped. Some members of my mother's family feared that my father may have been involved in more than marijuana in his past. But I never saw him use any drugs. Even though I knew that Dad was more than willing to get into people's faces and take a righteous stand, he was always tender and affectionate and never neglected his family. Still, seeing him bawling about the movie was really weird. Perhaps most oddly, he had never acted repentant before.

In the following weeks, Dad set to work editing his film. He showed Mom, Taylor, and me some footage of the group's protests, and I noticed that for the first time he didn't use his typical mocking tone when talking about them. The church members in the video each were carrying huge, poster-size signs with messages I found hateful. Mom was freaked out, too. "I don't understand this sign," she challenged him, pointing to one that read MATT IS IN HELL AND YOU'RE GOING TO HELL.

My mother's faith had taught her to believe that Judgment Day was when God decided who gained entry into His kingdom, and that no mortal would have knowledge of who was in hell or who was going there. According to Luke, there had been a thief on a cross next to Jesus being put to death at the same time. The thief had spent his lifetime stealing, and he knew he was going to hell. Jesus told him that forgiveness was available to everyone, no matter how a person had lived on Earth, and he would join him in Paradise.

Dad tried to explain to Mom the Westboro Baptist Church's position on the afterlife, which was based on unconditional election. God had selected who was going to be saved, and because his decision was foreordained, no amount of repentance would change His mind. I found it really odd that my father was serious, and actually sounding a little preachy himself, but Mom let him speak without interruption. She watched the videos and let him elaborate on the group's beliefs to us. My father was definitely acting like he was buying into their ideology, and I overheard my mother telling him that she didn't want him becoming caught up in another weird religion, like the one the missionary in Kansas had spouted. Dad explained how the church related current events to prophecies in the Bible, and he showed her examples and passages he was reading. This was the first thing that interested me about his newfound passion. For the first time, I saw the Bible in a contemporary context. Dad didn't seem to be overbearing or extreme in his commitment, which was a relief to Mom and me. We didn't talk about it, but I could tell that my mother was hesitant to get involved in this marginal religion.

Dad bought each of us a King James Bible—the translation used by the WBC—and we began reading the Bible as a family around the dining room table every Sunday. Mom, Taylor, and I were expected to have our heads covered during the sessions, a gesture of the female gender's subservience to God. In the WBC, women, girls, and even female infants had their heads covered during any church sermon. We would go around the table, and each of us would read a chapter from whatever book Dad had selected. I enjoyed learning the scripture stories—now that I was older, they intrigued me. They seemed profound and meaningful, nothing like the boring textbooks I was reading at school. My favorite stories came from Paul and Exodus. They read like mysteries or thrillers, and I eagerly awaited the next installment.

Mom tolerated religion returning to our home for the sake of Dad's spiritual life, but she wasn't nearly ready to embrace the WBC. She remained skeptical for quite a while, very worried about how her family would react to the church's well-known vitriolic fanaticism. Dad wasn't passive with her relatives about his religious positions, either. Mom's sister Stacy and her husband, Mark, who lived just four miles from us, weren't particularly devout, which was perhaps why my father would feel the need to go over to their house and talk religion. During one of our weekly visits to their house, Dad once again turned the conversation into a religious discussion. When nobody seemed to care what he thought, he just flipped out. He was a loud person, in general, and seemed to think that the more he screamed, the more likely he was to be heard. "I can't talk to you. You are not even on my level!" he shouted at Mark and Stacy. Taylor and I stopped what we were doing and stared at him in horror. He was enraged beyond control in front of my cousins, Dena, Amber, and Brennen. Luckily, everyone in the family had seen tamer versions of these kinds of outbursts before, so they weren't particularly agitated. This only made my father angrier. He demanded that Taylor, my mother, and I gather anything we had brought with us, and he stormed out ahead of us, too frustrated at the ignorance in the room to stay another minute. We drove the twenty minutes home, listening to him rip apart Mark and Stacy to my mother until he finally calmed down about a block from our house.

My father spent a full year immersed in the postproduction of his documentary. He needed my room to serve as his editing suite, so I shared a bunk bed with Taylor in her room. We were very close and I didn't mind sacrificing my privacy to bunk with her. Besides, I was rarely home, spending most of my days out with my friends at the pool, the beach, or the mall, or playing softball. Dad filled the suite with all sorts of fancy equipment—two screens, two computers, and a synthesizer for making music since he was doing the whole sound track himself. I was intrigued by his project—the church's pure fanaticism was pretty interesting, and I trusted my father's judgment that he knew what he was getting himself into.

Dad's assistant in the postproduction phase was a female friend of his from the University of South Florida. Again, the fact he was working with a college-aged female bugged my mother. This one was also funding his venture. The story he told us was that her father had died and left her a ton of money that she wanted to invest in something. She and my father had originally planned to do a film about a local artist, but my father convinced her that Westboro would be a better subject for a documentary. The woman seemed to flirt with my father, but he said he was only her mentor. She was going through a hard time and Dad was warm and supportive, so the relationship seemed to be mutually beneficial. Mom still didn't like it.

While Dad was immersing himself in the film, I was beginning to really like boys. Like those of most fourteen-year-olds, my hormones were raging. I started experimenting with makeup, wearing modest amounts of eyeliner and mascara, and I wanted to dress crazy and go to parties and school dances. A year earlier, before my first-ever school dance, Dad sat me down for "the talk." He told me the responsibilities that went along with being social at my age, and said that if I was thinking about sex, he wanted me to come to him and my mother so that they could get me on birth control. Dad also said I should go to them if I was thinking about experimenting with drugs, because buying them from a stranger was extremely risky, and he didn't want me to end up dead. He had been appropriately protective, but not overly so, and above all he'd been very open and honest.

But now, when I went to talk to my father about a particular boy at school named Will, I was shocked at his reaction. He said he had changed his mind about a lot of things and he didn't want me to date at all. Ever since Dad had come back from Topeka, he had become superstrict. There was no dating in the WBC, and he said I, too, needed to stay away from bad influences. My father thought Will was bad news, even though he was in my grade and from the neighborhood. I considered him to be cool because he had piercings and rode motocross bikes, but Dad said those things reminded him of himself as a teenager, and that he would never let someone with such a wild side date his daughter.

I had never heard these things from him before, even when he'd first embraced religion back in Kansas. He seemed to have gotten ultraconservative in his views. All of a sudden, when he thought I was being disobedient, he became very angry and aggressive. He wanted me to get rid of my friends and come home immediately after school every afternoon. I thought he was being way too overprotective, but I didn't dare let him know how I felt. Even though I wanted to keep our relationship open, he was becoming such a control freak that I found it was easier to lie if I wanted to do things that he wouldn't let me do, so I resorted to sneaking around in order to still be able to socialize with my friends. Never mind that I was a great student in all the honors classes, I played JV softball, and I never got in trouble—he was getting more and more overbearing. I knew it had to do with his growing connection to the WBC.

Dad started calling Shirley Phelps-Roper nonstop on the phone, but from what I could overhear from my room, the calls were now mostly about me, not the documentary. Upset that I was talking to boys, he sought Shirley's advice on the matter. She directed him in ways to correct me, telling him that as head of the household he had no choice. My father now wanted to control every aspect of my life, including my crushes. He knew high school was dangerous territory, at a time when so many kids took the wrong path. Shirley, his new confidante, warned him, "Do whatever you can to stop her. This is a war between the flesh and the spirit, and if you don't win, you are not the proper head of the household." Shirley told Dad there was hope for me, but he had to be forceful. If he waited too long, I would be too far gone. He was fighting for my salvation, and it was his fault that he had brought me to the age of fourteen without being a good Christian girl.

As he was getting harder on me, I noticed by the edits he was making that his film was going in a different direction. His original slant, that the group was a bunch of insane zealots, was entirely gone from the film. The new edit portrayed the Westboro Baptist Church as an organization with a sincere message and a maligned, misunderstood pastor. The signs at protests were hateful and provocative because that was the only way to get noticed, Dad explained to me. The picketers only had so much time to catch the attention of people in passing cars.

Dad told us that the church members wanted people to change for the good. They didn't want to see people sinning. They shouldn't be blamed for being the messengers; they were only trying to make an impression. He even compared them to figures from the Bible like Ezekiel, Jeremiah, and Luke, who had been compelled to resort to violence, like setting trees or idols on fire, to get people's attention.

I knew that my father's criticism of me didn't mean he hated me—we had always had a great relationship. I felt if he was going to act this irrationally, he must have a reason. I just needed to figure out what was going on with him and get our relationship back on track. And I couldn't afford to have him angry with me, because when he was, the whole house was filled with discord. He'd yell at me in front of Mom and Taylor, who would both just stare at us without saying anything. Taylor didn't understand it, and she didn't like it at all. She didn't pick sides, but as soon as the argument would cool, she'd try to change the subject or distract us. "Let's play a card game or watch a movie," she'd say, trying to make sure that everything seemed normal. On rare occasions, Mom would get involved. "Steve, stop! You're getting too loud. Be gentle on her," she'd say, defending me in a lukewarm tone. But my being a teenager seemed to scare her, too, so she would follow Dad's lead.

I knew that Will had a serious crush on me, and I liked him back, so despite the objections I knew my father would have, I started sneaking over to his house to hang out. The first time I visited, I was there for only about half an hour before my father showed up. He didn't say anything to Will's mother when she answered the door, just brushed past her rudely, grabbed me, and pulled me out of the house. Once we were home, he forbade me from ever going there again. The following week, I went again, but this time my dad didn't catch me. I knew I was defying him, but the forbidden nature of the rendezvous made it that much more exciting.

For my part, the real problem was that despite my parents' disapproval, I wanted to see Will. I even thought I was in love with him. Besides, it was impossible to avoid him. He lived on our street, rode the same school bus I did, and was in two of my classes. I flirted with him when I saw him in the hallway, and he would sometimes stay after school to watch me play softball. He clearly wanted me to be his girlfriend. He'd hand me notes before class, with cute messages like "I came in third place at my motocross tournament" or "I wish you could come to some of my events and meet my parents."

One day, I came home from softball practice to find Dad waiting for me at the front door. "You little whore," he raged, waving a stack of papers in his hand. "How dare you defy the Lord!"

I had no idea what was making him so angry, and when he said he had intercepted some notes from Will, I was even more confused. Apparently, Will had been writing me love notes and sneaking them into an outside pocket of my softball bag while I was on the field practicing. My father had found about twenty of them and started reading them to me one by one. I had never seen them before, and unlike the ones he'd slipped me in class, in a lot of them Will was describing his sexual fantasies. I thought they were slightly funny, embarrassing, and flattering, but my father disagreed.

"You whore! You whore!" he said over and over. He went on in a rage, calling me a long list of other names, scaring me with how out of control he was. "You cannot be anywhere near this guy anymore," he warned me.

I should have been the one angry with my father for violating my privacy, but here he was, calling me a chain of degrading slurs without even stopping for breath. I tried to fight back. "I didn't even do anything," I screamed, trying to get a word in. "I am not a whore!" It made no difference what I said. My father thought that I had been engaged in a physical relationship with Will, which wasn't true. I hadn't even known about the notes until that day.

To my horror, Dad told me he had already been over to Will's house with the letters and that when Will had answered the door, he told him he had better stay away from me. According to Dad, Will had been very snide, so my father had head-butted him and broken his nose. I couldn't believe that he had taken it this far and actually attacked him. "You ruined everything," I blurted out, which enraged him even more. Now, he began kicking and slapping at me, backing me into a corner. I was absolutely terrified. Mom and Taylor were home, but neither of them was coming to my rescue.

"You think you can disobey me, you little bitch?"

"Daddy, please stop," I begged. "We weren't doing anything."

I ran down the hall to my room and climbed up into my top bunk, with Dad following on my heels. Seemingly possessed by his rage, he pulled me to the edge of the bed and let me fall to the ground. His face was red and his temples were bulging as he hulked over me, practically spitting in my face. My father was a big, tall guy, and I was fourteen and weighed less than a hundred pounds. He unleashed a verbal attack on me for what felt like hours while I cowered on the floor, trying to protect my face from the spit spewing from his mouth. When his tirade was over, he stormed down the hall and out of the house, slamming the door behind him.

When I went to school the next day, I saw Will in the hallway. Several kids were crowded around him, asking him what had happened to his nose. I was mortified, and after making eye contact with him, I continued walking to my next class. A couple of days later, I saw him again at the community pool. He was way across on the far side, but when he saw me, he packed up his stuff and left.

Will's parents filed an assault charge against my father the day after the attack, and when my father got the notice, he filed a counterclaim against Will. I didn't attend the hearing, but apparently the judge took into consideration the lewd love notes Dad presented in court and ultimately dismissed the charges. My father even managed to get a restraining order against Will, preventing him from coming within twenty feet of me when we were in school and one hundred yards of me outside the school setting until I turned eighteen.

From that point on, Dad seemed to be mad at me for everything I did or didn't do. I couldn't figure out what to do that was right, but everything I did was wrong. Despite, or perhaps because of, my father's objections, I still had a crush on Will, and he still liked me, too. My dad knew I wasn't going to stop trying to see Will, so he watched me more closely than ever. He wouldn't let me take the bus to or from school anymore, insisting on driving me both ways. One afternoon, he arrived a little early to pick me up from softball practice and saw Will in the vicinity of the field. I had no idea he was even there—plenty of kids stayed after school, watching whatever practice was going on. When I got to the car, Dad said, "That's it, I am pulling you out of school!" He pointed at Will in the bleachers and said, "That son of a bitch is still hanging around you. You will never see that boy again!"

True to his word, my father withdrew me from school later that week. I was going to be "Internet-schooled"—home-schooled online—until I graduated, he told me. I couldn't do honors classes anymore because they weren't offered online. All the time I had dedicated to my academics had been for nothing. I couldn't play on sports teams anymore, even though the varsity softball team gave me more self-confidence and self-worth than anything else I did. My dad even forbade me to leave our street. Worst of all, I was not allowed to see a single one of my friends, even at my house. My father thought that they were invitations to temptation. If I was out with them, he thought I would have a chance to see Will.

In my father's newfound moral crusade, he wasn't picking on my mom or Taylor, only me. He started referring to me as the "evil daughter." He said that it was his mission as the head of our household to correct me. My salvation was all that mattered to him, no matter the extreme measures he'd have to implement to ensure it.

CHAPTER THREE

Ye adulterers and adulteresses, know ye not that
the friendship of the world is enmity with God?
Whosoever therefore will be a friend of the world
is the enemy of God.

—James 4:4

Slowly, I became used to being referred to as the "evil daughter." I could do nothing right, my father was almost always angry with me, and he was making my life a living hell. My mother didn't come to my rescue, which really hurt. She didn't like voicing any opinion contrary to my father's, especially when it came to me, and she agreed with his objective, even if she may have felt that his methods were a little extreme at times. But however desperately I wanted her to intervene and support me, she did nothing.

In 1999, I was a high school sophomore at the height of my adolescence, when peer relationships were absolutely critical to me. I hated not being able to go to school, play on the softball team, or hang out with my friends. I used to look forward to weekends, but now every day was the same. I felt like a prisoner all the time. Taylor was still attending public school, so I was home alone with my father for most of the day. When I'd still been at the high school, I had been able to sneak over to my friends' houses by riding their buses after school. I had gotten in trouble a couple of times for doing that, but now the bus plan

41

wasn't even an option. I didn't have a driver's license, just my learner's permit, so I had to have an adult with me if I wanted to use the car. All of the fun advantages of living in Florida were being taken away from me, one by one.

Somehow, I was still allowed to be on the computer, so I would talk to my friends online, using AOL Instant Messenger. They were upset that I had been withdrawn from school, and they understood that my father had done it to ground me, but didn't understand their role in it and why I was not allowed to see them anymore. That part was kind of hard for me to explain. My father now thought they were evil, too, but I obviously didn't want them to know that. Their parents just seemed to accept that I was being homeschooled for now.

Before long, I was cut off from AOL privileges, as well. My father found a conversation between me and a nineteen-year-old boy who had been a counselor at the summer camp I'd attended that past July. My father said it was highly inappropriate and again used the word *whore* before banning me from the Internet altogether.

The only communication I had now was with a few girls from the church. Dad had arranged for me to be pen pals and exchange letters with the ones around my age, all granddaughters of the pastor and cousins or siblings to one another. Shirley's daughter, Megan, who was fifteen, was the one I began corresponding with regularly.

Dad was extremely passionate about what he was doing for me and why he was doing it. In the beginning, I'd say things to challenge him, which also ended in wrathful rampages. After a while, I would try to hear him out just to keep him from raging at me. He wanted me to understand that God had a purpose for us here on earth, and that life was not all about doing whatever we wanted to do, and that included dating "heathen boys." And in the meantime, he had completely isolated me from every-thing and everybody. All I could do was sit alone in the room Taylor and I shared, all by myself, bored and miserable, trying to figure out ways to get back in his good graces, and back to my friends and my school. He was definitely trying to break me. Every time I told him I would do whatever he wanted as long as I could go back to school, he'd tell me that I was saying that because I hadn't given up on Will yet.

Any time I was defiant, his assaults went from verbal to phys-ical in nature. Oftentimes, they crossed the line into abuse, as far as I was concerned. He would shove me or push me or hit me to get my attention so I would stop whatever I was doing and listen to him. He'd try to hurt me when he hit me. He'd drag me off my bunk and slap me around, screaming ugly names at me and frothing at the mouth. It frightened me. But he re-mained adamant that according to the Word of God, corporal punishment was an act of love. "He that spareth his rod hateth his son: but he that loveth him chasteneth him betimes" was written in Proverbs 13:24.

The WBC backed up his belief in corporal punishment for children, preaching that physical inflictions woke a person up to bring him into instruction. It was good to hurt, and good to spank until it hurt. I was of two minds about this. I wanted to rebel because I was so mad at my father for being so harsh, but I wanted him to love me, so I was struggling to be obedient. I would be angry because my father was strict, and I would be obedient because I didn't want him to disown me. But on the other hand, I was still just fourteen years old, and I couldn't deny that I liked boys.

During scuffles with Dad, my mother would focus on my role in them, accusing me of causing all the strife in the house. Sometimes, she'd hesitantly say something like, "Oh, Steve, stop. You don't need to say that. The neighbors are going to hear." But that was the extent of her advocacy.

"This is what she needs," my father would respond. "I am supposed to be fighting a war. I have to get control of her!"

Even though my grandmother and my aunt Stacy lived in the neighborhood, I never saw or heard them trying to get my father to back off in any way. I knew Taylor overheard a lot of our fights, but at nine years old she probably thought it was too risky to defy Dad. She didn't get visibly upset, and she pretended not to be bothered by the arguments. I really had no allies.

On one occasion, Dad got so angry with me that I called Child Protective Services to intervene. He'd been in a mood, coming at me yet again and spewing venom about my wayward morals and my evil soul. I was so scared this time, though, that I brought the cordless phone outside to the front lawn, dialed Information to get the agency's phone number, and had the call forwarded automatically. It probably wasn't the best idea. They asked me all these questions about my situation, which I wasn't really prepared to answer standing on the sidewalk with my neighbors going about their business all around me and my father inside the house, steaming mad and likely to come out and catch me. I wasn't even convinced I wanted Child Protective Services to get involved. I just needed my father to know I was serious about defending myself from his physical bullying, and I was reaching my breaking point.

When someone from the CPS office called our house to say a complaint had just been phoned in, my father realized what I had done. He was livid, and he insisted that I call the office back and tell them it was just a prank and that I didn't realize the seriousness of my actions, then apologize for wasting their time and resources. I made the call with Dad listening in on a different phone. The whole thing was so lame. No one from CPS ever came to the house to speak to me or follow up in any way to be sure I was in fact okay. Unbelievably, my father had been able to shut the whole thing down. My punishment was already so severe, though, that there was little else he could do to me except make me feel guilty for having told on him, and brand me as a liar once again.

I don't know if my mother knew about the call. If she did, she didn't mention it to me. She and my father might not have agreed about how much physical punishment was too much, but they were in agreement about one thing: that my behavior was out of line. They both thought I was acting out, and if I did get punished, I deserved it. I wasn't a wimp, so it wasn't the physical pain that bothered me, but being controlled by my father pissed me off more than anything else. I soon came to realize that Dad's new mission was to watch every move I made to make sure I wasn't straying. I'd been punished so harshly at that point, I don't think there was much disobedience left in me anyway, but as far as my father was concerned, I still wasn't to be trusted.

Dad had grown tired of his Home Shopping Network job and had given it up to devote more time to the documentary. To bring in a little money, he was teaching religion part-time at a community college not far from our house. If he had to be in the classroom, he brought me with him. He made me sit in the back, but he could still see me at all times. I'd do my online homework on my laptop while he was in the front giving his lecture. My father was under the impression that this made me miserable, but I actually thought the arrangement was pretty awesome. He had really cute guy students in his class, eighteen-, nineteen-, and twenty-year-olds, and because I never left the

45

house except with Dad, they looked that much cuter. Any flirting, though, was only in my imagination.

At home, my parents often got into heated arguments, which kind of scared me. I knew I was the reason for a lot of the tension in their marriage, even though I wasn't always the topic of a given fight. My father's female friends were definitely an issue. Women, mostly Dad's students from the community college, would constantly call him or come up to him at school to tell him about their problems with their marriages and their personal lives, and my mother didn't approve. The two of them would go into a room, slam the door, and yell at one another for ten or fifteen minutes. They never got physical, as far as I knew, but it was pretty intense. Finally, my father would emerge a little calmer in his demeanor, leaving my mother behind to come out whenever she had collected herself. She almost always backed down.

Even if his religious fervor had a very angry aspect to it, one thing about Dad's new religion that I did like was his newfound self-restraint. He was still willing to get into arguments with Mom, but he didn't rage and carry on forever anymore. He'd make his point, then stop haranguing. When he was lecturing me, at least he was coming from a humble place. More often than not, he was even calm. Eventually, his peaceful delivery started making me feel like he was the best person there was to educate me about God's master plan for us. We were here for a reason, Dad said, but we had to adhere to the path of God. Dad was only trying to guide me along the right way. Slowly, his messages were beginning to have an impact on me, and I began to feel that I was really understanding faith. I took it to be proof that I was growing up.

Dad would give me lessons that went beyond scripture; he wanted me to embrace his new Westboro community with the same love and acceptance he did. "They love everyone, and they want to help everyone," he would repeatedly tell me. He said their zealousness came out of a fundamentally benevolent goal: to help the less enlightened people of the world to see. Even if I didn't fully get why a message of love had to be delivered with such hateful language, I could see by the footage of the church members' fervor that they were on a crusade that was spiritually driven.

I had been cut off from seeing my friends for more than two months when Dad told me about a picket in Jacksonville that he was going to be filming, and he invited me to go along as his assistant. He saw it as a chance to spend some time with the members and to introduce me to them for the first time. I was excited. The Jacksonville protest would be the first time I would actually get to meet Megan and my other pen pals from the church. The idea of getting away and traveling the 250 miles to Jacksonville was more than welcome. I also loved the idea that Dad and I were going to make the trip together, leaving my mother and Taylor at home.

Despite the video footage I'd seen, I had no idea what to expect. I was eager because the Phelps girls already felt like friends to me, and yet I was nervous about making a good impression on all these new people who were so important to my dad. Plus, I was curious about what had stirred such a strong spiritual reaction in him, ever since he had first come in direct contact with them back in Washington, D.C.

The way Dad had described it, the church was so connected to the truth that it was grander than anything he had ever experienced. I decided I wanted to be part of something that big, too, something that was definitely bigger than my life. I might not have understood the church's picket signs or why certain current events spawned their protests, but I wanted to grow spiritually and join my father's passion, especially since I would have his blessing.

During the four-hour drive, I found it hard not to succumb to Dad's infectious enthusiasm. Things had settled down significantly at home now that Dad felt I was on board with his new religion. It was great to be on the road, just the two of us. When we finally arrived in Jacksonville, I was fired up. As I jumped out of the car, I knew I looked like the epitome of a Florida teen, with bleached-blonde hair past my shoulders and extra mascara to show off my eyes. My father unpacked all of his film equipment, and we headed for Alltel Stadium, Jacksonville's huge football stadium. The event the church was picketing was a Billy Graham revival, a four-day "crusade" event, which would no doubt draw huge crowds of evangelical Christians. The revival and the picket were scheduled on what turned out to be a beautiful fall weekend in November 2000.

I had heard on the radio that the crowd was the biggest ever for a Billy Graham gathering, with more than seventy thousand people in attendance this day alone. There was a rumor that this crusade would be his last public rally due to his declining health. The crusade was pitched for a younger crowd, with evangelical singers and rock bands on the slate. I'd never seen so many people around my age in one place.

By now I was familiar enough with the people in the WBC, especially Fred Phelps, that I was able to recognize them in person. As we made our way to the protest site, I had no problem spotting the six-foot-four pastor. Dressed in an oversize cowboy hat and a Kansas City Chiefs football jersey, he was hollering at Billy Graham's most ardent devotees, "Billy Graham is in hell!" and "God hates false prophet Billy Graham and all of his parishioners!" He seemed to have no fear that seventy thousand Billy Graham followers outnumbered his handful of church members. He had a booming voice with a Southern drawl, but I didn't feel the least bit afraid of him. Rather, I was fascinated by his self-confidence, his charisma, and the boldness of his opinions in the face of such huge opposition.

The church's position—that Billy Graham was a false, lying prophet—was based on Graham's style of ministry. He liked to preach to the masses, and the WBC believed evangelistic megachurches like his turned religion into something really lazy. The pastor thought it was wrong for people to think they could do anything, or nothing, and still go to heaven. A certain lifestyle and procedure were required to get to God's kingdom, and simply attending a Billy Graham crusade once a year, clapping, singing, and praising the Lord, was not sufficient. The WBC also thought Billy Graham was a money whore. He was all about image and commercialism, not faith, and he would do or preach anything as long as he made money.

Pastor Phelps was holding up two signs. The first one proclaimed GOD HATES AMERICA—a direct jab at Billy Graham's favorite blessing, "God Bless America." The Westboro Baptist Church knew that God hated America because it was a fag-enabling country—so the pastor's other sign read GOD HATES FAGS. Activist movements that supported and mainstreamed gay rights were one reason for our recent accelerated descent into hell. The other was the cheapening of our religious convictions, as evidenced by these kinds of megapreachers and false prophets.

As Pastor Phelps barked out his message, he'd take pauses to chuckle and smile approvingly at Shirley and her daughter, Megan, who were imitating his style and shouting the same message with enthusiasm equal to his own. Shirley, Dad's friend and the fifth of the pastor's thirteen children, was so engaged in picketing, she barely had time to come over to greet Dad and meet me.

When she did make her way to us, she introduced me to Megan. The first thing I noticed about Megan was how pretty and bubbly she was. I was completely drawn in by her enthusiasm, and we bonded immediately. She was as friendly as anybody I had ever met, and she made me feel like an insider from our first embrace. On top of that, she was mature and intelligent, and she seemed more interesting than my old friends, with a deep knowledge about events in the world and issues that were being debated in the news, such as phony pastors and homosexual rights. I could envision us being friends.

I didn't feel that any of the Phelps girls were judging me harshly. Dad had told me on the trip up that they all were ordinary folks with a reasonable message. "These people are going out on their dime and time to protest something they think is important. They don't want people to be lied to." He said they were making it their life's work to spread God's truth: either obey or pay in hell.

When my father and I first mingled with the group, I only wanted to observe the picket or assist my dad with his filming. His still-unfinished documentary was no longer an exposé of the church's fanaticism, now that he had become totally indoctrinated. I was allowed to put the microphone on Fred Phelps, which was quite thrilling for me since he was a recognizable celebrity. Although I started out as mostly a bystander, over the course of the day, I began to feel a little more self-assured and got into the swing of things. I yelled along with everyone else, imitating Megan word for word when I wasn't exactly sure what I was expected to say. I held up a sign that read BILLY IN HELL; it had a photograph of Billy Graham's head with a pink, upside-down triangle on it. People were constantly streaming by and yelling biblical quotes back at us, things like "God hates those who hate" or "Judge not, lest ye be judged." Some of them stood in circles praying for us. I thought it was ironic that people would tell us not to judge them and then immediately judge us in return. My pet peeve had always been hypocrisy, especially in religion.

On the drive home, I told Dad how much fun the day had been. I hadn't seen anything wrong with what the church was trying to say. I was intrigued and wanted to learn more about their message and why they were saying it. Dad explained to me they were just trying to help people understand God's message. I could tell he was pleased that I had taken such a liking to his people and their cause. I was glad that my father was appreciating me, not thinking that I was worthless and useless. He said he would be sure to include me in the next picket event.

Megan and I wrote letters back and forth until the next protest we attended, which was in Manhattan two months later. Our whole family made the trip to New York. I had never been there before, and like many teens, I was excited to be going to an MTV event. The church was staging a demonstration outside the MTV offices on West Fifty-Fifth Street and Seventh Avenue, protesting the broadcasting of *Anatomy of a Hate Crime*, a made-for-TV docudrama about Matthew Shepard.

Shepard's death was the perfect hot-button issue to demonstrate the church's position against homosexuality. The brutality against Shepard had become so well known that he had become the poster child for antihomophobia groups around the nation and the world. However, for the WBC, he was the paradigm of God's hell on earth for fags, and in fact his funeral in Casper, Wyoming, on October 17, 1998, a little more than two years earlier, had put the Westboro Baptist Church on the map. Before the funeral, most of the nation knew nothing about the church. Its antigay protests took place in the Topeka area and made only the regional newspapers and local evening news shows. But because so many camera crews were covering the funeral, Pastor Phelps got the attention of the national and international media like never before. The news footage showed the pastor holding two provocative signs: NO TEARS FOR QUEERS and FAG MATT IN HELL.

The pamphlet the pastor had printed for distribution read "It is too late to rescue Matthew Shepard from the life of sin and shame into which he was lured by the perverted, depraved, and decadent American society into which he was born. All who say, 'It's okay to be gay,' have the blood of Matthew Shepard on their hands." The WBC was on to something—the bigger and sadder the story, the better the opportunity to spread the Word of God, that the world was doomed because of tolerance for homosexuality. Because the passersby reacted so violently toward the picketers, the pastor felt that the church did have something important to say—otherwise, the audience wouldn't be that angry.

After Matt's funeral, the Southern Poverty Law Center labeled the WBC a hate group. The pastor disagreed that we fit the definition, because the hatred was from God, not a personal dislike or an advocacy of violence toward others. However, he seemed to revel in the new tag, because he considered hate to be one of God's greatest attributes. He still organized a picket at the SPLC's headquarters in Montgomery, Alabama. The vocal and colorful pastor soon became almost as well-known as Matthew Shepard himself.

New York was extremely cold the January day of the MTV picket, but at least the deep freeze of the previous three weeks was over. Everybody in the city—except us—seemed so happy that it was forty degrees outside instead of zero, but temperature being relative, it was still really cold to me.

Although Mom had made the trip, she didn't want to picket, so she took Taylor shopping while I headed over with Dad. My father was filming again, still getting more raw footage for his documentary, even though he told me he wished he could just be picketing. Megan, Shirley, and a man from the congregation I hadn't seen before were at the picket site, very happy to see us and ready to start. Shirley distributed the signs. I proudly held a couple of GOD HATES FAGS placards whose flip side proclaimed FAGS ARE BEASTS. Shirley and Megan had MATT IN HELL and NO TEARS FOR QUEERS/FAG DIES, GOD LAUGHS combinations. Every once in a while, Dad would put down his camera and hold up a sign like NO FAGS IN HEAVEN from our pile of spares.

Just as in Jacksonville, we weren't there long before we started to provoke angry opposition. People walking by screamed at us that we, not Matt Shepard, were going to hell. Everybody seemed to think that Matt had been killed because of his sexual orientation. But the church didn't see it that way. Its standpoint was that people didn't get beaten up just because they were gay and that Matthew's murder was not a hate crime; rather, it was exactly what God had in mind for homosexual sinners. I now agreed with what the church members were saying and understood their logic. I thought that the people who were getting all upset with us were just ignorant.

I felt really confident on those midtown streets. I didn't feel the need to hang close to my father that day. If there was something I needed, I'd ask him, but for the most part, he held the camera and recorded the protest, and I was on my own. He'd walk around filming one of the four of us or some of the people who were hurling insults at us. I felt proud of how he played such an important role and handled himself so calmly.

About halfway through the three hours of our demonstration, Mom and Taylor came by to bring us something warm to drink. Mom was really nervous; I am not sure if it was because she was uncomfortable with the fact that people, many of them my age, were walking by and yelling violent things at us, or because of some of the messages on the signs. She still didn't like the idea that anyone besides God knew who was in hell and who wasn't. After just a few minutes, she took Taylor's hand and quickly pulled her off to do something else.

Taylor had wanted to picket. At ten years old, she probably didn't understand what the protest was really about, but she wanted to be part of it. There was always a bit of competitiveness between my younger sister and me, but it didn't usually get in the way of how much we cherished each other. I sometimes thought she was a little jealous of me because my father and I were a lot alike, both curious and outspoken. Before our crisis, I had liked grilling him with questions and getting his opinion on my school papers. We had fallen away, but thankfully, we were beginning to rebuild our close relationship. We'd had a lot in common before, like sports and music, and now we were sharing his church. Taylor was struggling to make sure Dad noticed her, too. But if Dad seemed to dote on me, my mother had a soft spot for Taylor. She had almost lost her to cancer, which no doubt made her hyperprotective. Plus, my sister was more soft-spoken and obedient than I was—of course, she was only ten.

At three o'clock, we packed up our signs and headed for the hotel. It had only been my second picket, but I could tell already that the Westboro Baptist Church was a community that I wanted to be a part of. There was something to it. We moved people to ask us a lot of questions, even if they screamed those questions at us. This meant we had some access to knowledge that they didn't. Just because picketing and provoking strangers was uncomfortable didn't mean we shouldn't do it. The whole three hours had been an intellectually stimulating experience for me. Whether or not I had it right, I hadn't been afraid. The group's seeming integrity was powerful, and they were really getting to the root of things, opening the eyes of their detractors to something profound, taking them to a new level of truth.

I arrived at the hotel exhilarated. My stereotype of a protester had always been an angry person saying something over and over, chanting and shaking a sign in somebody's face. In our group, we spoke calmly to people who were interested in engaging with us and asking questions. We had good points, substantive discussions, and strong arguments. I liked the high, happy energy on the picket line. None of the participants was mad or mean like I had thought they would be.

I liked the change in my dad from being a part of this church, too. His affiliation with them seemed to have brought out his humility. He'd so often been a jerk, especially to my mom. He always had to be the funny guy at the party, no matter at whose expense. Now he was less pretentious and didn't seem concerned with others' opinions of him; instead, he wanted to investigate something spiritual and do so with integrity. Dad was going in a good direction, and I felt hope for our entire family. I couldn't anticipate anything bad happening with this new religion guiding our lives.

CHAPTER FOUR

Praising God, and having favor with all the people. And the Lord added to the church daily such
as should be saved.

—Acts 2:47

Back in Florida, my father and I were managing to hold the
peace. Dad was really focusing on getting *Hatemongers* ready
for submission to the festivals. He'd retained the original title,
believing it was provocative and would stir interest, but he'd
added the subtitle *The True Story about Fred Phelps and the
Westboro Baptist Church.* He wrote his own sound track for the
movie, but I helped him with editing after he trained me on
the software and put me to work.

I still wasn't allowed to see any of my Bradenton friends at my
house or any of theirs. Despite how empowered I had felt at the
protests, I still really missed hanging out with them and getting
to be a teenager. I was on my best behavior, trying to get un-
grounded, but Dad was not budging. Instead, I had to resort to
doing everything with my sister. Taylor was still in public school
and often brought her friends home in the afternoons. I'd hang
out with them just for the sake of having company, even though
they were five years younger. On weekends, Dad let me go to
the beach, as long as I was with Taylor. When I complained that
I never got to see my friends, he'd encourage me to keep up my

correspondence with Megan and the other girls in Topeka, anticipating we'd be moving there sometime soon. They were all I had for contemporaries, even if they lived far away, and when I wrote any of them a letter, I'd get one back about a week later. And of course, our pen-pal relationship earned me Dad's approval, which was such a huge relief.

One day in March, my father got off his daily phone call with Shirley with great news. A very small house was coming available on "the block," the term church members used to refer to the homes surrounding the church building in Topeka. Shirley told him it was ours to rent if we wanted to move to Kansas.

When Dad mentioned a potential move to me, I thought about it seriously for a couple of days before I decided that I loved the idea. I was sick and tired of living in isolation in Florida, and I really liked Megan and the other girls, so I knew I already had a built-in community of friends in Topeka. I had already decided that Dad's new religion wasn't bad at all, and I liked that it had a grand purpose. He and I could spread the church's message together at pickets and finally be a team again.

Mom was not nearly as enthusiastic. Dad was in their bedroom reading scripture when she went to talk to him about it. "If you think we are moving to Topeka, you are out of your f——ing mind," she said, blocking the doorway. My mother was not one to swear. She used profanity only if she was really upset about something. We didn't have the resources to keep moving, she argued. The student loan payments were dragging down everything, and we were relying solely on one income in the house.

But this wasn't the only issue. She still had lingering questions about the church and some of their platforms, especially their view on the "chosen ones." Mom also didn't agree with the hard-line nature of their messages. Even though she objected to the homosexual lifestyle, too, she found the church's judgment overly harsh.

But Dad seemed to be full of answers for her. I overheard him tell her he was pawning my baseball card collection to help pay for the move. I had a signed Babe Ruth card in there that was very valuable. Dad had wanted me to save it for my adulthood so that I would have something to fall back on in case of an emergency. He never even mentioned it to me before he pawned it and the rest of my collection. I knew he had no intention of buying it back, but I didn't jump in and try to stop him. I was tired of fighting with him, and I knew that when he made up his mind about something, that was it.

Mom eventually did whatever my father said, so the argument about moving didn't last long. He'd been like this for so long that it was almost comical that she thought she had a vote. She would never entertain the idea of separating from him and splitting up our family. When he explained to her that this move was in my best interest, and would get me away from the heathen boys and bad influences all around me in Florida, Mom became much more amenable to the idea. She wasn't as tight with her family as when we'd first moved back to Florida two years earlier. My father had slowly been isolating her from them after he hadn't been able to convince them that his commitment to the church was serious.

She started letting her family know that a move back to Kansas was imminent. They knew that it had to do with the church, but they were also aware that if Dad had something in his head, my mother was going to go along with it. Uncle Mark was the only one who challenged them at all. "What the hell are you doing?" he asked my father. Dad tried to explain his theological reasons but quickly got angry and left.

In July 2001, Dad announced that the house in Topeka was

ready for us. We packed up virtually everything we owned. We packed Mom and Dad's queen-size bed, Taylor's and my bunk bed, the kitchen table and chairs, and our living room couch. Mom packed the linens and the dishes, and Dad packed up his camera, editing equipment, and all of our Bibles. The only things we didn't pack were my photos and keepsakes, which Dad confiscated, saying he'd return them later. But he never did. It was as if he was trying to erase our memories of life before the church. He also confiscated any of my movies, books, and music that he deemed inappropriate. Our two-year-old calico cat, Jesse, had to be given away, because Dad said too many people in the church had cat allergies, but luckily our adored pug, Buddy, was going with us. Everything happened so fast. In less than a week, we rented a small trailer from Budget Rent A Car to hitch to the back of our Toyota Camry and filled it to capacity. We loaded anything that didn't fit into the back of Dad's Ford F-150 quad cab. Dad, with Taylor in the backseat keeping him company, was the lead car of the caravan.

The trip to Topeka was almost fifteen hundred miles, twenty-four hours on the road. Dad decided to break it up into two days, with a one-night layover in a motel outside of Nashville. There, Dad smoked his last cigarette ever. Since his early teens, he had been a smoker, and I had been begging him for the last ten years to stop. He would strike deals with me—if I got straight As in school, he would quit. Over and over, I got the As and he still didn't quit, although he kept making me the same promises. But that evening in Nashville, he stopped cold turkey, knowing that smoking was not allowed in the church. This was his first test of will, and he was going to prove he could do it. He was such a sycophant. As gratified as I was that he had finally given up his disgusting habit, I still felt disappointed that he hadn't been able to do it for me, but rather for Shirley, someone he barely knew.

I was the primary driver of the Camry, the second car in the caravan. Mom rode with me, since she didn't really like long-distance driving. We filled the hours chatting, listening to Bible tapes, and discussing religion. The highway took us across Florida, through Georgia, Tennessee, Kentucky, Illinois, and Missouri before we finally reached Topeka.

We had been to Topeka quite a few times when we had lived in Lawrence, which was only thirty minutes east of there on I-70. For a city of only about 125,000 people, there were certainly a lot of places of worship, a church on seemingly every corner. The mainstream Christian religions, especially Baptist, Catholic, Lutheran, and Presbyterian, were very well represented, but there were a lot of Pentecostal and Eastern religious communities, too. Kansas's oldest continuous Baha'i community was in Topeka, right up the road from the Christian Calvary Motorcycle Ministry's house of worship. Of course, the one that interested us was the Westboro Baptist Church, with a membership of less than a hundred people.

When we pulled up in front of our new house, it was even smaller than I had been prepared for. It was painted a light green color and partially hidden by a great big shade tree. I could hardly see it, though, because of the thirty or so church members standing in front of it waiting to greet us. Everybody was superaccommodating, bending over backward to lend a hand. They were the most welcoming, organized bunch of people I had ever met. They started helping us unload the trailer and the truck, and they had everything inside and unpacked in less than two hours. They had already stocked the refrigerator and the pantry with all kinds of dry goods and supplies. Our new house was only five hundred square feet; by all appearances, only one person should have been living there. It had two small bedrooms, each one big enough for a bed that could be placed only in a certain direction. The tiny walk-through kitchen was connected to a dining room so cramped that it could barely fit our small table and four chairs. One small bathroom was going to have to serve all four of us.

The church, at 3701 SW 12th Street, was the centerpiece of the block. It was a big and very pretty building, typical of church architecture in the Midwest, with a kind of a faux-Tudor look of wood beams in the white plaster siding. Way up on one side of the oversize roof was a banner prominently advertising the WBC's website, godhatesfags.com. An American flag hung on the flagpole in front of the church, but it was purposefully displayed upside down out of disrespect for a sinful, fag-enabling America.

There were two entrances to the church, which was surrounded by a six-foot-tall, black wrought-iron security fence with spindles. Only visitors used the formal main entrance in the front, which was accessible from the street via a paved walkway. During Sunday services, two church members usually stood guard there to monitor the gate. There were times when members of the media who hadn't secured permission, or other suspicious people, had tried to get in, maybe even vandals, and the guards kept that from happening. Outsiders were welcome to attend Sunday services, but they had to have prior approval from Shirley. Church members entered through an entrance around the back, which actually took us through the pastor's kitchen into the sanctuary. Half the building was the church, and the other half was the pastor's residence. Above the kitchen was the master bedroom for the pastor and his wife, Marge. An inside kitchen door led to the sanctuary.

The sanctuary was large and simple. The walls were covered

with fake wood paneling, the kind installed from four-by-eight-foot prefab sheets. Lighting came from ceiling panels, and standard wall-to-wall carpeting covered the floor. There were two rows of twenty or so five-person pews for the congregation. The pastor delivered his sermons from the unadorned pulpit in the front of the room, with a map of the Holy Land pinned to the wall behind him and a poster elaborating the five points of Calvinism on a stand next to him. There were no pious statues or crucifixes on display anywhere, strictly following the policy against idolatry. Around the room, signs with messages such as Fags Are Worthy of Death and You're Going to Hell were displayed on easels. A few ceiling-to-floor drapes kept extra folding chairs or poster-size props out of sight. Above the sanctuary was the pastor's office and library, where many of the adult Bible study classes took place.

Back in the 1950s, Fred Phelps and his wife had bought a house there, and then had started buying up every house on the 3700 block of SW 12th Street for their children when they came up for sale. The street had slowly become the Phelps family compound. All of the members except Bill and Mary Hockenbarger lived on or near the block. Our house was technically across the street, but most people could walk from their houses to the church without having to use the street. The compound was set up so that all the backyards of our various houses adjoined the church property, creating a communal park, a gathering place for everybody of any age. Kids were always out there running around, while the teenagers hung out and kept an eye on them. The church had all the facilities of a park just for our use. There was a full-size basketball court, a 200-meter running track that bordered the inside edges of all the yards, a volleyball area, and a great big swimming pool surrounded by patios with outdoor furniture and picnic tables. We played football on a grassy knoll. A couple of trampolines, a big jungle gym with swings for kids of all ages, a few slides, and monkey bars had been installed for the kids. The churchyard and the ten private yards backing up to it were immaculate, always mowed and manicured.

I soon found out the kids and teens did all the landscaping and garden work. In two hours, we could mow, blow, and bag the entire communal property and all the yards. No one complained. Kids were expected to help; it was part of the discipline the church instilled. The sense of community was really impressive. When someone needed something, everybody was always there at a minute's notice. Each night of our first week in Topeka, someone either brought us a meal or invited us over for dinner.

After that period of isolation in Florida, being with so many people my own age was a huge blessing and a welcome relief. Megan, just as bubbly as she had been the first two times I had met her, gave me the warmest welcome, and her sister and teenage cousins were almost as effusive. Shirley had told Megan about all of Dad's complaints and worries about me and my behavior, so she knew we had moved there in part to save me. Before we relocated, she had sent me a letter that said she was optimistic about my potential, even though she knew I was currently on the wrong path.

One thing that surprised me was how modern and methodical the people in the congregation were. I had never seen a group of teenagers so keen on being current and informed. The Phelps girls knew the facts about everything going on in the news, so they always had something interesting to talk about. Next to the sanctuary, the church had an entire library of filing cabinets with neatly archived information about every organization the WBC had ever picketed. In each individual folder, marked with the time, date, and place of the picket, the pastor put the picket memo, the picket flyer, the reason for our picketing, and all the media we generated from the picket—the news articles, the video, and the e-mails we had received.

Another thing that surprised me was how tech-savvy everybody in the church was. The pastor liked to say the Internet had been invented so that the church could spread God's message. He also said that computers could be used for good purposes, although he believed most people used the Internet for bad and wasteful reasons. Ben Phelps, the pastor's oldest grandchild, and Sam Phelps, Shirley's oldest child, ran the church's many websites. Godhatesfags.com was the primary site, but because hackers were constantly trying to shut it down, there were plenty of others, too—godhatestheworld.com, godhatesthemedia.com, americaisdoomed.com, and priestsrapeboys.com—to name a few. If there was a new technology, the church had it first. The office was equipped with computers and fax machines, which were programmed to blast out the church's messages twenty-four hours a day. That way, even when members were sleeping they were doing a kind of picketing, spreading the Word of God.

The kids were superinvolved in the church community, and the church scheduled all of our activities—babysitting, day care, working in the church office, helping the elder members with chores, renovating property, picketing, and organizing church-only social events. Anything we were capable of we were expected to do, and nobody did the tasks begrudgingly. On the contrary, we loved feeling important. Everyone had a job. Some kids found addresses of organizations for the pastor's faxes, and others sent them out. Shirley often assigned the young people to e-mail duty in the church office. Anyone who was at least fourteen could answer the e-mails that came in from all over the country, as long as Shirley thought he or she had enough knowledge. We were supposed to use scripture to support whatever answer we were sending. If our answer wasn't up to par, someone else would forward a corrected response. Even little kids could empty the wastebaskets or perform other housekeeping duties. The operations always seemed to run smoothly with very few glitches.

If I didn't know something or was uncertain of a protocol, I could go to any of the church members for guidance. If I wanted an elder, I usually chose Shirley, but otherwise I would talk to Megan. She had assumed a leadership role among the girls my age and often led us at the picket line. She was considered the shining star of my generation.

Taylor had a harder time finding a cohort. She was at least four years younger than my group, and two years older than the next group down, which included Shirley's daughter Grace, so she was kind of caught in the middle. Being a bit of a tomboy, she didn't seem to mind hanging out with the five boys in her grade. I liked when she spent time with us, but I could tell that not everyone agreed. Shirley's niece Libby, in particular, seemed annoyed. As oldest in the group and the ringleader, she was a little spoiled and liked to be indulged. When she didn't want Taylor around, she didn't hide it. She loved being the center of attention, so when Taylor was with us, my sister took my focus away from her. I didn't think she particularly liked me, either, but I did my best to change her opinion of me by being especially nice and attentive when I was with her.

As much as I adored my sister, I encouraged her to find other friends. I hated shooing her away, but I needed to be in good standing with my group. One-on-one, the Phelps girls were intelligent and very nice, but as a group they made me nervous, and my circumstances felt too precarious for me to risk being shunned. I learned very quickly that we didn't spend any time socializing with anybody but one another. No one in our church made any outside friends, and I didn't need them when I had the Phelps girls by my side. Because only people in the church had enough spirituality to guide me to my salvation, befriending heathens was a frivolous waste of time.

CHAPTER FIVE

Favor is deceitful, and beauty is vain: but a
woman that feareth the Lord, she shall be
praised.

—Proverbs 31:30

If I had expected some sort of formal newcomers' introduction
into the ideology and practices of the Westboro Baptist
Church, I was wrong. There was no initiation; instead, everybody was expected to fall in, which was certainly overwhelming
for me. All these people had grown up in the church and
learned scripture before they could read. They could cite any
passage in the Bible without even thinking about it.

My foundation in scripture was adequate, but I was at a primary level of interpretation. I learned a lot more about the
church's rules and views when I had sleepovers with the Phelps
girls on the weekends. Our house was so small and cramped that
I loved the chance to sleep somewhere else, and I'd go as often
as I was invited. Usually the overnights took place at Shirley's
enormous house, which had two giant living rooms on its first
floor. One was a game room, the other a movie theater. Between
the two, there was everything imaginable: a wall-to-wall TV,
surround-sound stereo, Xboxes and video games, a Ping-Pong
table, board and card games, and big comfortable couches for
hanging out. The huge state-of-the-art kitchen had a center

island surrounded by at least a dozen stools. Shirley loved to cook. My favorite meal was her hamburger biscuits, a buttermilk biscuit baked with ground beef inside. For anybody who didn't like meat, she made a cabbage version. Either of them made a nice meal. The home-baked cookies on the kitchen island made that room the prized hangout for us teens.

Downstairs, the finished basement had even more bedrooms and a big reception hall, which was big enough to comfortably hold our entire congregation. Any big function, like the celebration after a baptism, was held there if the weather was too cold for an outdoor reception. Shirley's kids each had their own room on the second floor, all of them outfitted with a television and a computer. I loved Megan's room. It was large and comfortable, with a collection of framed candid photos of cousins and siblings, many of them taken at various pickets.

All the women in the photos had their hair down to their hips, uncut hair being an expression of obedience to God. Megan told me that none of the girls in our generation had ever had a haircut, because a woman's hair was a symbolic, religious covering that showed her submission to God and the church, according to 1 Corinthians 11:15. The angels could see whether women were good or bad by their hair. The generation before us had been allowed to have their hair cut, but at some point the pastor decided that it was rebellious and stopped letting them take scissors to their locks. We weren't allowed to color it or highlight it, either. Some women's hair never grew that long because of splitting, but it still couldn't be trimmed.

Most of the rules for women had to do with modesty and leading the godly life laid out for us in scripture. We couldn't wear makeup or paint our nails, either. We had to be modest in dress, although there was a lot of wiggle room for interpretation. When I first arrived, some of the girls criticized my wardrobe, telling me my shorts were too short and my shirts too tight. WBC women were supposed to be modest, being careful to not expose the "four b's": boobs, butt, belly, and back. I knew the Phelps girls had already heard I was kind of rebellious, and I didn't want to do anything that could be misinterpreted as a misstep, so I took their opinions seriously.

Mom started throwing away a lot of my clothes, even the ones I wanted to keep. Any lingerie other than sports bras went in the trash, as did any of my shorts cut above the knees and all of my bikinis. I thought that without my favorite clothes and makeup, I looked ugly and frumpy, but I got used to it quickly.

My mother had never been a flashy dresser, but in Florida she had been understatedly fashionable. She wore makeup, dyed and styled her hair, and wore nice clothes. I guessed that she probably enhanced her figure with padded bras, too. She stopped after we moved to Topeka. My father told her that he found her more attractive when she gave up even those minimal trappings of vanity. He said he was proud of her when she was obedient. According to him, everybody else was vain and whorish, and he was not attracted to the kind of women who were tan or wore makeup.

Mom settled into the house in Topeka with relative ease. A lot of tasks were communal, such as watching one another's kids and gardening, and Mom appreciated the support. But the other women, led by Shirley and her older sister Margie, made her understand she was not part of their inner circle. The two sisters would call each other to discuss matters large and small, such as who was worthy and who wasn't. They'd decide if a member needed to be chastised, or even removed from the church. The two women were the phone chain ringleaders for the community, and they never called my mother to ask her opinion about anything, although she was aware that the rest of the women all spoke on the phone regularly. It was important to have your voice heard, and my mother was anxious to be accepted on this level, but as she was naturally unassertive anyway, she knew not to push it. She was really intimidated by all of the Phelps women, but none more so than Shirley. I didn't know how much of it was based on lingering feelings of jealousy about how tight my father and Shirley were; I'd certainly had my own resentments about it, like when he stopped smoking for her.

The Phelps women seemed so intelligent and powerful, and many of them had law degrees. They had committed Bible verses to memory and used them to decry the sins and disobedience they saw all around them. Mom just wasn't as versed as they were in scripture and interpretations of Bible passages, and if she had a question, she was too intimidated to speak up. Sometimes she'd tell me how she felt like an outsider at church functions.

My mother was now under tremendous pressure to accept whatever Dad said. Before the move, she had been willing to be mildly confrontational with him when she didn't agree with him. Once we were established in our new house, however, those kinds of challenges were shut down, and she became his dutiful subordinate. She couldn't speak up when something troubled her or show that she ever doubted his judgment. One of the rules of the church was that a wife and husband were not to argue, as the Bible said arguing hindered prayer. She had thought of herself as a weaker vessel even before our move, and it was certainly reinforced now. According to the church, she'd spent her adult life thus far living wrong, surrounding herself with idols, and not serving God. Now at thirty-five years of age, and with no status in this new community, she was beginning again. The job she'd found as a dental hygienist at an office a few blocks from our house made for a respectable career, but it didn't carry with it the status of a lawyer. I thought she really missed her family back in Florida, too. She still wrote letters to them, but very rarely talked to them on the phone.

Now that we were in Topeka, my father was the happiest I'd ever seen him, partly because he had unlimited access to Shirley, whom he considered godly. He would check in with her before taking action on anything. The way she guided him, I often thought she was like the mother Dad never had, his own having been too self-absorbed to take an interest in him. Shirley seemed like a well-oiled machine. Her house was spotless; her school-age kids were straight-A students, eloquent speakers, and competitive runners; she was an attorney and a very active mom and homemaker at the same time; her family had the biggest house and the nicest car; and she was completely in charge of running the Phelps family law firm, the finances of the WBC, the picket schedule, and the daily media interviews.

Everyone looked up to Shirley, who, despite her extremist views, had a very kind, gentle, and caring manner. About a month after my family's arrival, I met with her one-on-one for the first time when I came by the house to see Megan. I had entered through the back door and was crossing the kitchen when Shirley motioned me into her large office at the back of the house. She pointed to a chair next to her desk, one of five large wooden ones in the room, and signaled for me to sit down while she answered e-mails and wrapped up a phone call. I was a little nervous, but I relaxed as soon as she finished her call and gave me a big smile.

"How are you doing, Lauren?" she asked. "How are you feeling about things?"

"Okay," I said tentatively, still wondering why she'd brought me in.

She said she wanted to explain to me what was expected of

a teenager, seeming genuinely warmhearted in her concern. "I want to make sure you understand that everyone is going to be watching your behavior. You shouldn't feel threatened or singled out. Every young person faces the same scrutiny. You might even receive an e-mail from me from time to time calling you out on a behavior, but I'm only trying to make you a better person."

I had already seen Shirley openly chastise her nieces Libby and Jael, so I knew what she was talking about. She did this with every teenager. I left the office in great spirits. Shirley continued to welcome me whenever I was around. "Come in," she'd say when she'd see me at the house visiting her daughters. Sometimes, she'd invite me to sit on the couch while she made iced coffee. There was always some kind of cookie in the oven, filling the kitchen with the aroma of chocolate or cinnamon, and lots of kids running around the house or the yard.

Shirley was forty-three, and when we got to Topeka she hadn't even had the last of her eleven kids yet. I was very impressed with her. She was so natural, with a beautiful smile and long, wavy hair with just a few strands of gray. She had intense blue eyes, which were always deeply focused on whomever she was talking to. She was possessed in an earth-motherly way, never out of control or raging, even when she was loud. She spoke without being condescending, as if she was a mentoring professor and you were a student. She made me feel so embraced and warm in her presence.

She was also very organized, and a good delegator, so she farmed a lot of chores out to her kids. All her children respected what she asked of them. Megan, her oldest girl, started helping her do the church's finances from the time she was fourteen. I personally had never seen such cooperation in one family unit.

Shirley managed everyone's tithes to the church. You had to

give 10 percent, no matter how young you were. Sometimes I'd make a little money babysitting for the children of church members, and whatever my earnings were, 10 percent went to the church. I'd get paid $5 to $7 an hour, so if I made $20 on a job, I'd give $2 to the church. I loved taking care of the kids. We'd take them on field trips, bring them books from the library, and teach them how to do chores like cleaning their rooms. I was happy to give my money to the church. I didn't need it, and giving it to the church made me feel responsible and a part of the community.

Shirley's husband was named Brent Roper. Brent was at least five years younger than Shirley. He'd been a friend of Shirley's younger brother, Tim, in junior high, and a few years later, when he was still a teenager, he fell in love with her. He actually approached her on a picket one day to ask her if she would like to start courting. By then, Shirley was in her early twenties and had a toddler son named Sam who had been born out of wedlock. I heard that she had conceived the child in a moment of weakness, when she had been completely stressed out from multitasking three enormous obligations—law school, the law office's books, and the church. She had acknowledged her fornication, atoned for it, and received forgiveness. She refused to say anything more about it or name the father of her child. After she and Brent were married in 1983, he adopted Sam, who was then about four years old.

Brent wasn't as convivial as his wife was. When he met people for the first time, he was nice enough, if a bit standoffish. He tended to let Shirley make the assessment if someone was worthy of a welcome. Often when I'd stop by on the weekends he was out in their garden, planting and pulling weeds. He was a long-distance runner, slight and in excellent shape. He loved being outside and enjoyed taking the teens jogging to the high school and back. During the week, he worked as a human resources manager at a big company in Kansas City and made a lot of money. I heard from Megan that he had been fired from his previous job after his employer saw a picture of him picketing on the front page of the *Kansas City Star*. When he sued his employer, he won and was awarded a sizable sum, 10 percent of which went back to the church, of course. He also wrote popular law and mathematics textbooks that were published and sold in bookstores.

Brent had used the settlement money from his lawsuit to make additions to their house. By the time the work was done, it had twelve bedrooms, six bathrooms, two living rooms, and a basement reception hall. He also paid for improvements to the church. But even though he had prevailed in his lawsuit, he never wanted to be recognized by his picture in the paper again. At the pickets he did attend, which were now only the out-of-town ones, he'd wear Oakley sunglasses and pull a hat down over his wavy brown hair, or keep a sign in front of his face to protect his identity.

When we were first settling in, my father was allowed to ask questions about the WBC's culture and lifestyle, and bring up things in the Bible that he interpreted slightly differently than the church did. After all, he was pretty knowledgeable in scripture, too, and thought he could add to the discussion. He frequently challenged Shirley, and at first she answered him enthusiastically, with lots of elaboration and details, but eventually she started to get annoyed with him. "He needs to stay at home and stop asking questions," Shirley said to me one day when I was at her house hanging out with Megan. "He needs to stay at home and read the Bible." I didn't have to relay the information to my father. Shirley told him herself, and Dad learned quickly that he was going to be humiliated if he didn't stop challenging her. Sometimes when he got angry, Margie would tell Shirley that he was being rebellious. Although he didn't consider his style combative, I think he realized that people were going to start hating him if he didn't conform, and he started to make an effort to curb his tongue.

Obedience was a cornerstone of the church. There was no human endeavor more important than obedience to God, and as for obedience to the church rules, a defined system was in place to keep people in line. It was based on making everyone accountable for his own actions, and when that failed, humiliating them. Church elders and parents were the highest order of disciplinarians. Parents had authority over other people's children as well as their own, which meant they had the right to correct them if they were doing something wrong. Shirley didn't mind at all telling Dad or me what I was doing wrong, and I appreciated her guidance and advice.

I still had trouble being accepted, despite my efforts to do everything that was expected of me. One time, when we were at Logan Airport after a Boston picket, Margie's son Jacob said to me, "I feel really bad telling you this, but Libby doesn't think you belong here." I was really offended. Libby, who was a little bit older and already through with high school, had not made much of an effort to befriend me, but I was trying to be as close with her as I was with my other friends. She didn't seem to like the fact I had come into her age group of cousins, Megan, Rebekah, and Jael. She had grown up with them, and perhaps she felt I was taking her place, or that they were leaving her out.

I was so ashamed by what Libby had said I found it hard to discuss, even with my father. But I needed to confide in him, since I wasn't sure I trusted anyone else. When I finally worked up the courage to tell him what she had said about me, he was nonplussed.

"You need to try to have a better relationship with her," he instructed me. "You need to work harder." He was suggesting the problem was with me, not her. That wasn't the kind of support I was looking for. He always seemed to be putting the onus on me these days. I knew my getting along with these girls was critical to Dad and to all the Drains, if we were going to be accepted, but I was doing my best.

I went to Shirley next. She recognized that there was competition among the teens, and that they might not trust me right away because I was so new. She told me I should take advice only from the elders. "Young people say and do stupid things," she said with a smile. "Don't listen to what Libby says." Shirley always had a way of making me feel better.

Because Dad was an elder, he was under the impression that he was in a position of authority over Shirley's children, too. Once in a while, he would admonish one of them, if he thought the child was acting inappropriately. For example, he would tell Megan if he thought she was speaking vainly or being a tiny bit arrogant when in fact she was. "Stop talking that way around the younger children," he would tell her. "They will pick up on that easily and think it is acceptable." He thought this was expected of him as an elder. However, the next thing he knew, Shirley was admonishing him in a church-wide e-mail, telling him he was trying to usurp her authority. She also denied that her children would ever behave in a way that needed correcting. So, after that he had to rethink his perception of his authority.

If he was being difficult, Shirley thought he was trying to assert too much power and control too quickly. That first summer, he wasn't permitted to have much say in terms of big ideas, like whom to picket, what signs we were going to use, or what slogans we were going to chant. He also wasn't allowed to approach the pastor when he was frustrated by a situation. But he was really trying. I could see that he was willing to do whatever it took to earn acceptance.

My father thought that going to law school might be the best path to gaining the Phelpses' respect and, from there, status in the church. Pastor Phelps and eleven of his thirteen children, including Shirley, had law degrees. Their law firm, Phelps Chartered, had been founded by the pastor in the 1960s. He had earned his law degree in 1964 from Washburn University School of Law in Topeka, but his reputation for being volatile and confrontational on a weekly radio show made it hard to find a judge to vouch for his good character, which was a prerequisite for admission to the Kansas state bar. The pastor supported his own case by presenting evidence that he had been an Eagle Scout in Mississippi, earned an American Legion honor, and received a letter from President Harry S. Truman. The proof was sufficient to allow him into the bar, and he was admitted that year.

Interestingly enough, the pastor said he had originally become a lawyer because he wanted to represent the disenfranchised, particularly the black population. He had been born and raised in Mississippi, and he believed it violated the Word of God to treat black people as poorly as he had seen them treated in the South. During his first years as a lawyer in Kansas, he took on mostly civil rights cases and won nice settlements for his clients. He liked to boast that he himself had systematically taken down the rigid Jim Crow discrimination laws in Topeka, winning discrimination cases against school districts and police forces.

In 1977, though, his right to practice law in Kansas was revoked. He had been preparing a case for trial and requested a
transcript from a court reporter, Carolene Brady, which she delivered a day later, but a day late. Even though the transcript
did not play a part in the outcome of the case, he sued the
woman for $22,000 in damages. He called her to the stand
as a hostile witness during her jury trial, where he badgered
and bullied her for a week, leaving her distraught. During the
cross-examination, he challenged her about her income tax re-
turns, her reputation, her competency, and her morality or lack
thereof. He alleged to the court that she was a slut, and to
prove his point, he subpoenaed ex-boyfriends of hers whom he
wanted to testify about their deviant sexual practices. Eventually, the pastor's case was thrown out. He immediately filed
an appeal, claiming under oath to be in possession of eight
affidavits from supporting witnesses, but when Brady's lawyer
contacted those witnesses, he learned none of them had provided the pastor with an affidavit. On the basis of that perjury,
the pastor was disbarred in the state of Kansas, although he
could still practice on the federal level.

Eight years later, nine federal judges filed a complaint against
the pastor, five of his children, and a daughter-in-law, alleging
the family had made false accusations against all nine of them.
It took four years for a settlement to be reached. The pastor
agreed to surrender his law license permanently in exchange
for leniency for his children, so he could no longer take on
any cases. Charges were thrown out against three of the children and the daughter-in-law, but his daughter Margie was
suspended from practicing in federal and state courts for one
year, and Fred Jr. lost his right to practice in both courts for six
months.

Nevertheless, the Phelps Chartered law firm was highly regarded and was always very busy with clients from all over northeast Kansas. The clients knew about the Phelpses' religious convictions, but they also recognized them as some of the best lawyers in town with a winning record. The firm also rarely turned down clients, even those who might have trouble paying. To collect their fees, the firm might work out a deal with a client to garnish his paycheck. There were clients they did refuse to represent, such as any couple seeking a first divorce, because the church believed that a couple should be together for life. Phelps Chartered would, however, represent a client getting a second divorce, saying that perhaps by divorcing, the client would reunite with his or her first spouse.

My father was under the impression that Shirley would be delighted to hear he was interested in being a lawyer, too, so he took it upon himself to apply to Washburn University School of Law, the pastor's alma mater, without consulting her first. He was accepted and offered a full scholarship. Even though he had never studied anything related to law, his LSAT scores were near perfect. When he got his acceptance letter, he proudly took it to Shirley, and was totally taken aback when she told him she forbade it.

"We don't need anyone else to be a lawyer," Shirley told him. She made it clear that if he went against her and decided to go to law school anyway, she wouldn't hire him at Phelps Chartered, because his work there wouldn't help the firm's bottom line; instead, they would just end up having to pay him for work they were doing themselves. She told my father to stop copying what her family was doing and find a career path more suitable to his talents. "Stop wasting your time in school. Your family needs you," she told him, referring to the fact that Dad had moved the family to Kansas to keep me from taking the wrong path, and he had to keep up his vigilance.

My father was really disappointed and upset. But, after some thought, he told the family that Shirley was right. Her guidance wasn't to be scorned or taken lightly; it was a gift. If Shirley told you anything, it was as good as hearing it from God. In this case, God was telling Dad how to help his family. "I need to stop being so arrogant," he said, and dropped the idea of law school altogether.

CHAPTER SIX

> Lift ye up a banner upon the high mountain, ex-
> alt the voice unto them, shake the hand, that
> they may go into the gates of the nobles.
>
> —Isaiah 13:2

People called us haters because the word *hate* was so prevalent in our protests. The rejoinders we heard most often from people trying to refute our message were: "God loves everybody" and "God is a loving, tolerant God." But as the pastor told us, these were perhaps the biggest lies of all. In truth, it was God who hated, not us. The pastor was God's mouthpiece on earth, and we were only the messengers. Most of our detractors thought that we went around spewing the same handful of lines from scripture and hiding behind a distortion and perversion of the Baptist faith. This couldn't be less accurate. The pastor might have called himself an "old school" or "primitive" Baptist, but the theology he preached was fundamental Calvinism.

Calvinism was not the least bit new in America. It had been the religion of the Pilgrims, the Puritans, and many of the Founding Fathers, and in one sense the reason why the Pilgrims left for the Promised Land in the first place.

Before John Calvin and Martin Luther, there really were no Protestant faiths. They were two spiritual leaders who dared to challenge the status quo, Roman Catholicism, and they were the leading forces in the Protestant Reformation in Europe.

In the early years of their ministries, they were considered as radical as our pastor was now. Martin Luther had dared to challenge the Catholic hierarchy with his Ninety-Five Theses. For that, he was excommunicated by Pope Leo X, and condemned as an outlaw by the Holy Roman Emperor. John Calvin was only eight at that time, but later made his own break from the Catholic Church in France when he published his *Institutes for the Christian Religion* in 1536. He, too, made lots of enemies, and many men in power condemned him. He eventually fled from France to Geneva, where his teachings became the foundation of Calvinism. He was basically a Christian apologist, with an excellent grasp of argument and logic. I could see this same trait in the pastor. There was no argument involving the logic of scripture he could not win.

Luther's and Calvin's biggest grievance against Catholicism was the hierarchical organization of the Catholic Church. They both thought every man had equal access to God through the scriptures. They were also opposed to the sacraments the Catholics insisted were required for salvation, especially since priests had become so corrupted, they were willing to sell indulgences to wealthy people to put them on the path to heaven. But for Calvin, the corruption was only part of the problem. He had the conviction that decisions about eternal life had been predestined by God, who had identified the people who would be saved before they were even born.

According to Calvin, no one could know if he was heaven-bound, because nobody understood God well enough, or was even capable of knowing God that well. However, there was the built-in presumption that if you lived your life like you had been chosen, with day-to-day, hard, honest work and rigorous moral standards, the chances were better that you lived that way *because* you were chosen. The assumption was that God wasn't going to bother creating people like that just to send them to hell. God's reward for the people he had prechosen was salvation and eternal life. But since there was still lingering doubt and no absolute certainty who was chosen, everyone still had to be decent and upright throughout his or her life.

The majority of the early settlers in New England had been either Calvinists or strongly influenced by the religion, and they didn't believe in God's overwhelming goodness and affection. The pastor preached about it in "1,001 Reasons Why 'God Loves Everybody' is the Single Greatest Lie Ever Told," available on the church's website. He said, "Before the 20th Century 'God loves everyone' was largely a foreign theology to the United States.... The Puritans that stepped off the *Mayflower* at Plymouth in 1620, and their progeny that inhabited the United States for nearly 300 years, largely did not believe that 'God loves everyone.'... They read the Bible daily and believed in the wrath of God and they feared Him greatly."

A hundred and fifty years later, many of the men who signed the Declaration of Independence or the Constitution were members of those churches. But during the 1800s, Calvinism was on the wane, and by the twentieth century, most people in our country had rejected the fundamentals of the faith outright. A lot of sincere Christians just couldn't accept that they were most likely going to hell despite the lives they led, so they threw out the rest of the Calvinist concepts at the same time.

The pastor was determined to keep the model going, even if he was only preaching it to a handful of us. On the easel beside his pulpit, he had letters from the word *TULIP* stacked along the left margin of his poster, which was the acronym for the five points of Calvinism. *T* stood for "total depravity," *U* stood for "unconditional election," *L* was "limited atonement," *I* was for "irresistible grace," and *P* stood for "perseverance of the saints."

"Total depravity" was an easy concept—every single person was born a sinner. Sometimes, it was referred to by the grimmer phrase "infant damnation." The idea was that after Adam and Eve's fall from grace, the rest of us were born innately evil. By no means did it imply we were pathological murderers or criminals, but because of original sin, we were all sinners. In fact, this was why men could not save themselves.

"Unconditional election" was the concept that seemed to rile people up the most. It was hard to buy into the idea that there was no chance you could earn your way into heaven, that you had to be chosen by God before you were even born. No amount of faith or repentance or righteousness would change your destiny. To me, the biggest misapprehension about Westboro was that we picketed to try to convince people to come to our side before it was too late, telling them "repent while you can." This couldn't have been further from the truth; we were just spreading the word that sinners were going to hell, because God wanted it that way.

"Limited atonement," or partial redemption, also caused a lot of consternation from other Christians. They were under the impression that a true, selfless faith in Christ would secure them a place in heaven. But limited atonement meant only the elect would be so graced. If you weren't a chosen one, you weren't destined for God's kingdom of heaven no matter how sincerely and how often you repented. There was no salvation for you. On the other hand, if you were one of God's elect, then atonement for transgressions was possible, because the error of your ways had really been part of God's master plan for you.

"Irresistible grace" was pretty straightforward. God's call was invincible, infinitely more powerful than hatred and hating hearts. Nothing could change the predestiny of the chosen ones, who were guided by God's grace alone. God would not forsake anyone he had chosen.

"Perseverance of the saints" was also known as "eternal security." Again, it didn't really have anything to do with man's life on earth but referred instead to God, who, having predestined people to His kingdom, would sustain them with faith until they got there.

It came down to this: Salvation was conditional, and election was unconditional. Salvation had to do with time, and election was God's decree, plain and simple, predestined without time or place. God's election was a mystery known only to Him. Every single person was guilty before God, and therefore deserving of His wrath. Certain sinners were chosen to be saved, but they were not saved yet. Without the elective intervention of God, salvation would be impossible. All sinners but the chosen few were justly and eternally condemned. The proof of everything the pastor said was written in the scriptures, but I was quickly learning that the ignorant were not aware of the message. The WBC was only spreading the Word of God.

On Sundays, the sanctuary would be pretty much filled to capacity. The atmosphere was always festive and energized. We weren't required to dress up for the service, although a few people liked to come in dresses or suit jackets and ties. Anybody who was just arriving from a local picket was usually dressed for comfort rather than ceremony. If it was cold, we'd be in sweat suits and layers, all of which were acceptable. The women had to have their heads covered, so most of us wore scarves, but a few opted for hats or bonnets.

We'd all take our seats in the pews. By habit, families sat together and in the same place each week. The Drain family pew we'd been assigned was the last one in the back on the right-hand side. Like all the families, we had a cardboard carton at our pew holding all the things we needed on a regular basis: pencils and notepads to take notes, extra scarves and head coverings, and our Bibles.

We all had the regular King James Bibles, each encrusted in gold leaf. The cool teenagers brought their electronic Bibles and their laptops with them, as well. That way we could look up passages from the Bible when we needed to or refer to any of the current events that the pastor would be talking about. The service always started with a song or two, straight from the traditional Christian hymnbook. Fred Jr., who sat at the upright piano in the front left of the church for the entire service, accompanied us while his wife, Betty, led the singing. The whole congregation, men, women, and children, were allowed to sing. Marge Phelps, the pastor's wife, dutifully sat directly in front of the pulpit to listen to her husband.

When we were on the final verse of the opening hymn, the pastor would enter through a door close to his pulpit. He usually wore a rumpled sports jacket and slacks. His long, wiry gray hair was hack-combed, giving him the look of someone who had just gotten out of a convertible. He was in his early seventies when we first got there and very fit. He loved to bike and run daily. Members of the congregation, even the ones not related to him, called him Gramps.

The pastor's first action after he took the floor each Sunday was to distribute a newsletter that he had written covering current events of the week. Then, he would begin his sermon in his distinctive Southern drawl. These sermons were the best opportunity for me to get up to speed on the opinions of the church. The first few weeks, I thought they were a little difficult to understand. The pastor presented them as if everyone knew every reference he was using. I understood them, but on a rather rudimentary level. I soon discovered they could be appreciated on many levels. They were layered. The more seasoned a Christian you were, the more you would understand.

The pastor led the entire service and delivered 90 percent of the sermons. On occasion, if he was sick or at an out-of-town picket, then one of the other elder men would take his place. Women were not allowed to deliver the sermons, let alone speak, when we were gathered in the sanctuary. Alternates filling in would base the homily on one of the pastor's hot topics. Nobody would want to usurp him by coming up with an independent idea, and the pastor never ran out of ideas. He was a cause monger, always with something on his mind. He read newspapers and monitored Fox News 24/7, trolling for issues.

The pastor would start a story at a regular volume, then crank it up a few decibels for dramatic effect before returning to his normal speaking voice. When he was specifying a sin, like a homosexual act, he'd grow more animated and make sure the words were clearly enunciated, not to be lost in the rest of the sentence. He was always very graphic, telling us that homosexuals were the type of people who would eat each other's feces, have sex with each other's feces, take "golden showers," and drink each other's semen. His sermon always connected a current event to a Bible story. First, he'd elaborate on a tale from the Old or New Testament, then demonstrate how it applied to his theme of the day. For example, he would equate George Bush with the Pharaoh of Egypt, saying that Bush viewed himself as America's best president, just as the Pharaoh thought he was the best leader of Egypt. He'd then draw parallels between all the bad things happening to America and the plagues that befell Egypt. I found his sermons fascinating, unlike any I'd ever heard at any of the churches I had been to. They were filled with the scary consequences of God's judgment. I loved that. I wanted to learn something new and be able to connect what the Bible was telling me to real-life situations. I thought that the pastor did that on a pretty large scale, and he drew parallels that I could follow.

Behind the pastor's podium was a big easel on which he'd display whatever current event was being discussed. If the subject was more specific than homosexuality or American politics, such as a recent natural disaster that had killed a lot of people or a catastrophic plane crash somewhere in the world, we'd learn that God wanted these people dead, and of course, they were in hell. The pastor had a lot more fervor and animation at the pulpit than he did away from it. Perhaps it was because all of his sermons were recorded and posted on the Internet, so he wasn't just preaching to us. Knowing that people outside of the church were going to be watching him, he wanted his sermons to be really dramatic, powerful, and memorable. If we were on an away picket, we'd take the time to listen to them on the Internet. They were organized by date on the website, so we could easily access the ones we wanted.

From the pulpit, the pastor would sometimes read us a letter or e-mail that had arrived at the church during the week from a complete stranger. The letter would confirm that we were not the only ones who thought God's wrath and violence against sinners were justified. Writers would congratulate the pastor for shining a light on these issues, saying the view of our church was correct and thanking us for having the courage to speak out against sins such as homosexuality. Sometimes they would have actually been in a crowd at a place where we had picketed, but hadn't had the courage to side with us. Even if it was a small voice somewhere, we had reached somebody.

During one sermon, the pastor read us a letter from someone

who had been homosexual and turned straight. The writer told us his life had been miserable until he heard our message and changed his sinning ways. Others told us how happy they were that we protested the Catholic Church on behalf of the victims of priest abuse.

There was a reason letters of gratitude were so rare. "There are only a few of God's people on earth who know the Truth," the pastor would say. That would explain why only one in a million letters we got would be a thank-you. The rest would be everything from threats on our lives to vile attacks on our souls. But that one thank-you would be enough for us to say, "Wow, someone gets it." Shirley would respond to the positive letters right away to show our appreciation for the endorsement.

Sometimes we'd have a follower who was rejuvenated by our message. He would join us for a Sunday service or a picket or two, and then he would fall away. We didn't mind if we never saw these people again. We were a very tight community, and we were spiritually connected to one another. We were not in need of any reinforcements.

After the pastor had finished his sermon, he would make his brief announcements. These were usually about local news events and the upcoming picket schedule. When they were finished, the service was officially over. At that point, we'd have a chance to greet the pastor and have a quick talk with him about anything we wanted. Megan, Rebekah, Jael, and some of the other girls would go up to the pulpit and hug their grandfather, but I preferred hanging back. He was so powerful that no matter how much I wanted him to think favorably of me, I'd inevitably tighten up when he was in my proximity.

For the rest of Sunday, we might picket again if there was something on the schedule. Otherwise, we'd do schoolwork, help out with jobs around the compound, or do something with our nuclear family. On the last Sunday of each month, we'd celebrate the birthdays of people who had been born that month. In good weather, the party was held in the yard, where we'd play volleyball and basketball; otherwise it was held in Shirley's basement. There was always lots of food and the singing of "Happy Birthday" to the guests of honor.

As I became more familiar with the pastor, I decided that the impression that most of the world had of him was wrong. I was aware of what people said about him, but he was not a vulgar, whacked-out, misanthropic crab. His truth was anchored in fundamental Christian theology, he didn't make it up as he went, and his passionate issue was that Christians underestimated the wrath of God. Within the church, the pastor was revered and respected by everybody.

I didn't know what the proper relationship I should have with him should be. He seemed so omniscient that I feared anything I said would sound dumb. I couldn't take my cues from his granddaughters, because as family members their rules would be different. I was worried that if I was too friendly, my behavior might be interpreted as disrespectful. If I was too detached, he might think I was bored or, worse, vain. I wasn't sure why I was scared to ask Megan, Rebekah, and Jael what they thought, but I couldn't. I just hoped and prayed that I was worthy to be in the church in the eyes of the pastor.

He was friendly to me, but not warm. "So, Lauren, how are you doing? How's everyone treating you?" he'd ask. "Do you like being here? Are you getting along well with the girls?" I felt mildly uncomfortable, but I thought he was genuine and sincere. One-on-one, he seemed gentle, humble, honest, and patient. Like the stereotypical gentle grandfather, he was very nonthreatening. He used big words and knew a lot of history and biblical concepts. Sometimes, I felt a little intimidated by his knowledge. He'd ask me a biblical question, and I would try to answer, but in my head, I worried that I was wrong.

I was probably being oversensitive, but I'd feel particularly awkward when the pastor would tell his biological grandchildren how much they meant to him right in front of me. "You're not going to leave me," he'd say, giving them a big embrace. I took these to be slights, a subliminal communication that I was an outsider. I was always on guard, wondering what he had heard people saying about me. Most cultures labeled people who talked about you behind your back as gossips, but in the church it was a way to keep people from straying toward evil. As time went on, the pastor warmed up to me. He would tell me I was like his real granddaughters, right there in his heart. Things like that made me feel much more included.

I could tell that the pastor's devotion to his church was genuine. He had founded the WBC when he was just twenty-six years old. The name he chose, Westboro Baptist Church, was a bit of a misnomer. The word *Baptist* in the title didn't mean it was aligned or associated with the Baptist world. Lots of Baptist churches were independent, because there were more personal freedoms outside it. Independence was good. The independent churches, usually more conservative and fundamental, could set up their own rules and govern themselves. I thought other Baptists must be terrified we'd be the bane of their faith. The disclaimer on the Primitive Baptist Church's website read "PB-Online and the Primitive Baptist Church do not recognize the ministry of 'pastor' Fred Phelps, nor do we have fellowship with the Westboro Baptist Church of Topeka, Kansas.... We find the actions of these people to be deplorable and against the very Scriptures they claim to believe."

As for the word *Westboro*, it was the name of a neighborhood that began just a block south of the church. It was a really cool residential area, filled with historic bungalows built in the 1920s and 1930s in the style of the famous "arts and crafts" movement. A local architect, L. F. Garlinghouse, had wanted to promote his home-building business by marketing floor plans to the bungalows in a catalog, so each month he'd put four or five floor plans into the catalog. The idea was that the rest of the schematic could be purchased if a homebuilder wanted that floor plan. He had a favorite designer who went around the country taking pictures of designs she liked. She brought them back to Topeka, the models were built, and the Westboro neighborhood was born.

The pastor's first church in Topeka was not the Westboro Baptist Church, where he gave his first sermon in November 1955. His first church had been the East Side Baptist Church, a traditional Baptist church across town. I heard a few competing stories about why he left, but whatever the true reason, he wasn't there long. Some members of the East Side congregation followed him, including two of our elders, Bill and Mary Hockenbarger. George Stutzman and his wife, whose name I never knew, were another couple who came with the pastor, although I never met either of them. Many of the East Siders who chose to follow him left his ministry pretty quickly. Only the Hockenbargers and George Stutzman remained. Even though his Westboro congregation was small, the few willing to give him a try believed in him. Then as now, his views were fundamental, extreme, and provocative; his sermons focused on scripture as it related to current events; and his presentation was always compelling and full of conviction.

I was in awe of the high standards the pastor set for himself and his commitment to his passions, especially to God. He had always been a high achiever. He once told us a story of how he had planned to attend the U.S. Military Academy, partly because his father had always wanted him to be a West Point cadet. To make that dream come true, he had worked hard at his public high school in Meridian, Mississippi. He made great grades, worked on the school newspaper, ran hurdles for the track team, was a star of the boxing club, played two instruments—the cornet and the bass horn—in the marching band, and belonged to the social fraternity. Not only that, he graduated sixth in his class at the age of sixteen. His focus and determination paid off, and he was accepted at West Point. However, under the Academy's rules, he couldn't actually matriculate until he turned seventeen. Around this time, the pastor had a huge change of direction and decided to pursue theology instead. He would have still been a teenager when he decided to go to Bob Jones College, a very strict, conservative Protestant college then in Cleveland, Tennessee; it's now called Bob Jones University and is located in South Carolina.

Students at Bob Jones were encouraged to do missionary work and plant evangelical churches in parts of the world that didn't have many, and the pastor said it was during a missionary trip to Utah with a friend that his life changed. During a tent revival there, he said the God of glory appeared to him, and he had his experience of grace. Whenever I heard stories of these kinds of spiritual awakenings in any of the elders, I could feel my insecurities coming back. Dad had had his own moment when he had gone to interview the pastor in Topeka for the first time. He had expected to find a snake oil salesman, but instead he found the truth about the Lord. I sometimes felt a little dejected that God hadn't come to me in such a singularly moving moment. Even though I had done my best to ignore Libby's comment that I didn't belong, I was still left with an insidious self-doubt that maybe she had a point: maybe I *was* unworthy.

Before the pastor's summer in Utah was over, he knew he

wanted to be ordained, so made his case before ten pastors at the First Baptist Church of Vernal, which had been sponsoring him, and he was baptized in a very cold mountain stream near Dinosaur National Monument in Utah. When he went back to Tennessee, the pastor was a seventeen-year-old minister, years younger than most.

The pastor stayed only one more semester at Bob Jones College. I'm not sure why, but he went to the Prairie Bible Institute in Alberta, Canada, next, then finally earned his theology degree from John Muir College in Pasadena, California. That was where he really started making sure he was loud and vocal enough to be noticed. He spent a lot of his free time preaching on the street corners of the city against the decadent behavior of students and teachers. His curbside preaching got him a cameo in *Time* magazine. The article that mentioned him was clipped, framed, and displayed in his office. The clipping was dated June 11, 1951, and titled "Repentance in Pasadena." I finished it with the conclusion that it didn't really have a bias either for or against the pastor. It said only that Fred Phelps spent a lot of his free time preaching against the decadent behavior of students and teachers, using the public sidewalks to condemn the weaknesses of profanity and filthy jokes. I thought the article was less about the pastor's values and more about his passion and his aggressive style of spreading his message. I realized that even then he had been willing to voice his opinion so boldly, whatever his audience thought of him. I was impressed that a person could be that fervent and courageous to speak his mind, even at the age of twenty-one.

From Pasadena, the pastor moved to Arizona to attend the Arizona Bible Institute. There, he met his future wife, Marge Simms, who was four years his senior but looked tiny next to him, at only four foot eleven compared to his six-foot-four frame. I really liked the very soft-spoken and kind Marge and enjoyed her company. The word was that she had been the pastor's one and only girl, and that he had never dated anybody else.

They were married in 1952 in Arizona. Within a year, the children started coming, one at a time for the next sixteen years. Fred Jr. was born in Arizona in 1953, and the rest were born in Topeka—Mark, Katherine, Margie, Shirley, Nathan, Jonathan, Rebekah, Elizabeth, Timothy, Dortha, Rachel, and finally Abigail in 1968. What's more, Marge didn't even start having children until she was twenty-eight.

I had never known a family with more than four kids and was amazed that anyone could raise that many children. Marge, one of nine children herself, said she raised hers with the same five rules that her own mother had used—keep the kids' faces clean, their hands clean, their clothes clean, the house clean, and feed them. She told me that in those days, she had two washing machines and two clothes dryers operating all day long. She did have the older children to help her with the smaller ones, but her biggest dread was that when one child became ill, all the rest would get sick as well.

From bits I heard, I assumed the huge Phelps clan had to live for quite a few years on very modest means. The pastor never had a big congregation, nor did he want one. But preaching didn't bring in enough money to support his family. I read somewhere that he sold vacuum cleaners and baby carriages door-to-door to make extra money in the lean years. I also heard that his children sold candy door-to-door after school and on weekends, from the age of five on up. The pastor would buy it wholesale and have them sell it retail, using the profits to pay the bills. He said he had never intended to be a minister for the salary, but preached only for the opportunity to spread the Word of God.

I thought that the amount of negative attention directed at him meant his message really did mess with the moral high ground of his sinning critics. Of course they were going to condemn him and call him a heretic and a lunatic. Even Jesus Christ had only a handful of believers in his lifetime. The pastor was only the messenger, no matter how unpopular the message. The words he spoke, which came off sounding spitted, violent, and despicable to the people not in the church, were all found in the Bible. Mainstream religion had so watered down God's wrath and guidance that the new myth was that God was a kind, benevolent presence and followers could do what they wanted. The pastor wanted that myth shattered. God was the One who elaborated on the cardinal sins and what would happen to the sinners.

There hadn't been any other pastor willing to tell the truth on a daily basis in the name of God. He certainly looked stern and angry when he was preaching, and he carried himself with a slouch, but that was because he was old. He really got himself worked up only when he needed to let God's people know they were disobedient. He didn't raise his voice when he was not picketing or preaching. Nobody in the WBC challenged the pastor, but we had no need to. He was our spiritual leader and was motivated only by our salvation.

If I was intimidated by the pastor, it was not out of fear but out of a sense of inferiority. To me, he was bigger than life. From my childhood in Florida and Kansas to my disrespectful, rebellious early teens, I could never have imagined myself so blessed as to be in the presence of and guided by such a holy man.

CHAPTER SEVEN

Cry aloud, spare not, lift up thy voice like a trumpet, and show my people their transgression, and the house of Jacob their sins.

—Isaiah 58:1

Although I had experienced the two WBC pickets in Jacksonville and New York prior to our move to Topeka, I had no idea how important this form of public activism was for the church. Picketing was the fundamental way to get God's Word to the heretics, and it was an activity with a higher priority than marrying and bearing children. There were daily pickets, noon pickets, and out-of-town pickets. There were bigger pickets that took lots of advance planning, and small ones, like the biweekly ones outside our school, which could be organized in very little time. The picket schedule would go up on the church's website, but it was also e-mailed out to families, so that everyone knew who was supposed to be where, and when. We didn't care if people outside of our church knew our schedule. We weren't hiding anything from anyone.

The pastor and the church hadn't started picketing until 1991, only ten years before we had moved to Topeka. Before then, the pastor had spread his message through faxes. He'd mass-mail them out the same way he did now, elaborating on some story that interested him and faxing them by the thousands on the church's letterhead. He'd write about current events, scripture quotes, new sign ideas, anything that came to mind as something relevant.

The WBC was extremely proud of its first picket ever, a May 1991 protest that took place in Gage Park in Topeka. It had started with Shirley. She said that she and some of her kids were in the park, a public space about a half mile from the church, when a homosexual who was also in the park tried to lure her son away from her. She was horrified. Gage Park, one of Topeka's largest at 160 acres, with a zoo, a miniature fifteen-inch-gauge railroad, an outdoor theater, and a beautiful rose garden, was getting disgusting.

The pastor, who always had a flair for provocative language, put the battle cry into a flyer he passed out in the park after Shirley's brush with danger: GAGE PARK—SODOMITE RAT'S NEST. Then he launched his Great Gage Park Decency Drive. For the first time, the WBC carried picket signs denouncing homosexuals. The Gage Park pickets became weekly events. By the time my family got to Topeka, the group was still picketing the park weekly.

The Gage Park pickets made the church visible, and the antihomosexual message attracted people who felt the same way. In fact, for quite a while, lots of Topekans outside the church supported the Decency Drive and joined in the pickets. They related to the pastor's printed literature about the situation, which read "Can God-fearing Christian families picnic or play touch football there without fear of contracting AIDS? HELL NO!" The handout described lots of upsetting, sinful behavior: "open fag rectal intercourse in public restrooms, in the rose garden, in the rock garden, in the theatre, in the rainforest, in the swimming pool, on the softball fields, on the swing sets, or the train—it's everywhere..." The language was so graphic that many couldn't help but feel disgusted by the situation. Maybe the pastor was too hard-core for his sympathizers, though, because by the time I joined the church, nobody in the public joined our ranks anymore.

The early church pickets started getting local press, and the pastor loved it. He showed up regularly on the front pages of the city's newspapers beaming his huge ear-to-ear smile. I saw lots of clippings from those days, with him wearing his white cowboy hat and holding an American flag upside down. So successful were the pickets that the church moved to local businesses next. The pastor chose the ones he thought deserved attention, like the ones that employed homosexuals. The Vintage Restaurant on SW Gage Boulevard was a famous target in our picket history. It was a popular dining spot in town, with lots of regulars from the political realm. Jonathan Phelps, Jael's father, knew the then manager, and he knew her sexual orientation. He also knew that the owner of the restaurant was Jewish. The WBC thought God hated Jews almost as much as He hated homosexuals, and the pastor never hid his opinion that it had been the Jews who had killed Jesus. The church started picketing the restaurant nightly with signs about God hating fags and Jews, and continued to do so for three years.

Everybody in the church knew the date March 26, 1993. That was the day a riot broke out on the sidewalk outside the Vintage Restaurant. Eight WBC members were beaten bloody and briefly hospitalized. The pastor pointed to the riot as a defining moment of our torment and our endurance. He blamed the police for allowing the riot and conspiring with the sodomites. Once again, the church prevailed, showing the world that no one could trample on the saints, the Word of God, or His judgments. We all celebrated the martyrdom of God's prophets every year on March 26, the day the membership stood up for God. The pastor used enlarged photos of the victims pasted to the picket signs at the anniversary protest outside the restaurant.

It was during the same month that the pastor took his pickets out of state for the first time. The first event was in Washington, D.C., a Gay Pride march similar to the one my father had videographed in 2000 for his documentary. The pastor got lots of national press there, and he began looking for big events outside of Topeka that could get the WBC in the news. He really was a master at getting himself into the spotlight; but it wasn't about him, it was about serving God. For a church this small to be recognized around the nation was quite remarkable.

However, receiving so much attention had a downside. I heard a lot about one of the bigger criminal attacks against the church, a pipe bomb explosion outside Shirley's house on August 20, 1995. Even more terrifying, her newborn baby, Gabriel, was asleep upstairs. Thankfully, no one was hurt, but Shirley's fence and the van parked in her driveway were damaged. The pastor insisted the bombers were the children of Satan. It turned out the bombers had thought Shirley's house was the pastor's house, and they had been retaliating against the pastor for his antihomosexual picketing at Washburn University and the law school. The perpetrators turned out to be two local men in their early twenties, and were turned in to police by a friend of theirs. One of the men was convicted of a Class E arson felony and sentenced to sixteen days in jail, which he could serve on weekends. He was also ordered to pay $1,751 in restitution and do one hundred hours of community service. The pastor still became outraged at the leniency of the judgment every time he talked about it. He thought trying to silence the saints was despicable, but the cowards would get their due in the judgment of God. The church's press release addressing the attack was prominently displayed on our website.

By 1995, the majority of the pickets were at the funerals of people who had died of AIDS. These were the ideal picket venues. The church could make its point that homosexual sinners died horrible, untimely deaths, and that God punished the dead and their loved ones with the judgment they deserved. Because these pickets seemed cruel to people who didn't follow the Word of God, they really grabbed attention and provoked angry responses. The press took note, and the pickets began to put the church on the national map. Matthew Shepard's funeral was where the whole world really began to know about the WBC, and the pastor couldn't have been more delighted to be so vilified. That was the way God wanted it.

The church's presence at the funeral made Michael Moore, the filmmaker, so angry that he began a countercrusade in favor of gay rights. He would occasionally show up at a picket with a busload of gay people, some of them dressed in drag as female cheerleaders. The bus, nicknamed the "Sodomobile," was painted pink and decorated with slogans such as BUGGERS ON BOARD and SODOM IS FOR LOVERS. At one picket in Kansas City, the bus came screeching around the corner and stopped in front of the pastor, who was dressed in a blue suit, red tie, enormous wraparound mirrored sunglasses, and white cowboy hat. The group got off the bus and mixed with the picketers, including the pastor's daughter Abigail and several children.

The pastor, waving an upside-down American flag on a long pole, watched in amusement as a busload of homosexuals danced to music blasting from the bus's sound system. Some of the men were using the top of the bus for a stage, and others used the sidewalk to perform a choreographed number they had clearly rehearsed. It was like watching the '70s pop group the

Village People dance to their most famous song, "Y.M.C.A." People from the bus were trying to intimidate the pastor by getting close and in his face when the pastor told them they had better not touch him. "You are heading to hell in a faggot handbasket," he said with a friendly grin. "If you keep living like you are living, you are going to die and split hell wide open."

Meanwhile, Michael Moore and a few others were badgering Abigail. When Moore asked her to sing "Amazing Grace" with them, she joked, "Who do you think I am? Karen Carpenter?" Moore and his group broke into a rendition of the famous Carpenters' song "Sing," and Abigail joined in, improvising some of the lyrics with "God Hates Fags." The picketers took to the church truck pretty soon after that, so Michael Moore declared victory in making them retreat.

He was incorrect. The church never looked at it that way. If picketers retreated, they did so because their job was done. We never lost at any protest, regardless of the counterprotest. We were preaching only to who was right in front of us. In Moore's case, the church knew he'd blast his video nationwide, thereby furthering its message. It was a win-win situation, as far as the pastor was concerned.

I never encountered Michael Moore, but from the first day we arrived in Topeka, Dad and I hit the ground picketing. Taylor was ten now, and she was really embracing the church's message, too. She was so happy that Dad was including her. It took Mom a little longer to warm up to the idea of being out in public like that, but after a couple of months she also joined in. After her initial feelings of intimidation around Shirley, she'd succumbed to her star power, and I could see on her face how excited she was to be around Shirley. If they were on the same picket, and Mom got to walk with her, she would glow. People considered being around Shirley a privilege, because they themselves became godlier in her presence.

The pastor was always reading the paper to see who or what we would picket next. But once he made his choice, Shirley took over the organization of the details. She would post the out-of-town picket schedule on the church's shared network, and in turn we would put our names under the ones that interested us. My new friends encouraged me to choose the same ones in hopes that we would be together. Once Shirley's decision was made, it was final, and she'd blast a church e-mail with the names of those who had been chosen. When I saw my name on a picket schedule, I felt I was like Elijah or Moses spreading the Word of God. There was status to being a picketer, also. It meant God was sending you somewhere and the angels were watching you. The minimum age and the number of picketers varied. For out-of-town pickets, she'd usually limit the number to five to keep the expenses down, and the minimum age was sixteen. In local pickets, though, we could have all eighty members, and kids as young as five were allowed to participate. It may sound small, but eighty people spread out along the sidewalk, each holding as many as four signs, looked impressive.

The protests usually were no more than an hour in length, and everybody was expected to be on his best behavior for the entire duration. There were plenty of rules about where to stand, how to hold your sign, and how to react to the people who insulted us. The young people especially had to make sure they were always holding their signs correctly. We had to turn them for the oncoming traffic, which meant adjusting where we were facing when the traffic lights changed color. If we were not paying attention, or if we were blocking foot traffic, we would be scolded by an elder.

Because so many of the church members were lawyers, by default we always had one or two with us on a picket to handle the permits and interface with the police. Shirley was diligent in ensuring that we were in possession of all the necessary permits, so that we could never be denied access to an event on some legal grounds. She also knew how to pick prime locations.

The biggest job belonged to the videographer, who had to make sure the camera was with us and fully charged in order to document the protests as well as any reaction from the crowd. Any physical assault or particularly ugly verbal tirade against us would also earn a place in our video collection on godhatesfags.com to show the world our martyrdom. Every moment 360 degrees around the picket line had to be recorded in case anyone, from the onlookers to the police, violated our right to free speech or caused us harm, because we would need the video evidence to win in court. If the videographer missed a shot, there would be an outcry from the other members of "Oh, my God! How could you miss something that important?" I dreaded the assignment for this reason.

Everybody else had a role at the picket, too. There was the sign bag holder, who made sure all the right signs for an out-of-town event were properly packaged. The sign bags were huge, literally the size of the signs. They were probably portfolio cases originally made for artist's paintings and drawings, and had zippers on both ends and handles at the top. We used signs without stakes or sticks on our out-of-town pickets, so that nobody could accuse us of using the picket sticks to hit or intimidate someone. We'd hold up as many signs as we could handle, giving the appearance that the number of people on the picket line was a lot greater than it really was.

Another job was that of the music book carrier. Oftentimes, we needed to defuse violence directed toward us, so we would sing loudly, like a church choir. We knew most of the songs by heart, but the music book carrier would still pass out sheet music for us to hold. One of the jobs I really tried to avoid was the "map-quester." The person with that responsibility always seemed to get reamed out. If you told the driver the wrong direction, or indicated the wrong place to turn, you were in serious trouble and everybody would start yelling at you. I was thankful when the church finally got GPS systems installed in the vans.

Watching the kids was my favorite job. I liked keeping them out of harm's way. Out-of-town pickets were generally not as predictable as local ones, so whoever was watching the kids had to keep them sheltered. Even if we spread them out, we'd try to have a couple of adults with anyone under ten. Of course, a lot of the pickets were restricted to members over eighteen, with the safety of the kids in mind. The pastor liked to get the out-of-town communities stirred up beforehand, so posting our upcoming pickets online to let residents know we were coming there was effective in making this happen. Our detractors might then blast threatening e-mails to the church office, and if there were enough threats, Shirley would pull the kids from the picket altogether.

Shirley was the memo queen. She would send out the memo detailing everybody's role, what time to be at the driveway, what to bring, and what to wear. If you were late or you didn't bring the sign bag or the video camera, you got chewed out. She was also the person who reminded us about crucial picketing protocol, such as never fighting back no matter how low some other people's behavior might become.

Megan was Shirley's right-hand person, and among other things, she was always the keeper of the receipts. For anything we spent money on—gas, food, lodging, rental cars—we gave her the receipt so that she could record it and we could write off the expenses on our taxes. Because we were a religious in-stitution, our expenses were fully tax-deductible. Megan also helped us prepare songs and chants for pickets. There were al-ways new ones to learn and practice. We had lots of parodies of patriotic songs, where we had replaced the traditional lyrics of America's favorite tunes with our own lyrics, written mostly by my father. Instead of "God Bless America," we sang "God Hates America." In "America the Beautiful," we substituted "O beau-tiful for spacious skies" with "O wicked land of sodomites." He actually wrote a couple of songs, too, including one about the Catholic Church that described priests raping little boys. We held rehearsals in the evenings after Bible study. There were some amazing voices among the members. Besides my father, Shirley, Margie, Abigail, and Sara, Libby's older sister, were wonderful a cappella singers.

Songs and picket signs were critical to delivering our message the best way possible. The signs, especially, were works of love. The pastor was the only person allowed to make them or decide what they were going to say. He would come up with the slogan and then put the message on the signboard by hand. He was particular about every curve in the lettering, cutting out the letters from construction paper with a utility knife and then attaching them to the poster. It was a long, labor-intensive process. Making even a single sign would take all day. The pas-tor soon recognized how creative Dad was and allowed him to have a small role on the sign-making team. He had seen his documentary, so he knew that he was creative in the film arena. The movie actually captured the pastor saying, "You are go-ing to make them real mad at you, Steve." The pastor thought Dad's depiction of the church was pretty true and accurate, and the members were all pleased with it as well.

When the pastor saw that Dad was able to render signs on

a computer instead of using paper and pencil, he asked Dad to show him what he could do. His system was much more efficient—he was able to create four brand-new signs in a day, as opposed to the pastor's one-a-day system. The beauty of the method was that if a current event occurred that necessitated a new sign, my dad was able to print several of them in a matter of hours.

The pastor was getting older, so he seemed open and agreeable to having my father assist with the task. Dad knew how to use Photoshop, so he could design the signs exactly to the pastor's liking. He and the pastor would then score and fold the prints and paste them onto the signs. Dad's role on the sign team became a source of great pride for my family. Sometimes, he'd let Taylor and me help create them. He'd print the various elements, and we'd all piece them together. Then we would wrap each one with packing material in a certain way so they wouldn't get ruined in the rain or snow.

It seemed to me like my father was always trying to impress the other church members. Dad had thrown himself completely into helping out with church pickets and propaganda. Flattered that they liked his creativity, he took on more and more of the artistic projects. At the pickets, he was loud, boisterous, and condescending, but also quick-witted, drawing the attention of both the media and people on the street. My mother was typically quiet and kept to herself, happy to let my father be the star, but even she began actively participating in meetings. She was still trying to be on her best behavior, of course, so she didn't dare step out of line and try to assert her opinion.

Pickets and protests were our chance to distinguish ourselves from the rest of the world, which was our constant driving force. When we staged protests, we were proving that we were right and righteous, and everyone else was wrong and clueless.

It was still a little confusing to me, because I didn't always feel right, but it was also a powerful feeling to be one of God's chosen ones. There was a sense of gratification in telling all of these sinners what they were doing wrong. I struggled with the contradiction of being humble, as the Bible teaches, with the ongoing pressure to separate and elevate ourselves from the masses. The church's teachings didn't always make sense, but I learned quickly that questioning our beliefs would not win me any friends within the church, so in the beginning, I did my best to keep my doubts private.

We picketed every day of the week, beginning on Sundays. Every Sunday before our own 11 a.m. service, we'd divide up into four teams, each of which would cover three churches in the area. We rotated the schedule. There were four hundred churches in Topeka, so we'd be sure to target the ones with the biggest congregations the most frequently. Some of the signs were giant, six to twelve feet high. Some of them we carried on wood sticks, but others we just held up at chest level. The messages we carried depended on our audience. For the church pickets, our signs would have messages like FALSE PROPHET, YOUR PASTOR IS LYING, YOU ARE GOING TO HELL, GOD HATES YOU, and LYING FALSE PROPHETS. We had special signs reserved just for the Catholic Church: FAG PRIESTS, ALL PRIESTS ARE PEDOPHILES, PEDOPHILE ENABLERS, and PRIESTS RAPE BOYS were the staples for those protests. The Catholic churches were the biggest and fanciest, and they were always crowded, with people of all ages, including families all dressed up, arriving at the cathedral doors in droves.

When we picketed their churches, the Catholics would shoo us with their hands and tell us to go home so they could enjoy their holy day. Theirs were my favorite houses of worship to picket because of the Catholics' hypocrisy. I found their disgust of us so ironic. I couldn't believe the audacity of these people who chose to ignore widespread crimes committed by their own priests against their own children. The documentaries and news stories about the huge number of victims had been all over the media. Parents were concerned about the sex offenders in their communities, but they didn't seem to care much about their deviant priests. To me, raping little boys was a lot more heinous than being homosexual.

Picketing was the way the church spread the word that sinners were responsible for whatever befell them, from small-scale tragedies to outright catastrophes. Because there were so many people who wondered why God had allowed such horrible things to happen on earth—why a single tornado had killed more than a hundred people, why a dozen coal miners had died in a mine shaft collapse, why a gunman had taken several lives in a mall—the WBC provided the answer. Homosexuality was at the crux of His anger. We had gotten so far away from God's message of obedience that we had it coming. Damnation in hell was a foregone conclusion.

The church was not looking for converts, penitents, or salvation seekers. We were not "witnessing" in the traditional sense of spreading the word, nor were we trying to change anybody's mind about what the Bible said. We weren't even trying to recruit anyone to our church. Instead, we delivered a message that we knew would be hated, and we thought it was our God-given duty to do so.

Very rarely did we encounter people who could challenge us on the specifics of the Bible, but when we did, we treated them respectfully. We all carried electronic Bibles, palm-size e-readers of the traditional King James translation, which we'd take out in order to very gently show them the verses that supported each of the points they chose to contend. Nothing anyone screamed at us shocked us in any way. We had heard every in-sult, projected in every tone and volume, before.

Others questioned us about who we were really representing. "Are you communists? What are you, Muslim?" people would ask. We'd say we were children of God who chose to obey His Word.

With freedom of speech on our side, the pastor staged pickets that were designed to generate a lot of anger. The way he saw it, whichever events would incite the most fury were the most important. Some places such as Gage Park, the Capitol, the city newspaper, and the courthouse had been picketed weekly for decades. Other situations called for a onetime rally, or maybe an anniversary picket, depending on the occasion. On St. Patrick's Day, we'd picket the annual downtown parade. On the Fourth of July, we'd head to Gage Park. On Christmas morning we'd picket the tons of churches that had made Shirley's list of wor-thy targets, based primarily on when we had last paid them a visit.

Shirley made sure we all understood that not following the rules at public protests could have legal implications against us. For example, when we were actively protesting, we were told to not step outside of our barricaded zone, stay longer than our permit allowed, or get into any physical altercations. Some cops were more contentious than others and seemed as if they would love to arrest us if they could find lawful grounds. They would act outside of their authority, telling us to put our signs away or we would be arrested. Sometimes, they would tell us not to speak at all or they would arrest us for "fighting words."

"What's the reason?" one of us would ask.

"Just do it, or I will arrest you!" would be the curt reply.

Because every picket had an attorney present, our lawyer would step forward and confront the officer. "We have the permit, we have already contacted you, and you are violating your duties," our representative would say, trying to be reasonable.

A lot of times our signs would target fag-enabling cops, and the officers wouldn't be able to control themselves, causing them to abuse their authority. If it became apparent that they were not going to back down, we'd have to pack up our signs and leave, but we'd use legal means to address their unconstitutional treatment of us later. One of our attorneys would inevitably file a lawsuit on our behalf.

Sometimes we would get support from cops at a protest, who would thank us and even express an interest in our religion. "I have never seen such a strong church who knows the Bible like you do," some of them might comment. Other people would also say things that would confirm we were legitimate and not crazy, that we had intelligence and Bible knowledge.

Despite the fact that our picketing often had risks, most of us weren't afraid. Mothers with new babies would go to the local pickets, bringing their toddlers strapped into strollers with them. Little kids held the smaller, lighter signs. Old men and ladies, midlifers, teenagers, and younger kids often shared the same small piece of sidewalk. It was not unheard of to see nine- or ten-year-olds on the edge of the sidewalk next to a street of high-density traffic holding up one large sign. Sometimes, people driving by would scream out "child abusers," referring to the little ones so close to traffic. One time, Shirley's six-year-old son, Gabe, was struck in the head by a fast food restaurant drink hurled from a passing car during a picket we were staging along a busy road in Topeka. Shirley cleaned him off, hugged him, and made sure he was okay, but the picket continued.

I truly loved picketing with my friends. We thrived on being productive, upstanding kids who used our time and money to make a difference, and who made our parents proud. If there was an early morning coffee run on a picket, we'd be the first to volunteer. I never felt obligated or pressured to be on the picket line. I thoroughly enjoyed participating and did so freely and willingly. The enthusiasm and intensity on the line provided us all with an uneasy thrill. We actually flourished as the sentiment against us grew. When we were on the picket line, we were so empowered that we became almost possessed. It was as though God was with us, and His presence manifested itself in a passion that was visible in our eyes.

As I became more acclimated to the church culture, I was eligible to attend out-of-state pickets. In time, I went to WBC protests in nearly every state, from New York to Florida and from Alaska to Massachusetts. Picketing at all these locations was very expensive. I had to pay my own way to get to them, but that was part of the responsibility of earning my place. I was able to make some money working off the books babysitting the kids in the church and helping Shirley at the law office. Our travel budget was huge. Shirley told any reporters who asked that the WBC spent almost a quarter of a million dollars a year.

To get to a picket, we would prefer to drive to save both money and hassle. We'd usually send one van full of church members. Almost every family had an eight-passenger Honda Odyssey minivan with a drop-down DVD player for entertainment. Whether we were driving or flying, there was rarely time for sightseeing or exploring. When we did fly, sometimes we'd stay on the ground only long enough to stage the scheduled picket, then fly home the same evening, which cost us as much as $400 each for a round-trip ticket. Sometimes, we'd stay overnight, which was fabulous. In the motels, my girlfriends and I would share our own room. We were now too old for the conventional childhood sleepover, so our picket nights on the road were our new teenage version of that social event. During the day, we were single-mindedly picketing, with all the procedures that entailed. When we'd get to our destination, we'd unpack our signs, picket, stir up the audience, which gave us great satisfaction, videotape the event from start to finish, pack our signs, and move to the next destination.

I was too young to attend one picket we staged in Canada—only people eighteen and older were invited—but I heard about it later. The picketers were attacked shortly after they crossed over the border into Canada, and all their signs were ruined or ripped to shreds. Everybody had to make improvised signs out of cardboard or poster board, which they bought at a local CVS. When the group returned to Kansas, the pastor was very inflamed about the treatment they had received. "I think we are done in Canada. We have already told them so many times and they don't get it. So we won't give them any more warnings," he told us in the next sermon he delivered. However, he later changed his mind and went on to stage more pickets in Canada, despite the Canadian border patrol's attempts to confiscate our signs at the border.

On the church's godhatestheworld.com website, the pastor talked about another incident, in which members had been arrested at the International Airport in Ottawa on their way to picket Canada's Parliament, which was passing legislation in favor of homosexuality. At another picket in Alberta, Royal Canadian Mounted Police ordered picketers to put away their GOD HATES FAGS signs, saying it was against Canada's law to incite violence against an identifiable group. Still, the WBC members managed to burn the Canadian flag in protest of the country's approval of same-sex marriage. Back in Topeka, the pastor raised the Canadian flag in the upside-down position, where it joined the American flag on the pole outside the church. Canada was now an equally doomed nation.

The pastor believed that we, as God's representatives, were doing a community service by spreading our message there. The places that we selected to be picketed were going to be graced with a visit from God's messengers. The people we were picketing didn't necessarily see it that way. We were taking the time, money, and effort to go there with a very important warning, but they looked at us as the enemy. We didn't care. Our primary motivation was to let people know God hated them, but we weren't trying to convince them we were right. Time was running out, so even if we had traveled a long distance so that only one person in the crowd might change his heart, it was worth it. We weren't inviting anyone to join us. We *were* encouraging everybody to see God's truth. Someone who we would never see again might come away from an encounter with us with a new awareness of the wrath of God. However, if we were done with you and weren't coming to your city or your country anymore, then there was no more hope for your city, nation, or continent. You were even more doomed than you had been before.

Lots of times, people would stage counterprotests, some of which I actually found really funny. GOD HATES FIGS was one sign we would see at college campuses. People holding those signs said the message was also from scripture—in Matthew 21:18–21, Jesus cursed a fig tree, which made it wither and die. Other times, homosexual counterprotesters would engage in simulated sex acts right in front of us. They'd tongue-kiss and embrace, and practically have sex within inches of us. We were trained to be really unflappable about it, and sometimes we'd joke around right with them. On occasion, we'd put false notices about future pickets on our website, ones that we had no intention of staging, just to get counterprotesters to use their resources going somewhere we wouldn't be.

We were expected to be cool and collected at all times, in any scenario. There was no official training in how to behave, but we were told it was imperative to defuse a situation that was getting out of hand. If someone wanted to talk, we knew it was okay to engage him in conversation, but if he started to argue, we were supposed to ignore him. We learned by trial and error on the picket lines. We didn't shy away from any passersby who wanted to mix it up with us. We always tried to be friendly to the people who talked to us, because we didn't hate them—God did. One of our attorneys was always there to guide us through a heated moment. "Don't say anything, record everything," he or she would remind us.

The first time I saw a weapon was during a picket in Kansas City, Missouri. We were outside the Kemper Arena, where Cher, one of the world's most popular singers but, more important, a celebrity mother of a lesbian, was giving a sold-out performance on her Farewell Tour. Toward the end of the picket, a woman came up to us flashing a knife and threatening us. We were only a group of five: four church members in their midtwenties and sixteen-year-old me. James Hockenbarger, who worked as a prison guard back in Topeka, was able to talk her down while the rest of us headed to our car. In that instant, I realized that the weapon had been flashed because of our message, but I felt more power than fear.

Another time, we were at a regular weekly picket of a favorite target when a truck drove slowly by us, then circled the parking lot and came back. The driver flashed a gun, then started driving toward us fast, yelling out the window that we were Communists and Nazis. We were used to people yelling and driving fast, and our tactic was to ignore people to show them that they were not going to get a rise out of us. But when we saw he had a gun, it was a bit shocking, and someone made the executive decision to cut the picket short and pack up.

Over the years, we had Gatorade bottles thrown at us, BB guns shot at us, and people threaten us with guns and knives. A lot of people drove their cars recklessly toward us, heading first in our direction before swerving away. But still, none of those things scared me. I believed that God would protect us in all circumstances as long as we obeyed and held those signs.

Something did happen at a picket at Washburn University that caught me completely off guard and made me more fearful at these kinds of events. It was one of our typical pickets, where we had about thirty members spread out along the sidewalk for two or three city blocks. We were holding tall wooden signs bearing the usual messages: FAG ENABLER SCHOOL, YOU ARE GOING TO HELL, and GOD HATES FAG ENABLERS. The signs were directed mostly at the cars driving by, but there were also a few pedestrians walking along the sidewalk. I was situated in the middle of the picket near Rebekah, Jael, and Megan. Typically, the teenagers carried the largest number of signs or the really big ones.

On this particular day, Bill Hockenbarger, one of our oldest members at almost eighty and a member of the WBC since the 1950s, was standing near his wife on the far side of the picket. Suddenly, I heard fellow members shouting my name. I was the videographer that day, and they needed me. "Lauren! Get down here and film!" they yelled. I couldn't see what was going on, so I handed off my sign and darted down the picket line with the camcorder. I heard the church members yelling, "Call the police! Get off of him! Cowards! God will punish you for this!" But I still didn't know the extent of the problem. All I could see were college kids, crouched over and pummeling someone on the ground.

Soon, the men ran down the picket line to the scene, scaring off the college kids. I finally saw Bill lying on the grass with his face covered in blood and one of his eyes swollen shut. I burst into tears. How dare someone beat up an old man! He was an elderly gentleman exercising his right to freedom of religion and freedom of speech. I knew we angered people, but that didn't mean they could physically assault someone for his beliefs. That was truly against the law and against any ethical standard. Denying one person's right to free speech was essentially denying that right to everybody who takes that freedom for granted. We saw and heard things all the time we objected to, but we never resorted to violence. I felt knots in my stomach that somebody had dared to mess with us on such a cowardly level and that they had then run away. But I knew God would have the final judgment on these bullies. We were God's only people.

I was on the picket line because I wanted to please God. These people so upset at us were not Him and had no power over my soul. I didn't take anything they said to me personally. They said horrible things: "ugly bitch," "ugly virgin," "jealous whore," or "miserable lesbian." They were just validating what I had been taught: that prophets are often abused. As the pastor said, "If you're preaching the truth of God, people are going to hate you. Nobody has the right to think he's preaching the truth of God unless people hate him for it. All the prophets were treated that way."

Closer to home, though, things were more peaceful. The neighbors on our block who weren't in the church never harassed us, usually preferring to ignore us. They knew that our right to free speech was protected under the First Amendment. Plus, when we weren't picketing, we didn't seek any attention at all. Once, our signboard in front of the church was defaced with "God Hates the Phelps" in permanent paint and a couple of times people put bullet holes in it, but none of this scared me. If God wanted something to happen to any of us, then it was His will. The pastor installed security cameras and left it at that. Anyone could find us. The address of the church, as well as the addresses of the families in the congregation, was available on the Internet or in the Topeka phone directory. People strongly opposed to us even posted compiled lists of our names, addresses, and phone numbers on their own websites in order to facilitate pranks and harassment by our detractors.

But we weren't trying to hide behind high, thick compound walls or establish an isolated settlement in the desert. God was on our side. He protected us, and that was all the protection we needed. We were God's gifts on earth, His messengers and His angels.

CHAPTER EIGHT

But they mocked the messengers of God, and de-
spised his words, and misused his prophets, until
the wrath of the Lord arose against his people, till
there was no remedy.

—2 Chronicles 36:16

In August 2001, I entered Topeka West High School filled with
optimism. The school was just past the enormous Mount Hope
Cemetery, about two miles from my house. In the month since
our family had arrived, I had become close enough to my three
best friends that we had affectionate nicknames for each other.
I was called La, Jael was Jay, Megan was Meg, and Rebekah was
Bekah. At Topeka West, Jael and I were going into eleventh
grade, Megan was going into tenth, and Bekah was going to be
a freshman. The school had about eleven hundred students in
the four grades, so Jael and I were with almost three hundred
other juniors.

Having friends gave me confidence as I returned to public
school for the first time in ten months, but the transition was
still challenging. Everybody knew who the Phelps girls were,
since they even picketed the high school. Therefore, not only
was I a curiosity as the "new girl from Florida," but I was also
associated with the WBC, which came with its own negative
presumptions and prejudices about me.

As much as I put my trust in God to help me navigate the

first few days of school, I put equal trust in my friends. The four of us never took the bus, choosing instead to have Megan drive us in one of the Phelps-Ropers' cars. We were exclusive and inseparable, from our studying to cross-country running to weekend amusements. My first week at Topeka West, I ran into one of my old elementary school friends from Lawrence in the hall. I was really happy to see her until Megan let me know I shouldn't associate with her anymore, saying, "She's a whore." I avoided her, and eventually she got the hint.

It didn't take me long to adopt the same mind-set as my new clique, that anyone who was not from our church was confused and had been brought up wrong. The Phelps girls had the advantage of being born and raised in the church, however, so they hadn't been putting themselves ahead of God all those years during which I hadn't even known about His fire. I hid my fear that I would be rejected by them since my upbringing had been flawed. I was joining a righteous club of His elite, and with that came the panic that I could be cast out at any time. I was so outnumbered by blood relatives of the pastor's—including Libby, whose doubts about me were no secret—that despite their reassurances, I'd still sometimes feel paralyzed by a sense of overwhelming inadequacy. I'd think I was like the wicked, with no purpose and not serving a good, truthful, or obedient life. I had no specific reason to feel this way, but I'd just feel doomed. I made it my mission to work on improving myself so much that I'd never fall out of their favor.

The Phelps girls had similar characteristics—clear, fair skin; wide, toothy smiles; and high, chiseled cheekbones. Megan was beautiful, with gorgeous, dark, curly hair that fell right past her shoulders. No one would have guessed that she wasn't allowed to cut it, since you couldn't tell how long it was unless it was wet. At five-nine, she was three inches taller than me. She was one of the prettier girls in our foursome, a spitting image of Shirley as a young woman, with piercing blue eyes and a slender face. She had an outgoing personality and thrived on being in the spotlight, the perfect character assets for her in her role as the junior spokesperson for the WBC.

Bekah was also tall, slender, and athletic. She was pretty in a plain way, but not as dazzling as Megan. Her straight blonde hair was down to her waist, but she had a lot of split ends that just kept splitting, keeping it from getting exceptionally long. Bekah was more sheepish than Megan and didn't carry herself as confidently, either, seemingly resigned to being her sister's runner-up.

Jael, the tallest in our group, had dark brown hair that she liked to wear in a tight braid. She was a warm person with a great sense of humor, and the two of us hit it off the moment we met. Like me, she had a bit of a paranoid side. We both understood predestination—that we were either hell-bound or we weren't—but we had in the back of our minds that we could fall from grace at any instant. Jael was particularly worried about timing. She was convinced that God was returning any day now. If you're not careful, He will come when you are in a bad spot, she'd say. That freaked me out. I'd say to myself, *If the Lord comes tonight, I am doomed and going to hell forever.* It was not that I had done anything in particular that was bad. I just didn't think I was worthy of the glorious kingdom of heaven yet, whether I was elected or not.

My friends and I dressed like all the other teenagers at school. We shopped at the malls and wore clothes that were in style. Megan dressed more provocatively than the rest of us. Our mothers looked down on wearing anything revealing, tight, short, or low-cut, but in my opinion, Megan's standards were questionable. Shirley never seemed aware that Megan's clothes would have been unacceptable on another WBC girl. Megan would wear something kind of risqué and then would complain about the attention she got from boys, because she knew male attention was against the rules. All of us were as fashionable as the rest of the girls in our high school. Really, the only thing that distinguished us from the general population was the length of our hair.

I was surprised that the environment at school wasn't as tense as I thought it would be. One reason was because our classmates had become somewhat desensitized to us. They'd have their chance to berate us when we took them on in our heated, biweekly school pickets, but otherwise they basically ignored us. Two lunch periods a week, the Phelps girls and I would go to Megan's car, get our signs, and start our twenty-minute protest outside the school building. Everybody knew one another, so sometimes it was really odd. One minute, I'd be in math class sharing calculus problems with the kids in the class, and the next minute I'd be picketing with Megan, Bekah, and Jael, and our classmates would be flipping us off, cursing and yelling that God didn't hate America, that God loved America. They'd call us whores and throw their lunch trash at us. I thought it was hilarious. They didn't realize God was on our side. Afterward, we'd put our signs back in the car and head to our next class. The three days we weren't picketing the high school, we went off campus for lunch. We never ate in the cafeteria, preferring to get fries and chicken nuggets at Burger King or Wendy's rather than sit with everyone else.

The other reason there wasn't much tension at school was that we were such capable students. The pastor's grandchildren and I were all very academically inclined and always at the very top of the class. With well-rounded insights into lots of different subjects, we could not be accused of being brainwashed or being bumbling idiots. If anything, we were just the opposite.

I spent a lot of time on my homework, because getting good grades was a high priority. My dad would look over the papers and homework that Taylor and I had completed, making suggestions and corrections where he thought they were needed. Unlike the experience of many American teenagers, our culture actually embraced bragging about our accomplishments and our grades. We thrived on knowing the headlines in the news and talking about them in a way that was above everyone else in class, demonstrating how savvy and worldly we were. On the rare occasion that one of us did get a bad grade on an assignment, Shirley would come to the school and speak to the teacher about it, getting in his or her face.

From the time any Phelps kid entered kindergarten, she made sure every teacher they had knew who she was. When she complained, she used very litigious language. If she thought a child had been graded unfairly, she'd send e-mails, using the term "religious discrimination" to threaten lawsuits. Copies would go to every principal, superintendent, and school board member in the district. If we missed school for a picket and a teacher objected to our absence, Shirley would write a letter claiming religious discrimination on that occasion, too, and we would be officially excused. No teachers wanted to deal with her, although the ones in the elementary schools seemed more intimidated than the secondary school teachers. By then, most of them knew not to grade us lower because of our beliefs, because we were really good students in our own right.

The pastor also had a lot invested in our intelligence. He encouraged us to maintain large vocabularies and use advanced words in order to sound erudite. This way, when we were defending our views, people would look at us and say, "What is that word?" We were proud to be well-spoken in both biblical and secular matters. There was no way our detractors could say, "These people are uneducated." The pastor groomed us to come across as reasonable, sensible, and intellectual. We were expected to maintain a very smart and professional demeanor, and then if anyone dared to say anything bad about us, we were always above them.

We were also very diligent about abiding by the school's code of conduct. We were always on time to school. We never cut class or broke other rules. We weren't drinkers, smokers, back-talkers, or delinquents. We certainly couldn't be criticized for being lazy or underachieving, because we were hard-working and studious, and proud of it. There really wasn't much about us that could make teachers mad, except for our religion.

Being with my girlfriends helped me start high school with confidence. I was smart, I had friends, and by virtue of being in the good graces of God and the Phelps family, I was entitled. Whenever I could forget my insecurities, I felt very blessed.

I knew I wanted to stay with the church. I felt superior and righteous by being involved, and so many people showed me support. The kids in my grade who flipped me off didn't have any of the focus or understanding that I had. I was using my passion and energy to promote something grand and purposeful, something spiritual. I discounted anyone who said we were a cult. I knew about real cults and how they operated, quashing the free will of converts through brainwashing and isolation. But that didn't apply to us. Plenty of people had strong religious convictions, and that didn't mean they were part of a cult. I took my beliefs very seriously and was offended by mindless insults that used the word *cult*.

The teenagers in the WBC were not sheltered from the modern world. If anything, the older church members wanted us to be regular citizens of Topeka. We could hang out at the malls after school, go out to eat at restaurants, or go to the movies at night once in a while on a rare splurge. We were not forbidden to watch TV shows. In fact, when it came to the media, my parents probably did less censoring than more conventional parents, who were often afraid of the language and content in the network shows. My girlfriends and I enjoyed watching *South Park* on Comedy Central. We loved the show's crudeness and its parodies of other religions, especially the episode that lampooned Scientology. I thought that the fact that we were teens who were out in the world and not tempted by evil proved to everyone that we were truly God's example.

Sleepovers at Megan and Bekah's house were the perfect times for us to follow our favorite sitcoms together. When we tired of television, sometimes we'd look through the latest *Chevalier*, Topeka West's yearbook. Since I was so new there, it was even more exciting to see the kids I would be in class with. We loved looking at the cute boys and would pick out the one we thought was the cutest. Sometimes, we'd watch a movie and comment about the cute boys in the film, too. I didn't like to share my opinion about who I thought was cute, though. I felt awkward when I did. I knew Megan and Bekah had the same urges that I had, even though we didn't use terms that suggested anything about sex. We'd just giggle. I figured we were suppressing our hormones mostly for our parents, so that they wouldn't look down on us if they ever found out.

It was a little bit confusing for me, though. I knew they were aware that my interest in boys was a gnawing, obsessive concern of my father's. Yet here we were, fantasizing about boys. I desperately wanted to get it right, not talking too much about boys, but not scoffing over the idea that I was interested, either. I still wasn't sure if Shirley's daughters were hanging out with me as friends, or if they were spies; if they liked me, or they were just pretending to like me. I was paranoid about it. On occasion, things I told them privately came back to me through Shirley. *Oh, my God,* I would think. *They're telling on me.* I never dared bring it up. I just wanted them to like me. The craziest part was, I was only doing the same things my friends were. All I really wanted was genuine approval from them.

It seemed no matter how pleased I was with my efforts and accomplishments, I wasn't able to rid myself of my anxiety about my acceptance. I was truly enjoying reading the Bible and learning about the WBC's beliefs. I had positive conversations with the pastor, Shirley, and my dad, and I felt like they were all proud of me. Yet, lying in my bed at night, I'd think about what else I could do to make myself perfect in the eyes of all those who judged me: my peers, my parents, and my God.

CHAPTER NINE

Or those eighteen, upon whom the tower in
Siloam fell, and slew them, think ye that they
were sinners above all men that dwelt in
Jerusalem? I tell you, Nay: but, except ye repent,
ye shall all likewise perish.

—Luke 13:4–5

I had been in school for less than a month when one morning in
class I heard that two planes had crashed into the World Trade
Center in New York City, another had attacked the Pentagon,
and a fourth plane had fallen into a field in Pennsylvania. The
news seemed so surreal that nobody at school even reacted right
away.

When the pastor saw the fire raining down from the sky after
the attack on the World Trade Center, he saw the light about
God's true message. He was thoroughly convinced that God
was sending a fair warning to sinners. Osama bin Laden and
al-Qaeda's catastrophic attack on U.S. soil was really a message from Him. "Look what God did," he said triumphantly.
The September 11 attacks were God's punishment for America's tolerance of homosexuality. Gays were the reason God was
so angry. His judgment against them was evident everywhere,
even if the ignorant couldn't connect the dots.

The pastor wanted to get to Ground Zero as fast as he could
to share God's message, and he assembled a group of five or six

adults to fly to New York. My father went along as the videographer. When everyone got back to Kansas, he told me that the protests had been a huge success. He had captured great footage of the group standing in front of a row of police barriers and holding some of the church's newest creations: THANK GOD FOR 9/11; TOWERS CRASH, GOD LAUGHS; NYPD FAGS; and FDNY SIN. The bottom of the last two signs had stick-figure pictograms of two men having anal sex. My father seemed so proud that the church had let the rescuers know that those who had been killed in the attacks had died because of God's will. The church also planned to protest at the funeral of David Charlebois, a copilot on American Airlines Flight 77, which had crashed into the Pentagon. The pastor believed he was homosexual, and picketing homosexual funerals was a standard practice for the church. The military got word we were coming and kept Charlebois's funeral plans under wraps just to keep us away.

The pastor's hatred of homosexuality was long-simmering. He considered it to be the basis for all of God's judgments against mankind. Of course God did horrible things to people on earth. Everybody was either a fag or a fag enabler, and homosexuality was the worst of all sins, the furthest a sinner could go from His grace. There was no hope for salvation for this population. They would burn in hell through eternity. The pastor often said he thought homosexuality should be a capital crime, often quoting Leviticus to demonstrate his point. In Leviticus 20:13, God said homosexuals "shall surely be put to death; their blood shall be upon them."

The day of the attacks, my father sat in the printing room making picket signs that read THANK GOD FOR 9/11, and we started protesting in Topeka with our new signs the very next day. People hated the THANK GOD FOR 9/11 sign more than any other we had ever displayed. They hated that we were celebrating the deaths of ordinary Americans and delighting in their pain. The pastor, however, thought it was about time the nation opened its eyes.

Standing on the street corner on September 12, I didn't realize how much raw pain our message was causing. I hadn't had a chance to step back and look at the big picture. I was so anxious to be accepted by everybody in the church that I focused on what they thought of me rather than how outsiders saw me. I was still trying to earn my father's recognition and pride, as well. I didn't think I had it yet, and if I couldn't make him proud, I thought he would disown me. At the time, I was too young and childish to care about and consider the feelings of people I didn't know.

That Friday, our church, like so many others across America, held a special program for September 11. The only difference was the other services around the country were held to mourn the dead, and ours was convened to praise God for his judgments. In the pastor's sermon, he said, "Those calamities last Tuesday are none other than the wrath of God, smiting fag America.... How many do you suppose of those hundred and thirty soldiers died [sic] in the Pentagon last Tuesday were fags and dykes? And how many do you suppose were working in that massively composed building structure called those two World Trade Center buildings, Twin Towers? There were five thousand or ten thousand killed and, counting all those passengers in those airplanes, it's very likely that every last single one of them was a fag or dyke or a fag enabler, and that the minute he died, he split hell wide open, and the way to analyze the situation is that the Lord God Almighty, pursuant to His threatenings and warnings, killed him, looked him in the face, laughed and mocked at each one of them as He cast each one of them into Hell!...

"God hates America, and God demonstrated that hatred to some modest degree only last Tuesday—sent in those bombers, those hellacious 767 Boeing bombers, and it was a glorious sight. What you need to do is see in those flames—those sickening, twisting, burning, life-destroying flames, brightly shining from every television set around the world! You need to see in those flames a little preview of the flames of Hell that are going to soon engulf you, my friend. Burn your soul forever."

The September 11 attacks didn't change our message, but they did become our symbol of God's wrath, and from that point on, we really ramped up our message and our pickets. When we held our signs THANK GOD FOR 9/11, GOD HATES YOUR TEARS, BUSH KILLED THEM, and GOD SENT THE PLANES, we always provoked really angry reactions. People would swear, throw things at us, cry, tell us we were horrible, say that we were going to hell, and call us communists who needed to leave the country. I had already developed a sort of tough exterior to get through any aggression that might flare up at a picket, but things were definitely starting to heat up after September 11. Even at our weekly local pickets, we noticed an increasingly violent reaction to us. But I had such a strong sense of entitlement and protection that I quickly overcame any sense of fear. I was also told that it was good to have the whole world hate you. It made you a better Christian.

Because the attack was a sign of God's wrath for a nation that tolerated homosexuality, we had to remind everyone that God hated fags, and anything supporting or enabling them. The country was corrupted by evil. Anyone who supported a country that supported homosexuals was a sinner. The pastor believed there was no longer a fundamental religious community in America, which was why it had strayed so far. According to him, the country had started out right, as a melting pot for citizens from many nations who were escaping religious persecution in their own homelands. He said it used to be the best place in the world, founded on godly principles and guided by a Constitution with a lot of protections for religion. No other country had freedom as we had established it here. Freedom of speech and freedom of religion were the cornerstones of our liberty.

The pastor didn't think that God had always hated America. He said for three hundred years, from the time the Pilgrims landed forward, the population had been God-fearing and had lived obedient lives, until the tolerance of homosexuality became its undoing. He liked to cite Alexis de Tocqueville's book *Democracy in America*. In it, Tocqueville referred to homosexuality as the worm in the American apple. The pastor agreed, believing when homosexuality ran rampant in our country, the fruit of America would go bad.

The pastor said that when you had God at the center, evil was kept at bay. But now, Americans either didn't care about God anymore or practiced a fake religion, one in which a distorted God loved everybody. When prophets like us, who spoke only for God, were persecuted, our country was doomed. God was punishing it with various catastrophes. God was also willing to punish anyone who lived in a country where His prophets were vilified or attacked. Sodom was the pastor's ideal example of retribution. In the time of Abraham, Sodom had become so overrun with sin and sinners that God chose to eliminate the city entirely by raining down fire. The word *sodomy*, the sin of deviant sex and homosexuality, was derived from Sodom. God's destruction of the evil city was a precursor of what he had planned for the modern world.

Despite the fact that God hated America, the church used to celebrate traditional patriotic holidays along with the rest of the country. The pastor thought that there were still enough good Christian leaders preaching against homosexuality that God still had hope. Our family had moved to Topeka a few days before the church's annual Fourth of July celebration, when everybody had gathered together in the churchyard for a communal picnic of fried chicken, potato salad, coleslaw, watermelon, cookies, and pies. Kids had been diving in and out of the pool and jumping on the trampoline until evening, when the older ones had mischievously set off small firecrackers and Roman candles. After September 11, 2001, however, the pastor realized just how angry God was. He canceled future Fourth of July celebrations and any other holiday that celebrated America, like Memorial Day, Veterans' Day, and Labor Day. In fact, the Fourth of July became a major day to picket Gage Park and a few large parades. The Thanksgiving holiday was celebrated for a year or two more, but eventually it was canceled, too. The pastor said it was a pagan feast that had been created to allow the governor of Massachusetts a chance to "lust after the semi-naked bodies of the Indians he invited." Also, we thanked God every day for our blessings, so we thought it was disingenuous to do it once a year.

After September 11, Shirley, Margie, and Dad created new mockeries of patriotic songs. "America the Burning" being especially fitting. Megan, Bekah, Jael, and I used the new material in our biweekly high school lunchtime pickets, which of course, incited even more rage from our fellow students. We just laughed in their faces, our usual response to hostility. We were trained to treat everything as though it were a joke, because then our attackers wouldn't be able to engage us. September 11, as supersensitive an issue as it was, was no exception. We were probably the only ones in the country who believed God had acted properly and justly when he caused so much carnage, death, and destruction on that day. Everybody else thought it was terrorism, but we knew it was the wrath of God.

When the United States overran Afghanistan with American armed forces a few weeks later, the pastor used the invasion to talk about his outrage that homosexuals were allowed in the military. He loved when soldiers were killed, saying that God agreed with him that the military was infused with perversion, and that fighting men deserved to die. He had celebrated when soldiers died in action even before September 11, but he became more hard-line after God showed him His unmistakable wrath.

I had heard accounts that the pastor started really loathing homosexuality in earnest somewhere around the time of his high school graduation. He had been prepped for a military career from the time he had been very young. His father had had high hopes of him being a military man; he had risen through the Boy Scout program from a Cub Scout all the way to an Eagle Scout, its highest honor; and his congressman had written him a letter of recommendation for West Point. However, he never enrolled. According to the story the pastor once told us, he went to an orientation weekend in the summer of 1946 and came out of it with a change of heart. He said he had been really excited about his trip to upstate New York, but something must have happened during his visit. He never said what sparked his religious epiphany there, but after that weekend he made a total about-face and decided he was going to be a preacher rather than a soldier, and he has hated homosexuality and the military ever since.

The pastor insisted that there were homosexuals at every level of the military. Sometimes, interviewers would ask him if he had ever engaged in homosexual activity, and he would always get outraged, stop the interview, and refuse to continue on any line of questioning.

I always found it odd that whenever the pastor had a pulpit, his most vicious attacks against homosexuals seemed to come when he was talking about the military. I knew precisely where and how many times in the Bible God said He hated homosexuals. I wasn't quite as clear as to why the pastor also found military men abominable. The pastor didn't like being called homophobic, either, because, he said, he had no fear of homosexuals. But his intense hatred seemed more personal. He never seemed to mind talking about the details of his personal history, but any discussion of his weekend at West Point seemed to hit a nerve. I often thought that something in particular had happened there, but it was nothing more than a hunch.

Picketing funerals of soldiers killed in Afghanistan and Iraq didn't begin in earnest until 2005. Of all the pickets we did, none of them excited the pastor as much as the protests at the funerals of fallen soldiers. They were his most satisfying protests. To me, this seemed like an overreaction, but we all got into it, like we did at every kind of picket.

As far as the pastor was concerned, fighting for a country that did not have godly principles was not honorable. If the laws of a country were bad, such as the law allowing homosexuals in the armed services, then it was only a matter of time till God would punish that country. The population was throwing itself on its deathbed, because God would turn His back on everyone, sinner and sin enabler alike, just as He had in Sodom. God had sent America many warnings before September 11, so many forebodings in the form of natural calamities and smaller deadly incidents, but America hadn't changed its ways. It was just getting weaker and weaker, more and more evil. The pastor said it was the church's duty to tell our countrymen they were doomed, not to save them but to open their eyes.

CHAPTER TEN

For by one Spirit are we all baptized into one
body, whether we be Jews or Gentiles, whether
we be bond or free; and have been all made to
drink into one Spirit.

—1 Corinthians 12:13

We had been in Topeka only a few months when I decided to
be baptized and become a permanent member of the church. I
made my decision in the afternoon of a regular school day in
October. I had just come back into the building after picketing
outside with my friends, and I was feeling especially moved and
excited. September 11 had shown me how temporal and frag-
ile life on earth was, especially when God was feeling vengeful.
I believed in hell; I wanted to be baptized, and I wanted it
to happen fast. The members of the WBC were the only true
Christians left in the world, and things were so much better at
home now that I knew God was telling me my path to spirituality and fulfillment was through obedience. Mom and Dad
seemed a lot happier with me and even a little proud.

Baptism was an irreversible decision. Every child brought up
within the church had to decide if he or she would commit to
a lifetime in the church through baptism. Once baptized, your
membership in the church was sealed, save for a fall from grace.
Dad had been baptized during the summer. His ceremony was
held outside by the swimming pool, with Taylor, my mother,

135

and me joining the rest of the congregation around the pool's edge. The pastor recited a verse from John the Baptist, then dunked my father in the pool. Every member of the congregation was there—in fact, baptisms weren't performed unless everyone was able to attend. I knew this rite of passage was a turning point for our whole family now that my father had made his life commitment. Now my own baptism was going to be the true testament of my belief.

The evening after I'd made my decision, I broke the news at dinner. Mom, Dad, Taylor, and I were seated around the table in our tiny dining room off the kitchen, where Mom had just served us her fallback midweek meal of pot roast, buttered noodles, and something green. Mom wasn't a fancy person. She usually set the table with washable place mats and practical, heavy green plates. Her better stuff, like her wedding china, was displayed in two china cabinets inherited from her grandmother, but we rarely used it. I could see the hideous duck-and-chicken border of the kitchen from my place at the table.

Dad stopped eating and immediately started asking me questions about my decision. "What is your reason for wanting to become a member?" he began.

"I believe in God, and I believe in the church," I answered sincerely. "I feel this is where I want to be."

He explained that I would have to speak with the elders, who would question me and assess the validity of my request, but he was really excited for me. Mom and Taylor were also over the moon. Mom, always taking things more slowly than anyone else in the family, hadn't made her own commitment yet, although she was certainly moving in that direction.

Babies weren't baptized in the WBC. You were allowed to participate in the sacrament of baptism only if you were serious about your commitment, and you made a formal request. The process was laborious and thorough. After you had made the request, you had to be interviewed by the elders of the church. They would ask questions like "Why do you want to be baptized?" and "Do you know what it means?" They'd challenge you on the Bible and on your behavior. I had to make sure I wanted to be part of their fellowship as much as they wanted to include me.

Four of Shirley's eleven kids, including Megan and Bekah, had already been baptized. A couple of the Phelps cousins had been baptized as young as age six. As long as someone could intelligently answer questions about his or her faith, he or she could be baptized. The commitment was a big deal and not to be taken lightly. Jael still hadn't even done it. She said she was too nervous about the consequences. "What if I get baptized and then I mess up?" she asked. We both knew that after baptism, a serious mistake guaranteed you infinitely more excruciating torture in a hotter place in hell.

Not everybody who asked to be baptized was granted permission, but Danielle, one of Tim's daughters, was the only one I heard of who was denied. The membership felt she was requesting it only because the other kids her age were, not because she was committed to joining. But she was allowed to make the request again when she felt she could prove her commitment.

As soon as we finished eating, Dad called Shirley and told her that I had something really important to discuss. Shirley hosted a dinner for our family a few nights later. She always had room for everybody, between her huge open kitchen island crammed with dining stools and her dining table for ten. The younger kids sat at the island, and the rest of us were at the dining table, Megan and Bekah on either side of me. Everybody seemed genuinely enthusiastic about my decision, which was a great relief.

I knew I wanted to be baptized, and I thought my friends were happy for me, but I didn't want to give the impression that I was being rash or self-indulgent or just trying to impress everybody.

In my case, twelve elders, one from each family, had to interview me before I could make an appointment to speak to the pastor. I was very nervous during the series of one-on-ones, but for the most part they seemed to go well, and I proceeded to schedule an interview with Pastor Phelps.

Our meeting took place on a late October afternoon in the wood-paneled library of his home. The walls were lined with bookshelves crammed with historical and theological texts. I could see the spines of *Absolute Predestination* by Jerome Zanchius, *The Five Points of Calvinism* by R. L. Dabney, and *Sinners in the Hands of an Angry God* by Jonathan Edwards popping out from the rest of the collection, as if they had been read recently.

I wore nice pants and a T-shirt, making sure I didn't look too dressy. The last thing I wanted was to look fussy, fake, or vain. When the pastor came in, I realized this was the first time I had ever been alone with him. Our few conversations before this were always in a group setting with his granddaughters. He sat down at his mahogany desk across from me and gave me a warm smile, which put me only slightly more at ease.

"Why do you want to be a member?" he asked, right after our brief greeting.

I was so nervous, I could barely speak, but I managed to say, "Well, I believe in God, I believe in hell, and I don't want to go to hell." I immediately started tearing up at the thought of writhing in pain forever, but he didn't seem to notice. He asked me for my interpretation of a verse or two in the Bible, and about what kinds of things the other elders had been asking me.

There were only a few questions but I felt like it went on for hours. I was so intimidated in the presence of such a devout man, wondering if he was skeptical or excited about my confession of faith.

Finally, he got to his last question: "Are the rest of the members happy with you joining?"

"They seem to be, yes," I said sincerely. Even Libby, who still hadn't warmed up to me much, hadn't objected to my petition to join.

Once the pastor was satisfied with my commitment, he asked everyone else who had interviewed me what they thought, and then made the decision to admit me through the sacrament of baptism. Shirley and Dad told me the good news. I was really anxious for it to happen right away, but it kept getting pushed back because of the picket schedule and work conflicts. It was always hard to pick a day when everybody could be present. The delay scared me, because we preached that God would return any day, and I was terrified he'd come before my baptism and that I'd be sent straight to hell. Finally, a date was decided by the elders.

My baptism took place during a Sunday service in late fall. I was wearing a frumpy tan-and-black business suit from the 1980s that Mom had hanging in her closet. The outfit wasn't my style, but I was trying to look formal, conservative, and grown-up, and I loved that Mom lent it to me. My hair was two shades of blonde, now that my natural darker blonde roots had pushed my golden color from Florida a good way down the side of my face. I wasn't allowed to cut off the dyed portion, and I wasn't allowed to dye the roots, so I was now half and half. I was too excited about my baptism to even think about it.

Dad was really proud of me that day. He hugged and kissed me before I took my place in the front of the church. The pastor quoted verses that talked about being born into this life in sin, about baptism washing away the old sins, about being immersed in the water and coming back pure. There were two baptismal fonts: one outside, which was the swimming pool, and one inside, the size and shape of a bathtub, behind the pulpit and hidden by a curtain. My baptism, a full immersion style, took place inside because of the time of the year. The pastor opened the curtain behind the pulpit and summoned me to come with him. He blessed me and dunked me. When my head came up, I started crying. I was in awe of being a full member of the church and one of God's chosen few. I felt truly blessed.

The reception was in Shirley's basement. Fred Jr. played hymns on the piano while we ate a delicious spread made up of various potluck dishes brought by the members. Everybody congratulated me and welcomed me into the fellowship. I didn't think it got any better than this.

Once I was baptized, I became a real part of the community. I was now going to be held to the strictest standards of the church. I knew I had an even higher responsibility to my fellow church members than before. If I saw somebody doing something wrong, I was expected to report it. Likewise, I was going to be more accountable to them. More than ever, people would inform my parents if they witnessed something out of line on my part—maybe if my shirt was too short, or if I was acting lazy. I lived in constant fear of disappointing my parents and other members, of the embarrassment of being called out for "transgressions," of going to hell, or even of being banished from the church.

Internal policing was an effective way of keeping us all in check. Anything anyone did wrong was a transgression, and to be called out on one was a huge embarrassment. The pastor employed a system of humiliations. The mildest level was being scolded, being told something sternly. If you were facing the wrong direction at a picket or wore something too short, you were disobedient and you were scolded. Anyone older, college age or above, could do the scolding. It was a sanctioned method to keep the young ones in line. Older people were duty-bound to be overseers and spiritual guides. The elders were not only looking out for themselves, they were looking out for others, which was an act of charity and love.

Scolding was designed to humiliate, and it almost always succeeded. When it didn't, and the behavior continued, someone would tell your parents, or it would be broadcast in an e-mail written by an elder and blasted to everyone in the congregation. The e-mail would be long, saying you were doing this and this wrong, and pointing you to appropriate passages in the scriptures you had to read to understand your errors. Sometimes, someone would call you on the phone with the same message, but with a little bit of a threat added. If things didn't change, no one was going to stand by you, no one was going to hang out with you at a picket, and people were going to outwardly turn their backs on you. You might even have a job or role taken away from you as punishment. Shirley knew that I loved babysitting the kids at the day-care center located in the basement of the law office, so she might temporarily take away that privilege or assign me to a solitary task if she needed to chastise me.

The highest level of humiliation was an admonishment that was taken right to the elders of the church. Admonishments were very demeaning and designed to make you feel like a lesser Christian. By then, the whole church community was involved and already shunning you. Privileges that involved trust, such as handling finances on pickets or in the law office, were revoked and replaced by really menial tasks like shredding papers or weeding the communal garden for hours. Your Christian status was diminished in the eyes of God, as well. You learned that you should fear going to hell. Even worse, you could be banished from the church, which would be a living hell before you died and went to real hell. We were taught that God would kill or harm those who left the church.

If any member's behavior or beliefs were called into question, there was a process the church followed. First, one person went to the wrongdoer in confidence and asked him or her to change. If the behavior continued, three members went together to confront him or her. If that still didn't change anything, then those three people presented the matter to the church leader and the entire group discussed it. The wrongdoer was given the opportunity to repent, but the membership ultimately had the power to decide if someone should be removed. It reminded me of when I played on athletic teams back in Florida. If you were no good, you were going to get cut. There was no room for people who made you look bad and who weren't carrying their weight.

If a member was in a bad situation, maybe wearing something ungodly or acting disrespectfully, and someone else brought it to everyone's attention, that person was in the spotlight. Members would say, "I just don't feel like so-and-so belongs here, I just don't get a good vibe from her or him." One of the respected elders, typically either Shirley or Margie, would receive these "feelings," "intuitions," or "messages from the Holy Ghost" regarding a particular person's sin. The intuitions were so supernatural that we would wait to hear the women's prophecies with acute anticipation. Shirley might intuit that someone was an unrepentant sinner, living disobediently and unwilling to make atonement. She would pass on her intuition and everyone else would embellish her suspicion with other sins they had observed, such as gluttony or vanity.

On occasion, Shirley would get her intuitions in dreams. She would have visions that something was going to happen, or that such-and-such a picket was going to be dangerous. Other times, her feelings would come to her when she was reading scripture. Usually, though, they were intertwined with a sense of anxiety. "I am stressed out, and there must be a reason," she'd say. "We need to check on so-and-so." Then, we'd all obsessively focus on that person looking for possible transgressions. "I know this child is not going to make it into God's kingdom," she'd say about somebody else's kid. "I know this child is evil, I can already tell. The devil is in him, and he is not going to make it." She said it about Timmy, Fred Jr.'s youngest child, and her prophecy was fulfilled when Timmy left a few years later.

From the beginning, I endured my share of criticism. I heard that a lot of members were saying things about me that were really harsh, like that I was too vain. Their criticism played with my mind a lot. Not only did I disagree, I didn't think I was pretty enough to be entitled to vanity. The church members made me doubt my intentions and my motives for many things I did regarding my appearance. I would hear the elders, and the pastor in particular, complimenting all his granddaughters with praises of their beauty. Sometimes, he would tell me I was almost as pretty as them, a very awkward compliment. Once in a while, I confided in my father that I didn't feel attractive, hoping that he would reassure me. Instead, he told me that it didn't matter, that it wasn't important.

Being the target was the most horrifying, creepy feeling. If I was the center of the discussion, I felt like I was losing my identity, my life, and my eternity. I felt like no one was ever going to be on my side. The intimidation made me feel unworthy. *Am I really this person? Am I letting the devil take over my mind?* I would think. I really struggled to understand how so many people could share an opinion of me that I thought was incorrect. Shirley, Margie, and even my parents would interrogate me with questions like "Do you feel like you belong here? Are you sure? Do you feel like you belong with God? With good Christians? With people who are going to heaven? Or would you rather be with people who hate God?"

I wasn't used to being spoken to this way—these weren't the kinds of questions I had heard from people in Florida. I had a hard time remembering what Shirley had told me about not taking the questions too personally, that everyone was scrutinized. The way certain people posed them made me think, *Wow, maybe I* don't *belong.* Sometimes, I would feel paralyzed by the thought that I was, in fact, that lost. Margie, in particular, had many complaints against me. Because she thought I was a troublemaker, she made a lot of issues bigger than they were. For one, she thought I was too close to my father. When I would visit her, she would say, "You really don't need to be so close with your dad," adding her opinion that our relationship was weird. "Nobody can separate you two," she'd say reproachfully. "Why are you so close?"

Margie, Shirley, and Shirley's son Sam would all tell me to stop asking my father for things. They told him he treated me like a princess, but that I was just like any other member of the church. Those kinds of criticisms affected Dad more than me. Even though I listened and tried to act obediently, I could not distance myself like they wanted me to. I was closer to him than to anyone else. My father, on the other hand, wanted to prove himself to his community, so he tried to make it appear that he was not as close with me as Margie, Shirley, and the others perceived.

I had witnessed how Dad had struggled to be accepted as a valuable person, and how in time he was looked upon as an asset to the church. He was an eager worker with great ideas and useful skills. He made the church run so much more efficiently than it had before we got there. Not only was he an important member of the sign-making team, he created and managed several church websites that supplemented godhatesfags.com, and he was the go-to guy for photography and video work.

He started producing tons of video shorts with hip versions of the church's message inspired by pop culture. Sometimes, Taylor and I would assist him, whether it was filming the videos in the basement of the Phelps Chartered office or helping him edit at home. A number of us would create the parodies, changing the lyrics of top-of-the-chart pop songs to words that contained the church's message. Along with these, Dad also made one-to-three-minute music videos called "sign movies." Each one featured one or two church members and their favorite church message from our picket signs. Anybody who was interested could tape one, and we were given the freedom to say what we wanted. The message I chose was "Prepare to Meet Thy God." I started to write my script, but my father, who always wanted me to be the best, intervened to make it "better." After several retakes, he still didn't like it. His criticism made me so nervous that there was no way I could do a good job. Meanwhile, he was telling everyone else how proud he was of them and what a good job they were doing, which of course made me feel even more horrible and inadequate. He took out so much of my wording, replacing it with his own, that I barely recognized the finished product. I preferred making movies with a lot of people in them, so I wouldn't have to feel so personally humiliated. They could be a lot of fun when they were made that way. Everybody took a bit part and stepped out into the spotlight to jive and tell God's Word like a rap star.

Dad's sign movies were a hit, but he still needed to find

full-time employment in Topeka. He found a job as a creative services director for a local television station, where he wrote the commercials for local advertisers. He was so good in that position, he won many "creativity in advertising" awards in the state of Kansas. He filled up an entire wall of our house with honors and plaques. In one year, he totally rebuilt the creative services department at the station. Then, in his second year he was abruptly fired when somebody from the administrative office deliberately left a newspaper with a front-page photo of my father protesting on his desk. It was taken at a Topeka city council meeting, where my father and other church members had gone to voice their opposition to a ruling that would define homosexuality as a civil right. The photo showed two men escorting my father out of the meeting for being disruptive. He had not tried to hide his church affiliation from his employer, but two people from human resources came to let him know that the company couldn't have the creative services director on the front page of the paper, causing a scene on such a sensitive topic. Shirley's husband, Brent, had been fired under similar circumstances. My father opted not to sue, however, and collected unemployment instead. After that, he couldn't find work for nearly six months.

Just as he and Mom were seriously beginning to panic, he was hired as a manager for an insurance company. Within a year, he was promoted first to senior manager and then to vice president. Even though he had never taken business courses and had no background in finance, he was a natural businessman and made the company a lot of money. Shirley credited his new employment to the good work of God. "God is blessing you; he is promoting you," she told him.

The church had a way of justifying everything that happened, good or bad, as an act of God. When my father was

unemployed, Shirley had said it was because he wasn't committed enough to his beliefs. When he found work, that was also
God's choice. It was a direct reward for his faith. "Your dad sub-
mitted himself to the church, and look what happened," Shirley
said to me. That was the reason you didn't really question
things. Everything Shirley predicted always ended up coming
true and making sense, so why challenge it?

In addition to Dad's salary at the insurance office, he made
money working for the church. He was self-taught in remodeling, so he took on the task of improving the houses on the
block. One by one, he renovated them all. He also helped the
Phelpses remodel their law offices in downtown Topeka. Under my father's tutelage, the younger guys in the church became
skilled as well. Boys started getting tools for their birthdays so
they could apprentice, and I assisted whenever I had time. After
a while, most of the houses on the block seemed like they were
four times bigger. One-story, two-bedroom houses grew into
two-story, four-bedroom homes. Kitchen makeovers turned everybody's little galley kitchen into something out of a magazine.
Our own renovations were more modest and done only after
everybody else's were completed, since Dad was mostly interested in impressing the elders with his abilities and work ethic.
Shirley still had the biggest house. Of course, she also had the
biggest family.

Mom was shy and insecure, so she didn't get as involved in
the church business as Dad did. She worked Monday through
Thursday, and sometimes she worked Fridays, too, to make
overtime. She went back and forth between wanting her Fridays off and working on Fridays. A lot of it had to do with
our growing family. I was sixteen and Taylor was eleven when
we learned that Mom was pregnant again. The news was
shocking at first, because my sister and I didn't know that our

parents were thinking about having a baby. But we were all excited.

The church prohibited the use of birth control, saying it interfered with God's plan for natural life, and was extremely adamant in its position. In fact, if you were married and hadn't had a child within a year, they'd suspect you were using it and might even throw you out. I heard a story about one of the members who had given a young couple "evil" advice by telling them if they were not feeling up to starting a family yet, they could always "spill on the floor." The couple told on him, and he was chastised.

Mom hadn't known about this rule when we were still in Florida, but it was a huge bone of contention between my parents once we got to Kansas. I would often hear them arguing about it when I was in my room. My mother thought she was too old, and she was done having children. My parents had other loud, frequent fights, on anything from frivolous spending to me. They were always nervous that I wasn't representing the Drains well enough. The oldest child had the burden of walking sin free, so anything I did out of step reflected poorly on them. The irony was that the church considered it a sin to argue, so their arguing about me was their sin. Kids were supposed to report their parents when they argued, but I didn't dare to report Mom and Dad to the pastor or Shirley, although I knew I should. That behavior was unacceptable in the church, but I couldn't bring myself to do it. I was tormented. I didn't want to get them in trouble, fearing the whole family would be kicked out of the church if I said anything. But I didn't want to be evil by withholding information about somebody's sins.

Just when I thought it couldn't get any worse, Dad came to me and told me I needed to talk to Mom. "Your mother is a contentious woman," he said. "All she does is start arguments."

My father said to do it for my mother's sake. Nobody else knew about the fighting but Taylor and me, and Dad knew it was my duty as a newly baptized member of the church to report the rule-breaking arguments that I witnessed. "I want to spare your mother the humiliation of being publicly admonished if the church finds out," he instructed me. "Please just tell her to stop."

I found Mom when she was alone in the kitchen cooking dinner. I was embarrassed and scared that she'd be mad at me, but I knew I had to do it. "Mom, I need to talk to you. Dad wants me to talk to you about something."

Turning toward me, she looked like a deer caught in the headlights, sensing that I obviously had something important to discuss.

"Dad's been worried about you for a long time," I told her. "He asked me to talk to you in hopes that it would help. He feels you are way too contentious, and if you don't change, he will have to tell someone in the church."

The conversation was incredibly emotional. I was crying as I told her that she was not allowed to bring things up against Dad anymore, even in the privacy of our own home. Mom was upset and angry, but I told her that Dad had asked me to speak to her because he was afraid that if things didn't change, she was going to be humiliated in front of the congregation. I hated being caught in the middle. Dad was putting me between him and my mother, and he was also making me a conspirator in his sin by asking me to keep their arguments secret. After that, in my mother's eyes I had taken Dad's side, so she seemed to favor Taylor.

The arguments continued, even after that. However, I honored Dad's desire to protect Mom. To be in full compliance with the church's standards, I would have had to bring up my parents' arguing to the elders. Then, Shirley and Margie would have suspicions about the conduct in our house, which would then call into question both of my parents' memberships. I knew I should be telling on them both, knowing the consequences of my secrecy might be an eternity in the part of hell reserved for evil coconspirators like me. But that was the risk I took.

Though I wasn't able to take much of anything with me when I left the church, here are a few photos which are the only physical mementos I have from my childhood.

Dad and Mom married on May 5, 1983, just after turning eighteen.

Mom and Dad just married.

At age five with two babies: Taylor is on the left, a cousin is on the right.

Taylor and me dressed up as bunnies for Halloween before trick-or-treating with our parents.

Family Christmas photo taken at a portrait studio in 1993.

Opening presents on Christmas Day in Kansas (from left to right: Mom, me, Taylor, and Dad).

Family Christmas portrait at home with our dog, Buddy, 1995.

Taylor and me at an indoor adventure park.

With my mother's side of the family one Christmas (from left to right: Mom, Grandma Stout, my cousins Dena and Brennen, Taylor, my cousin Amber, and me).

At age thirteen at a family Christmas party.

At my Grandma Stout's house
(from left to right: Aunt Stacy,
Taylor, me, Brennen, and Mom).

Collage I made of pictures of
Taylor and me.

Hanging out with our cousins at Disney
World (from left to right: Amber, Taylor,
Brennen, and me).

At the hospital with my family on the day
Boaz Abel was born, August 8, 2002.

CHAPTER ELEVEN

But sanctify the Lord God in your hearts; and be
ready always to give an answer to every man that
asketh you a reason of the hope that is in you
with meekness and fear.

—1 Peter 3:15

Throughout high school, I lived a tightly controlled life.
Teenage girls not in the church experimented with makeup,
looked at cute boys, went on dates, and danced at the prom.
The teenagers within the church were expected to focus on
daily picketing, school, and part-time jobs. We were also supposed to help our parents by contributing to the family finances
and babysitting the younger children. At first I resented it, but
eventually suppression started to feel more like support. Most
of the church members seemed so cheerful and friendly in their
judgments of me that it didn't feel like they were condemning
me, and I really was trying to learn the right ways. Compared
to my house arrest in Florida, I felt like I had a lot more freedoms now. I could go to the movies, have a cell phone, borrow
the car, travel to pickets without my parents, and hang out at
my friends' houses. These freedoms came with heavy monitor-
ing, but that didn't really bother me. The longer I was there, the
more I bought into the concept that if I needed to be corrected,
these were expressions of love. Sometimes I had a fleeting wish
that I could have a boyfriend, or at least talk to some of the guys

in school, but I wouldn't have traded anything for my support system in the church.

I loved sports and being athletic, so the fact that physical fitness was a priority in the church was great. The pastor demanded that we respect our bodies like temples, as stated in the Bible. At one time, the pastor had been overweight himself, but he had overcome what he'd seen as a weakness of character and was now a health nut who insisted everybody in the congregation partake in an exercise program of some sort, although I noticed that different people interpreted this regulation differently. As evidenced by the range of body sizes among church members, the fitness program was self-administered, not official.

Megan and I frequently exercised together, from practicing in front of an exercise/belly-dancing DVD in her bedroom to running a five-mile loop from the house to the high school football field and back. If we didn't have much time, we'd do laps on the track in the yard, where sixteen laps made a mile. We liked to run every day because we were cross-country runners on the high school track team. We traveled with our teammates on the school bus for the meets. Nobody bothered us about being Westboro members, and we didn't try to incite controversy unless we were picketing. Sometimes I'd run five to ten miles on my own, loving the freedom of just being out of the house for a while. As long as I carried my cell phone, Mom allowed it. The pastor, Fred Jr., and Shirley's husband, Brent, were marathoners. Fred and Brent would take anyone who was interested on cross-country runs in the park areas of Topeka on the weekends, sign us up for local races, and help us keep fit.

Except for the girls on the track team, Jael, Megan, Bekah, and I associated only with one another at school. This had an upside and a downside. I liked having a close circle of friends, but I still felt they treated me like an outsider in many ways.

The fact that they were all related to one another but not to me left me feeling their loyalties didn't lie with me.

Another thing that made me really insecure was when I found out that members of the church had been meeting for group Bible studies that excluded the Drains. Those times that Dad, Mom, Taylor, and I had been meeting for family Bible studies, the rest of the church members were having community Bible studies, but nobody had taken the initiative to include us. I didn't know if it was just an oversight or a deliberate lack of goodwill, but my insecurity had me leaning toward the latter. It felt kind of mean to me. Certain older members of the church never warmed up to my family; they just ignored us, even on Sundays when we were in the sanctuary.

We were the only family that had ever come from a distance. In fact, we were one of the only outside families to ever arrive. The feeling was that we would probably be the last. Two other Topeka families, the Hockenbargers and the Davises, had joined in the early years of the church. Everyone else in the congregation was a child of Fred Phelps, a spouse, or one of the pastor's forty grandchildren, including my friends Megan, Libby, Bekah, and Jael. The Phelpses had resigned themselves to the belief that no one else was coming. On the other hand, we were the chosen ones, predestined for God's kingdom, so whoever else was on the outside, let them be damned. God's tree had been shaken, and all the bad leaves had fallen off.

Eventually, after the congregation trusted that we were sincere, most people accepted us. We started going to the church-wide Bible studies in addition to our regular family Bible study. I joined the community group without any resentment about not being invited sooner. I didn't want to raise the issue that I'd felt left out, because I didn't want to be criticized for being envious. Besides, I really enjoyed the group study. A whole bunch of us would get together according to age. The young people went to Sam's house on Wednesday evenings after dinner. Sam, Shirley's oldest son, was a cool guy with his own house, so that was fun. Megan, Jael, Bekah, and I joined the other young people in his living room and discussed passages from the Bible. The oldest male in attendance was always the first to read, then we'd go clockwise around the room with every person reading a chapter. Sometimes, Sam would serve us snacks, but usually, we just studied the Bible.

I looked up to all the Phelps girls, even though I was sometimes uncomfortable when they overemphasized their status as the pastor's grandchildren and became boastful and entitled. As a strategy, I tried to model my behavior after theirs, figuring that would be a good way to keep myself out of trouble, but some of their actions perplexed me. For example, Megan and Jael both dressed more provocatively than I thought was allowed, which confused me. If they hated boys, and they hated attention, then why were they wearing such revealing clothes? Megan would wear tight, low-cut shirts and then get upset about the reaction. "Some boy called me hot today," she would complain. "I hate when boys do that. It's so nasty." Sometimes Jael would wear tight pants and heels to school. The church didn't have a dress code, but *modesty* was the operative word. Some of the clothes the girls wore might not have seemed inappropriate to other people, but they weren't modest.

My mother took it to the extreme, considering anything tight to be immodest. My shorts needed to be at least to my knees, my pants needed to be baggy, and if something I was wearing showed even an inch of skin or revealed my figure, my mother would throw it out. Church people would complain about certain outfits they saw us wearing. Sometimes it was Megan. Sometimes it was Jael, and sometimes it was me. My mom would freak out if people commented about me. She needed me to be perfect.

Meanwhile, Megan would talk about her body and the size of her breasts. She was always working on her abs. At school, she was quite the exhibitionist, wanting to exercise in the hallway in some tiny exercise outfit or show off some of the belly-dancing moves we had learned at her house in front of our classmates. Sometimes, I'd join in at her urging. She would also walk the line by wearing low-cut or snug tops, and she was always fussing with her hair. The church mandated that we were not supposed to be focusing on our outward appearances, so this seemed to me like a pretty flagrant violation, but she got away with it. It always struck me as unfair that she pranced around worrying about her looks and being on television, either caught on camera at a picket or at a scheduled interview. Maybe I was jealous of her. She told me once that sometimes she felt competitive with me because we were the same age, both ran track, and took the same classes.

Megan and I liked shopping for clothes together, and we shopped at the same stores, Target and Walmart. At Megan's urging, we bought a lot of matching short skirts and tops. She'd spend a lot of time in the dressing room, sizing herself up in the mirror. I loved Megan, but I was beginning to think she was a little vain. One time, she wanted us to wear wedge heels and identical shorts to school. She had picked them out at the store and bought them for us. Shirley found out about it and came to me very upset, telling me I was such a bad influence on her daughter. She said Megan would never wear anything like that without my encouragement.

Shirley didn't seem to think a kid of hers could ever do wrong, so if we were wearing something inappropriate, it had to have been my idea. Megan knew her mother was scolding me for something that was her fault, but she didn't step in to take responsibility. For once, my father defended me. "It's not that big a deal," he told Shirley. "They're wearing shorts, but they are not that immodest, as long as they're covering everything." But Shirley would have none of it and still blamed me.

This favoritism was really starting to bother me. Shirley didn't seem to have the capacity to humble herself enough to see faults in her own children. Every kid got reamed out by her, except her own. She would rip me up in public and in private, telling me to be less vain, more humble, less conceited, more obedient, less selfish, and more worthy. She'd accuse me of wanting guys to look at me. Meanwhile, her daughter's cleavage would be sticking out of her blouse as she flirted with guys who approached her at pickets. I kept my issue with it to myself, deciding that I would most likely be scolded for being jealous if I said anything.

Soon, Mom and Dad both started cracking down on me. No spaghetti straps, no push-up bras, no tank tops, no shorts. My mother was still throwing away clothes that she didn't like, even sometimes hunting in my closet for forbidden items. She'd make sure I saw what she had taken by leaving them at the top of the wastebasket in my room. It was so unfair. Taylor's wardrobe was safe, because Mom bought all of her clothes, but the one last thing in my life I could possibly control was my wardrobe. I couldn't cut or style my hair, paint my nails, date boys, or have any time to myself except on my runs. My clothes were all that was left, and my mother took that away from me, too.

My parents monitored everything: my e-mails, my Internet use, even my cell phone history. Every single second of my day was monitored. Any time I drove anywhere, I had to carry my cell phone so my parents could call me. If I wasn't at school, I was doing chores for the church or my family. The chores increased substantially after my brother Boaz was born.

We were ecstatic to welcome him into the family. Dad, Taylor, and I were in the hospital room throughout Mom's labor and delivery, so we were part of Boaz's birth experience. Dad was so excited to have a boy. I always thought he wanted me to be a boy, since he had signed me up for every sport possible, he taught me to be supercompetitive, and he wanted me to be interested in all the guy stuff he loved—rock and roll music, construction, basketball, softball. If he liked it, he wanted me to like it, too, but now he had Boaz. I wasn't jealous in the least—instead, I was more happy for my father that he had finally gotten his boy. My baby brother looked exactly like Dad from the moment he was born.

Not long after we brought Boaz home from the hospital, we had to put down our dog, Buddy, who'd moved with us from Florida. He was getting senile, and he was snapping at Boaz. Nobody else in the family wanted to be in the room with the veterinarian, so I volunteered to be by Buddy's side to comfort him while the doctor gave him the injection. It was a pretty emotional day, and I was sad for a long time afterward.

Taylor and I loved having Boaz around. He was a really funny kid and he never whined. My mother used me as her main caregiver, which was really stressful for me. The moment I picked up Boaz from the church's day care, I was on duty. He had a delightful disposition, but he was really active, so I had very little down time. I had to feed and change him while I was doing my homework.

Taylor wasn't expected to help as much as I was because she was younger. She spent most of her after-school time in our bedroom reading or watching television. During the week, I couldn't expect much relief with Boaz when Mom and Dad came home from their jobs, either. Dad was now a vice president at his firm, and after his long workday, he'd want to head straight to his editing suite to work on church videos, which he considered to be a relaxing pastime. Mom was always exhausted, so if I tried to have her take Boaz, she'd get offended. "Why don't you want to take care of him anymore?" she'd ask. "Why are you annoyed?" I wasn't *annoyed*, really—I was simply overwhelmed.

On weekends, too, Mom wanted me to take care of Boaz's needs. One time, when Boaz was a toddler, he came down with the rotavirus. He had been suffering from extreme diarrhea and dehydration and was hospitalized for two days. He became so dehydrated that he needed IV fluids and medication. He was pale and weak, but I knew he would pull through. I stayed by his bedside for hours, rubbing his arms and back, and trying to make sure he felt comfortable. I brought him a DVD player from home so he could watch movies. I was helping the nurse, answering her questions about how he was doing right up until he was released.

I was still coming up short in my struggle to win my parents' approval, and this overwhelmed me with anxiety. I was babysitting Boaz while doing the household duties, running errands, and doing the grocery shopping. Every two weeks, I was given $300 and a list. I'd go to the local Walmart where all the church members shopped, a fifteen-minute drive from my house. My route to the store was determined by my parents, and I could not deviate from that course in the slightest. I had a time allotment, and if I ran even five minutes late getting home, I would get a phone call asking where I was. If I took a left instead of a right, I was steering into evil.

I loved having Taylor with me on these shopping trips and took her as often as I could. In the store, she and I would load up the cart with everything on the list but nothing else, no impulse items. My purchases could not exceed $300, so I focused on generic store brands and sale items. We had to be so careful. Taylor and I spent an entire hour just shopping. When we got home, Mom would review the receipt and the purchases. If I forgot a loaf of bread, it had been a failed mission. "I can't count on you for anything," Mom would say. "You didn't check the list. We printed the list for you, and you still didn't bring home bread." If I brought home a jar of mayonnaise, she'd say, "We already have mayonnaise. Why do you think we need two jars when we already have one?" She'd always focus on my mistakes instead of praising me for the things I did right.

I couldn't seem to please my father, either. He gave me more positive feedback than my mother did, but usually only when I did things for him and the church. Taylor and I helped him a lot with his editing, spending countless hours working with him on his videos of the pickets. I also helped him design and build the picket signs using Photoshop. On top of that, I apprenticed with him for his remodeling projects. I would get a sense of pride from our accomplishments, but he was often backhandedly critical. "That's helpful, but this is how I would do it," he'd say, shortchanging me. "You take twice as long as I do" or "This isn't up to par" were two more direct complaints I'd hear from him. I couldn't impress him, no matter how much I tried. "Why can't you pick it up? Why can't you just get it?" he'd scold.

These nitpicking comments would make me so anxious that my mind would go blank, and I couldn't absorb what he was trying to teach me. I would forget steps or just get them wrong. Of course, Dad would then call me flighty. "Where's your head?" he'd ask me. "Your head is in the clouds."

I was always being compared to the Phelps girls. Both my parents required so many adult responsibilities of me, but they never complimented me or said thank you. Instead, my mom was constantly calling me rebellious, which made me resent her. She was a very passive person, except when it came to me. Like a lot of teenage girls, I could get upset at my mother more than any other person in my life. Sometimes, it annoyed me that she wasn't stronger or more willing to show passion or an opinion. She never wanted to stick her neck out for me. She and Dad had moved me to Topeka, practically the dead geographical center of the United States, to save me, and she still didn't give me credit for all I had done to save myself.

"Why can't you be more like Shirley's girls?" she'd say. "You're so vain, Lauren. You always stir up strife or look to start an argument." All the while, she'd have nothing but praise for Shirley's girls. "They are so obedient, and they love their mother." I cried when I told her that I wanted to be as close with her as Shirley was with her daughters. Just as she wanted me to be like Megan and Bekah, I encouraged her to be more like Shirley, who really indulged her girls. She gave them first dibs for pickets and interviews, made sure they were financially set with everything, and bestowed them with praise.

I couldn't help but compare Mom to Shirley, who was the only person giving me the supportive kind of attention I craved. If Shirley was critical of me, she somehow ended her critique with guidance, whereas Mom's takedowns were just plain hurtful. My mother lacked Shirley's confidence and self-assurance, too, the qualities I wanted to emulate most in my own life. I started to feel that Shirley was more vested in my salvation than my own mother was. Shirley seemed to genuinely care about me, and we were becoming very close. She would talk to me about school, show a lot of interest in all my classes, and offer to help if I needed it. She managed the schedules of every kid in our generation, which meant she was responsible for

166

about forty people. She knew where everyone was every minute of the day. She knew if I had an hour free, if I could help with lawn maintenance or the law office, if she could send me to a picket. But somehow, she found time to know about everything going on in the world, including every event in the news.

Mom was so busy she didn't seem to mind my growing relationship with my new mother figure. The more Shirley treated me as if I were another one of her daughters, the more I respected her advice. Many people outside the church directed their wrath exclusively at her, but that was the price she paid for being the spokesperson for a controversial organization. Shirley always took it in stride. To me, it seemed like she loved it. When she did interviews on television, she was often criticized for smiling when she was talking about horrific events, but she said she was just misunderstood. She always responded with a line from scripture, and on the rare occasion that she raised her voice a little or engaged in the bickering, it was only because the question was so ignorant.

Meanwhile, my insecurities were constantly challenging my self-confidence. No matter how hard I worked to convince myself that the Phelps girls considered me to be on their level, I still had lingering doubts about their sincerity. I tried to do little things I thought would endear me to them. I zoned in on a craft project that Shirley's only daughter-in-law, Sam's wife, Jennifer Hockenbarger-Phelps, had done. Jennifer had made a kind of doll out of metal. It was a flat metal profile of a person with its hands extended up, was about a foot tall, and was propped on a doll stand. It was holding a to-scale picket sign made of magnetic material so it could be stuck onto the doll's hand and the messages changed out. Everybody admired it at Bible study one Wednesday evening, and Jael and I decided to see if we could make the dolls. I wanted to give one to each

Phelps girl as a gift, customized with her favorite picket slogan. Megan's had GOD HATES FAGS, Bekah's read YOU ARE GOING TO HELL, and Jael's said GOD HATES AMERICA. I made one for myself with my favorite sign, PREPARE TO MEET THY GOD.

Of course, no sooner had I handed them out than I began worrying about how they would be viewed. Idols were forbidden, and therefore making dolls might be sinful. I had trusted that Jennifer had known what she was doing, but I'd become so paranoid that everyone seemed to have an evil eye. I was almost too paralyzed to do anything that hadn't been approved. Luckily, no one said anything about making an idol, but I was still nervous until each of my friends had hers on display in her bedroom. Even then, I still had lingering expectations that down the line I was going to hear from someone that the dolls weren't allowed. It was probably all in my head.

I trusted Shirley, though, and when she liked the dolls, I relaxed. I was usually completely comfortable with her. She didn't make me feel dumb, like other people did. We talked a lot about the Bible. We had been reading Revelation, and there were a few chapters that were bothering me. We were always talking about the "end of the world," which Revelation described in great detail, but some of the timing didn't make sense. In Revelation, the end of the world came soon after the seventh of seven seals was broken. After it was broken, there was one half hour of silence; then seven angels appeared, each receiving a trumpet. At that point, the world came to an end, with God pouring down his wrath on all the sinners and escorting the chosen ones into His kingdom. Our church embraced the belief that the end was nigh. Our whole existence was waiting for the end, being prepared, and knowing what to expect.

The point I wanted to make to Shirley was that there was an urgency to study the events in the Bible in order to be ready.

I believed that the end of the world could be determined with more certainty if we knew more specifically where we were in time. For example, the Bible said Satan was locked up in a bottomless pit, where he would remain for a thousand years. Knowing *exactly* when God had cast him there would give us a huge advantage in predicting when he would return.

We were always focusing on verses about the "end of the world." We read them over and over to make us feel we were more knowledgeable about those verses than any of our detractors. We would be the most equipped to describe it and preach about it at pickets. This was the reason my questions were so pressing: I needed to know for sure what I was talking about. If I was telling someone else his soul was going to hell, I couldn't just be spewing it without scriptural basis.

We read Matthew 24 often. The chapter wasn't as elaborate as the Book of Revelation, but it had stunning imagery about the end of the world. One image in particular was causing me some confusion, but nobody could ever tell me exactly what it meant: "And knew not until the flood came, and took them all away; so shall also the coming of the Son of man be. Then shall two be in the field; the one shall be taken, and the other left. Two women shall be grinding at the mill; the one shall be taken, and the other left. Watch therefore: for ye know not what hour your Lord doth come."

My confusion was about which was better: to be taken or to be left. The verses always seemed to be interpreted differently. Sometimes, they were referred to as the "fly away" or "rapture" doctrine: that at the end of the world, God's people would "fly away," or be swept up into the skies *before* the destruction on the earth, and therefore they would meet God in the skies *before* they died. However, the pastor said the only ones "getting raised up into the skies" were already dead, dead in the grave, dead in Christ, dead. They would then rise to heaven instantaneously to meet God. According to our interpretation of scripture, people were either in heaven or hell *upon the moment of death*, and if that was the case, they couldn't possibly rise for the rapture. He wasn't 100 percent sure about meeting God in the skies.

It was so confusing, yet the pastor insisted we be correct and fully informed on all things biblical. I would get very frustrated when I met with what I thought was a refusal to investigate possible contradictions in the text, even the contradictions that might be a little sensitive because they conflicted with what the church said or taught. We scrutinized every other religion, after all. The pastor was obsessed with reading what other people of other faiths said they believed. He would read books, watch the news, or see something on a website related to faith, and then the whole congregation would analyze and dissect his discovery. He'd even send out a press release disputing the claims of other believers, especially when it came to God's return.

We studied all the apocalyptic visions in the Gospels, including those of Mark, John, and Luke. The book of Jude was so important for its vision, the pastor had us memorize the whole thing over one summer. All the kids who could read had to memorize it and know how to recite it. We would all read it aloud to one another and recite it at the pickets. At the end of the summer, we had to recite it in front of Shirley and all the other kids to prove that we had learned it. Kids as young as seven and eight years old could do it.

I didn't want to bother the pastor with my problem of Matthew's vision because I didn't want him to attribute my question to a weakness of faith. The older he was getting, the less approachable he became. I had been on only a handful of pickets with him in three years. He was starting to get paranoid that someone might want to assassinate him, so except to preach on Sundays, he mostly stayed in his own living quarters. For his daily exercise, he either used his indoor stationary bike or walked the church's track. I felt honored when Shirley told me to stand by while she went to discuss my conflict about the end of the world with him. She was very enthusiastic about my question and wanted to know the answer herself. Shirley had a way of saying things that sounded better anyway. She located the pastor walking laps around the track and joined him for about fifteen minutes, while I waited at the picnic tables. I couldn't hear what they were saying, but they seemed to be caught up in an earnest discussion.

When she came back, she told me the pastor didn't have a light on that right now. I accepted that, but her demeanor was now angry and frustrated. To my surprise, she started scolding me. "Gramps told me that you are not supposed to question things that you don't know, and you are not supposed to tell God when to tell you stuff. Beg for understanding when you don't get it," she warned me. "I don't have the answer. Don't ask me anymore, and I will tell you when I know. We are not investigating this or doing a study on this right now."

I was taken aback that she was running out of patience with me. I thought I was being sincere by coming to my elders and talking to them about this. I was very disheartened and never heard anything more about my scripture question again, although it still bothered me. I couldn't figure out why I didn't understand something the church said proved our point, nor why I didn't have the right to get answers to my questions. Even though I was discouraged, I had to accept it without a challenge.

Shirley's scary side came into evidence whenever she wasn't supporting you. She had so much power and authority, she could reduce you to "worthless" with one slight or "how dare you" answer. I knew I shouldn't take her shutting me down about the specifics of the end of the world too personally, because she chastised everyone, constantly keeping us in check with Bible quotes of her own and letting us know she had power over our membership in the church. She was the mother of the church. If she got mad at you, she won. If you thought there were two sides to a story, everybody believed her, not you. Her word was sacrosanct, and nobody dared to refute her.

I never got into the minutiae of scripture with the pastor. After Shirley told me that she and he were done with my silly questions, the pastor and I stayed pleasant and superficial with each other. He was no more and no less standoffish than he had been before, so I was still left wondering what was going on in his head.

He definitely had a propensity for manic habits. He had periods when he abided by an extreme diet that he had started in his fifties, which featured bowls of yogurt, blueberries, and full cloves of garlic. The girls and I would joke that Gramps had garlic breath because of the cloves he ate every day. He drank eye droppers full of oregano oil, exceeding the daily recommended maximum of four drops, but enough to just fill the back of his mouth. He had a fig tree in his backyard, because figs were in the Bible. He didn't drink anything stronger than his daily "vitamin C cocktail," which was vitamin C powder diluted in a combination of Diet Pepsi and water. His only "junk food" was veggie wraps from Subway. He didn't have a single health issue, even into his seventies, and he wasn't on any medications.

I would often get groceries for his wife, Marge, and clean their house. The whole house was really dated. They had a '70s-style kitchen with linoleum countertops and well-used appliances. The blue carpet in most of the rooms was worn in the heavily trafficked parts and looked practically new at the edges. Framed Bible passages and famous quotes from Alexis de Tocqueville and some of the pastor's other heroes decorated the walls. The couches in the living area had floral designs, and the pastor's La-Z-Boy swiveled instead of rocked.

I loved doing errands for Marge. I wasn't as intimidated by her as I was by the pastor. She might have been the warmest person in the whole church. Just as we called the pastor "Gramps," we called her "Gran." All the girls had a role in keeping house for the two of them. Since I was planning to be a nurse, I'd do small medical things for the pastor and her, like check their blood pressure or heart rate. I could even use the hours I spent helping them toward my community service requirement in school.

No matter how kind and generous the Phelpses were to me, things in my head caused me enormous tension. I didn't know if they were doubts about the church or just my own insecurities. I needed clarification on scripture and church rules so often, but after the conversation on the track between Shirley and the pastor, I wasn't sure if looking for answers would be taken as a strength or a weakness. I was completely on edge. If I caught somebody at a bad time, I'd get a snippy answer to my inquiry, but if I caught that same person at the right time, I would get a thoughtful explanation. It always seemed to be a gamble.

As a spokesperson for God, I was often conflicted about what was expected of me. It was a strange feeling. I'd ask myself what I was supposed to be doing. I didn't want to be judged, so I didn't ask too many questions. I just wanted to get it right. I didn't want anyone else to know that I was doubting myself. I would bring a Bible to the pickets and start reading it, but then I would get self-conscious. Was I reading it to show off, or was I really reading it? I would get anxious and start second-guessing myself.

I would question my own motives. *Am I doing this because I want to, or am I doing it because I feel like I want the other church members to see me and be impressed?* I'd seen the consequences of substandard behavior on the pickets. I just felt really unsure, and I didn't want to get kicked out like other people who had done things wrong. But sometimes I was overwhelmed with fear. I thought I was living my life for God and I was going to heaven, but the church let me know that I could fall from grace at any moment. I was consumed by the desire to get it right.

CHAPTER TWELVE

Ask, and it shall be given you; seek, and ye shall
find; knock, and it shall be opened unto you.
—Matthew 7:7

During the weekly Bible study that was open to anyone, I was
still willing to ask questions, and I was convinced my questions
were impressively deep. I thought everybody knew my intentions were coming from my heart, and I wasn't trying to waste
anybody's time. There was just so much to learn. Dad was often
in attendance, and sometimes he led the group. He would happily answer my questions until people like Shirley and Margie
started calling me divisive. They thought I was causing trouble
and going against authority. I was just trying to straighten out
the contradictions. I used to point out some of them during the
sessions, such as why people needed to repent if they weren't
going to heaven anyway.

In my understanding, nothing the church preached could
change anybody's destiny, since everyone but us was still going
to hell. I wanted to know why we were telling outsiders to
obey if salvation was only for the elect. Dad might say, "Good
question," but then the other members would criticize him for
indulging me, accusing him of showing me favoritism. It upset
him when they started blaming my behavior on him, so he just

shut me down. The oldest child was considered the reflection of how well a man was running his household, and he needed me to conform and submit. After this happened, I made sure not to ask him anything in front of other people, because I knew he would try to make me feel inferior or tell me I was screwing something up.

The problems and inconsistencies went beyond the ones I'd found in scripture. I noticed a lot of hypocrisy—some people seemed to get away with a lot more than others. Taylor might agree with me, but she would never bring it up or acknowledge that it was an inconsistency. She might say to me that something wasn't fair, but fair or not, she'd accept it rather than get in trouble. She didn't like being accusatory. People admired that about her. She was easy to get along with, a go-with-the-flow kind of person who stayed away from pricklier issues.

I handled the criticism the best I could, taking the suggestions I thought would make me a better person. The church elders expected us all to figure out what career we wanted before we went to college. The policy was a good one: nobody should waste time and money in college after he or she got there. The idea of squandering money was extremely distasteful, especially on something as expensive as an education. We didn't have many career choices, though. My parents told me the best options for me were to be either a dental hygienist or a nurse. Between the two, I decided on nursing, and Jael did, too. We had a shared purpose—to get a really good nursing job, to give our parents money as soon as we could, and to still be productive members of the church.

By the second semester of my senior year, I was splitting my day between Topeka West and a technical high school, where I was earning credits for my nurse's aide certificate. I'd spend the first half of the day at Topeka West, then drive to the tech school for the rest of the school day. I wanted to get the certificate so I could earn money as an aide to put myself through college and nursing school. Nurse's aides could make almost twice the minimum wage that most after-school jobs paid.

At the tech school, I noticed that there was always a sporty red Camaro parked next to my car in the afternoons. I also couldn't help but notice its owner, Brian, a really cute boy who was about my age. He had brown hair, green eyes, and a nice white smile. We started chatting briefly before classes every afternoon, and he told me he was taking photography classes there. Some days, I'd be eating lunch in my car while he was outside having a brief smoke. Our conversations were superficial, but it was my chance to flirt. One day, he walked over to me and told me I was beautiful. He said that he had a crush on me and leaned into my car to kiss me, my first real kiss.

After class a few days later, when Brian asked me to come over to the house where he lived with his parents, I hesitated. I was so scared, knowing how completely forbidden it was, but I had really liked the kiss, and so I followed him there in my car. When I parked at Brian's, I noticed that one of my tires was a little flat and needed air. I didn't worry about it, figuring I'd fill it on my way back.

Neither of Brian's parents was home, so we skipped lunch and went straight to his bedroom. We sat on his bed talking for a few minutes, and then he put his lips to mine. His kiss felt so good, I didn't want him to stop. He was really hot, and I was turned on—but after an hour, I knew I had to go.

By the time I got to my car, my tire had gone completely flat, and Brian had left a few moments before. I tried to drive as far as I could with the flat, but I got only a street away. I was starting to freak out when my cell phone rang. It was my mother, wanting me to pick up my brother from day care. I told her I couldn't. When she asked why, I was forced to explain where I was so she could come pick me up. Her interrogation began the moment I opened her car door. She asked me if I had been visiting a boyfriend. She demanded to know how I met him, did I have sex with him, was there a chance I had gotten pregnant, why did I do it, did I want to go to hell, did I hate God, was I a whore, and would I rather be a whore or a Christian? She upset me so much I cried, but even worse, she told my father. He was furious. "I feel like I should hit you," he growled. "But it won't do any good. I will humiliate you enough to be memorable." He proceeded to tell everyone in the church about my transgression.

Nothing could be kept hidden once it was in the church's pipeline. About fifty church members had to come and talk to me and ask me if I still wanted to be here and question why I did what I had done. Megan said my obsession with boys would ruin my life. Jael reminded me that the devil was always lurking to offer us temptations. The body language of members after they were through talking to me distressed me more than the lecturing. It was almost unbearable. They avoided me at pickets. If I was standing on one corner, they would walk right by me and stand somewhere else. They'd laugh in my general direction and sneer at me. They wouldn't joke with me, or even say hi. Pickets used to be an opportunity to socialize. Instead, I'd have to endure thirty to forty minutes of being shunned, even by my best friends.

Shirley, however, was surprisingly gentle. She sat me down to talk to me. "When I was young, I made mistakes and ended up getting pregnant," she said. She didn't want the young people in the church to make the same mistakes she had made. She said the best way to avoid danger was to stay busy. She gave me as many chores as she possibly could to make sure every moment of my day was filled. I weeded the yards, mowed the lawns, emptied the wastebaskets, cleaned the floors, and did anything else she could think of.

Margie, who had never liked me much, wanted to instill guilt about what had happened with Brian. "This is never going to happen again," she admonished. "If you can't stop thinking about being in a relationship, you are a weakling. Grow up and get over it." She wasn't done with me. Next, she took me with her on an out-of-town business trip about a legal matter. The most embarrassing part was that she brought her son Jacob along, too. He was close to me in age, making it all the more awkward and embarrassing. "We are not going to tolerate this," she said, as we drove along through the cornfields of central Kansas, a pair of eyeglasses perched at the end of her nose. "Next time, you are out. I hope you realize the seriousness of what you have done." For the next two days, she chastised me in front of Jacob, telling me that it was not right to lust after boys.

I wished I hadn't gone to Brian's house, only because it wasn't worth the humiliation. I felt embarrassed and really insignificant, and I thought that if I died, nobody would even care. When Margie and I got back, people in the church gave me horrible looks. They talked about me behind my back, saying I didn't belong, warning one another that being with me would cause you to sin and have sex, and that wanting a boyfriend was evil, worthy of hell. Members would call me over at a picket to talk to me about what I had done. "Do you realize you are tempting God and tempting hell? God can kill you any day for doing things like this," some of them told me. I found it hard to believe that I was the only girl who had ever felt this way about boys, but that was the way it seemed. I hadn't known I was going to be stranded by a flat tire and get caught. Now, I knew my car crisis had been a message from God expressing his disappointment in me.

My parents said they were done with me and sick of answering my questions, which they thought were just attempts of mine to find a loophole and do as I pleased. They grounded me and didn't let me out of the house for anything other than pickets, chores, and school. I had to check in constantly if I was out of the house. Mom monitored everything I did at home. Anything involving trust, even driving unsupervised, wasn't allowed. There was little chance I'd be earning the trust back any time soon.

I was still allowed to go to Topeka West, but my father pulled me out of the technical school one month before I was supposed to get my nurse's aide certificate, which meant I couldn't be certified and had to wait until the second semester of nursing school to get it. This was the second time my father had withdrawn me from school over a boy. I was really upset about it. I told him I hadn't done anything, but he said I had been tempted by evil, and therefore I was a sinner in his eyes. No matter what I did, there was bound to be humiliation, phone calls, people having me to dinner to tell me what I had done wrong, all the adults, all my peers, all criticizing me relentlessly, but out of love. As for Brian, I never saw him again.

That was a turning point in the way I was accepted and viewed in the eyes of the church and my family. In the WBC, you got only three chances for everything. After three strikes on the same issue, you were done, thrown out. I was now in a probationary situation. After this incident, I was still a member, but they had me on watch. I was caught between two incredible extremes, the natural hormonal curiosity about the other sex and then this guilty, nasty feeling for being curious, so I tried to suppress any kind of impulses I had.

For a long time, I didn't have any more incidents with boys. Jael was always with me, having been told to make sure I didn't do anything wrong. She had to carpool with me to keep an eye on me for the rest of high school. Jael wasn't sanctimonious toward me, which I really appreciated. She understood that people made mistakes. She gave me advice, but she wasn't judgmental or ruthless. She was one of the only people who tried to cheer me up, suggesting we play volleyball or do something fun in the yard if I was really down. If we talked to a boy at school, she wouldn't say, "Are you thinking about sex?" She relieved some of my anxiety by making me feel I was worth something.

She didn't feel like a chaperone. We'd cry in front of each other and share our fears. She would open up to me about when her parents argued, or when she caught her brother watching porn. I had every reason to believe that we were good, loyal friends. I didn't dare step out of line, so Jael really didn't have any dirt on me to report back to anyone. Besides, I didn't want to put her in the middle, knowing that she had a duty to tell on anyone who broke the rules. I didn't entertain escaping the church, either. I would never have wanted to live without my family, and there were too many things I didn't like about life on the outside. I didn't have much self-esteem anymore. My hair was ratty, my clothes were wrinkled, and I wasn't taking good care of myself. I felt insecure and ugly. Maybe I was subconsciously making sure I wasn't attractive. But whatever the reason, I didn't want to get in trouble.

I still talked to boys, but only when it was about church business and therefore sanctioned by Shirley. We were interviewed all the time by college students, some studying religion and some in filmmaking classes looking at us as a good subject. Lots of the film students were interested in making documentaries for their classes, and of course the church was very eager for its members to be interviewed. Shirley liked us to be the representatives of the church for these projects, because we were the "young faces" of the WBC. We were the same age as these guys, so we couldn't be written off as old-fashioned, out of touch, or dark-age dinosaurs.

I still had a natural inclination to look attractive for the interviews, so I still tended to get a little dressed up when I knew cameras would be present, but I now took extra care to look conservative and appropriate and act the same way. My girlfriends liked flirting with the college guys who were interviewing us. I thought Megan and Jael sometimes teased boys too much, using big, coy smiles to punctuate their arguments. "You are going to hell because you didn't obey the Lord your God," they'd say, batting their eyelashes and smiling their dimpled smiles. In the girls' thinking, it was all innocent, because anyone with a brain in his head had to know they were unavailable. I found this a little hypocritical: flirting while talking about church activities. They claimed they were doing what they were supposed to be doing. They loved the media and being in the spotlight, and they were getting attention nonstop, like celebrities. I was not as high-profile as the Phelps granddaughters, so luckily I wasn't as sought after. There was too much risk in having anyone think I was taking my flirting too far.

The girls definitely weren't crazy mean to me about boys. They tried to be really good influences, letting me know that boys were my biggest threat. "That's your weakness, that has always been your weakness," they'd warn me. The church commonly identified members by what that person's weakness was, and mine was vanity, which was paired with being a whore. Margie's weakness was wanting babies, so she was deemed "selfish" and "fleshy," as opposed to spiritual. My father's weakness was arrogance. Taylor's weakness was laziness—she never wanted to move an inch. I'd get annoyed with her, but I personally thought that was how she kept out of the crosshairs. As long as none of us acted on our weaknesses, though, we were okay. "Some people here don't have that problem of being attracted to boys, but you do, it is obvious," the girls would insist. I'd get shot down if I hinted that they flirted, too. "Some of these girls are stronger than you and don't go off and do this," they'd say back to me.

They didn't shy away from using the *whore* word against me. "You can go be a whore if you want. That's what you are if you don't stop thinking about boys. You're a whore." That word was used so much around me and in that culture that I almost got desensitized. My father had started calling me that systematically when I was trying to flirt with the motocross boy in Florida. Back then, I would fight back, saying, "No, I am not." But now, I'd become so desensitized to it that it was like saying someone was an "idiot." I wasn't particularly caught off guard or superoffended anymore. I knew that if someone so much as wanted to kiss a boy, that made her a "whore."

The church had the logic that once you were Christian, everything about your life changed, and you couldn't go back. Dad was not a Christian until he was baptized into the church at age thirty-five, so he had gotten to experience a wild side in his adolescence and young adulthood. I became a Christian when I was fifteen, and now I was trying to lead the righteous life expected of me. Slowly, I began to stop being so hard on myself and did some harmless flirting on the level the Phelps girls were doing—smiling and laughing with boys, but nothing more. After all, they weren't classifying their behavior as whorish, and they had to know the standard. For their entire lives, they had seen their older siblings and cousins manage these delicate matters.

Because there was no dating in the church, flirting was technically harmless. We didn't use the word *dating*, because to us it was a term loaded with implications of fornication and sexuality. Instead, when two people were interested in marrying each other, they "courted."

The system of courtship was based on a set of unwritten rules. Only when we were through with college could we be in a courtship. It was acceptable to court someone only when both people had an established career and the male had set himself up with a home, so that both parties were mature and fiscally responsible. Young women in the church, though, lived at home until they were married. There was no possibility of women going away and living on their own when they graduated from college; only those who had reached their thirties without marrying could live on their own.

The opportunity for the members of my age group to marry, however, was becoming scarce to nil, especially as the rigid marriage rules changed frequently on the whim of the pastor or Margie. At first, members could marry anyone, as long as the mate was willing to be baptized in our church and become a committed member. Of the pastor's nine children who were still in the church, four of them—Fred Jr., Shirley, Jonathan, and Tim—had married outsiders who were now members. Two—Becky and Rachel—had married members. Three—Margie, Liz, and Abigail—remained unmarried and lived in their own households.

Ben Phelps, the oldest of the pastor's grandchildren, was supposed to be the last person allowed to marry someone who was not already a member of the church. He had met his wife, Mara

Jones, at the University of Kansas, where he taught courses in information technology. She had been one of his students and had expressed interest in his religion. Mara cared enough about Ben to get baptized into the church before the two started courting. They had been married by the pastor nine months before our arrival in Topeka.

After Ben and Mara's marriage, the pastor made more restrictive rules. A person who wanted to marry could choose only someone who was already a church member. This made the prospect of growing the church through marriage and babies pretty impossible, since there certainly weren't any people knocking down the church doors looking to join.

Sam Phelps, who was three years younger than his cousin Ben, had two choices for a wife within the membership: Jennifer or Katherine Hockenbarger. Everyone else his age was related to him. He chose to court Jennifer, who at twenty-four was two years his senior. He owned a home, and he and Jennifer both had college degrees and careers, so the pastor gave them his blessing to court. This was the one and only courtship I ever witnessed, and it was fascinating.

Courtships were a very old-fashioned regimented ritual and weren't necessarily designed to help you decide if you liked somebody. Once you began a courtship, the expectation was that you were going to marry that person. It was a total arrangement to be entered into no more lightly than marriage itself. It seemed backward and weird, but that was the rule. But in the case of Sam and Jen, they really liked each other even before they started courting officially, so that was good.

Couples in a courtship had to have a chaperone with them whenever they were together. Once in a while I was a chaperone for Sam and Jennifer. Sam was six years older than me, but it wasn't weird to be his chaperone. Both Sam and Jennifer were already my friends. We went to pickets together, ate together, and did schoolwork together. When I chaperoned them, I was really just hanging out with two people who happened to be courting. We'd go to the mall, walk around, and grab a bite at the food court.

I wasn't sure if there were actual rules for chaperones or behavior on their part that I had to be on guard for. Were they allowed to kiss? They didn't try to do anything physical, but I wasn't sure if I was supposed to report back to Shirley if they did. I knew people who courted were allowed to talk on the phone, but they weren't allowed to be alone together in person. After six months, Sam officially proposed to Jennifer. They were allotted five minutes alone together, enough time for him to pop the question, her to accept, and them to give each other a peck. Even after they were officially engaged, they couldn't be together without a chaperone until they were married.

Six months later, on August 10, 2002, the wedding took place. It was a festive celebration, with all of the elements of a traditional Christian wedding—the church service with an exchange of vows, the pronunciations of man and wife offered by the pastor, and the reception immediately following. Shirley had the reception in her basement, with lots of donated potluck dishes, soft drinks, photos, toasts to the bride and groom, and dancing. Consuming alcohol was frowned upon, so there was no booze.

I wasn't at an age where getting married was a pressing concern, but probably like any other teenage girl at a wedding, I fantasized about what my future had in store for me. Being a WBC member made getting married particularly problematic, but if I asked how to bring someone into my life, I got either "You are such a whore for focusing so much on boys" or "God will bring someone to you." The whole system seemed so filled with inconsistencies and bent rules, all depending on the circumstances.

My friends never expressed much of an interest in getting married, except for Sara. She was Libby's older sister, another daughter of Fred Phelps Jr. She was four years older than me and two years older than Libby. She was petite, with an infectious, bright white smile and green eyes, and a loud, beautiful singing voice, which she loved to use on the picket line. One day I heard Sara tell Shirley that someone was flirting with her at work, which she said made her realize she wanted to get married. She added that she was feeling vulnerable and had wanted to flirt back, but she had stifled the urge. I wasn't sure if she was asking Shirley for advice on how to handle it, but Sara did say that she didn't think anyone was ever going to join the church just to marry her. "I am glad you are realizing that," Shirley said with great satisfaction.

Shirley thought she and her niece were in agreement, but then Sara started bawling her eyes out at the thought that she was never going to get married. A day later, after she had settled herself, she made a complete about-face. She told me that she had come to realize how evil marriage was, how it brought you down and away from your true purpose. Marriage was hell and fire, and celibacy was a singleness of devotion to God, she said, so it wasn't like you were really alone.

"You have to find focus in something else, put your energy into something else," Sara told me, explaining her rejection of marital dreams. I wasn't convinced she was fine. I thought she was probably just suppressing her desires. She feared being humiliated for flirting, so she had decided to forget the whole thing.

The marriage system was so arbitrary, though. Some of the members hadn't courted people in the church. How were they meeting someone outside the church at all? Wasn't it frowned upon to talk to outsiders of the opposite sex unless they were at a picket listening to our message about God? If the standard for a marriage partner was going to be whether or not the person agreed with our religion, then how come anyone wasn't allowed to find someone on the outside who was willing to join our religion?

I couldn't make sense of it. If I was going to marry someone in the church, I occasionally thought about who that might be. I wasn't daydreaming or fantasizing about anyone in particular; I was just trying to understand in a concrete way. Some of the boys in the church were my age, but I had grown up with them over the past few years, so it would be like marrying my brother.

Jael had three brothers whom I was friendly with, but they were closer to Taylor in age. Paulette, Jael's mother, was funny about my interactions with them, though. "I have teenage boys to protect," she'd say to me if I arrived at their house dressed in baggy boy shorts and a tank top. "Wear more layers." I'd say okay and add a T-shirt, but she made me feel like I was causing problems. I was too young to worry about it and just did what she asked.

Shirley's son Joshua, who was about two years older than me, and Margie's son Jacob, who was my age, were my only real prospects. Joshua was really nice, but he was already through high school. There was the tiniest bit of something between Jacob and me. I knew that he had always liked me. He used to ask me loaded questions. "When are you going to finish school?" he'd say. "You can't get married unless you finish school." I hadn't even had the time to question if I could ever have feelings for him. Every minor action had to have such long-term consequences. The "community involvement" filled anything and everything with so much pressure that I didn't know how to act. I didn't know if I should be reserved, forward, coy, naïve, uninterested, or anything else when I was around him. He was nice, but I hadn't been sitting around thinking *I wonder if he would be a good match for me* until the pastor's announcement banning outside marriages. Then, I started asking myself questions. Should I like him because he was the only one available to me? Did I have options? Did I want to be married? I thought I did, but sometimes I wondered if WBC marriages were more like arranged marriages and not based on love. Going on about something as important as who I would marry, with the community weighing in, felt so unnatural. Sometimes I thought it might be better to deny my hormones and forget boys forever, like the nuns, just to let God know I could conquer mortal feelings if I tried my very best.

CHAPTER THIRTEEN

Thou hypocrite, first cast out the beam out of
thine own eye; and then shalt thou see clearly to
cast out the mote out of thy brother's eye.

—Matthew 7:5

I still had more questions than anybody in the congregation was
willing to answer. Certain verses in the Bible seemed contradictory to so many things we were preaching at the pickets, but I
wasn't able to get explanations as to why. I thought people who
challenged us deserved honest, straightforward answers. One of
my biggest problems was trying to reconcile the scripture with
our message, especially when it came to death. A lot of people
at the pickets wanted to know how we could make definitive
statements such as "Thank God for September 11" and "Thank
God for dead soldiers." I wondered, too, how we could say these
things with such authority when Ezekiel 18:32 says, "For I have
no pleasure in the death of him that dieth" and Ezekiel 33:11,
where he says, "I have no pleasure in the death of the wicked;
but that the wicked turn from his way and live: turn ye, turn ye
from your evil ways; for why will ye die, O house of Israel?" People at the pickets would ask me, "God wants us to go to hell?" I
really didn't feel like I knew the answer.

The church had taught me to put my doubts in a certain context if I was having trouble with scripture, but it still didn't add

up for me. I didn't want to fight, though, so I accepted that certain things were fundamental beliefs of the church, but I never felt satisfied. My name was already associated with words like *tension*, *strife*, and *contention*. Church members liked to say that I stirred up strife. They thought I was trying to change the rules, that I was up to no good, and that I was trying to find loopholes. I was not intentionally trying to be contrary or malicious. I was just trying to logically understand when things were okay in the WBC, what our religion was, and why we were allowed to do some things and not others.

Sometimes in a Bible study I just couldn't keep myself from posing what I thought were probing, intelligent questions or bringing up inconsistencies about things like unconditional election, eternal damnation in hell, and Judgment Day. I would read a verse in the Bible about a catastrophic disaster, then say, "This doesn't seem to match up with what we tell everyone about calamities and tragedies." We were telling people at our pickets all these prophecies, but I was reading something different. At the very least, I felt the biblical events were open to interpretation. God wasn't always straightforward, and His references didn't necessarily mean the same thing in every verse. The church was trying to make everything black and white, but I didn't see how we could be that certain.

There was nothing I could do about what the church members thought of me. They misunderstood my curiosity as skepticism. I wanted to be a good Christian, and having my questions answered was important. Nevertheless, Shirley dismissed me. She told me, "Nobody else asks questions, not like this," and she said the pastor was in agreement. The part that bothered me the most was that everybody else was also asking questions that were seen as sincere. I thought mine should be, too, and I wasn't sure why I was being singled out as a contrarian. Doubting Thomas, one of Jesus' twelve apostles, had asked questions about the verity of the crucifixion, and he had later been sainted. I just wanted to know how to explain passages that seemed contradictory to me. If someone asked me, "Why would you thank God for killing our soldiers?" I wanted to have a dignified answer. I didn't think that saying "because he didn't obey" was sufficient. There were examples in the Bible where a person dutifully obedient to God was severely afflicted, like Job, and other people who had led disobedient lives went unpunished on earth, like Pontius Pilate.

My passion for studying the Bible was falling off because of the way I was constantly rejected. If I couldn't ask questions, I couldn't move forward. I still knew how to respond to people in public who would hammer us by asking how we could be so cruel and unpatriotic, or by telling us to move to another country. I knew the scripture inside out and many passages word for word. In terms of being passionate and being involved in the ministry, however, I was stuck and very frustrated.

I was feeling irrelevant, because I wanted to be in the church, but I heard rumblings that people were beginning to say that I didn't belong. I wasn't sure if there was a ringleader who was undermining me. Church members didn't mind sharing their intuitions with me, no matter how much they hurt my feelings. "Oh, you don't belong here," or "I'm not sure the church is for you," they would say. The intuitions did not come all at once, but throughout the years. They weren't always spoken. Sometimes they were in the way people acted. They didn't want you near them, or they didn't want your influence or opinion. They didn't want to take your advice anymore. They didn't want you to babysit or to come around for dinner. Everybody seemed to be drifting away. I felt that it was them against me, a very unpleasant, paranoid feeling.

My feeling of being excluded got even worse after I was involved in three little fender-benders. I admit I wasn't the greatest driver, and my constant anxiety about doing something wrong didn't help. One time, I rear-ended someone with a broken taillight in the rain. Another time, Taylor was with me while I was pulling Dad's big-ass truck into a parking space, and I scraped a parked car. I was so freaked out that I left the parking lot and stopped around the block to call my mother. She told me to go back to the parking lot and find the driver. When I got back, however, the car was gone, and I never heard anything more from the other car's driver. The third time was the scariest because I had young passengers. I was transporting two of Tim's kids from a picket, and as I was getting into traffic from the shoulder, I was sideswiped on the driver's side. After that, nobody asked me to drive their kids anymore, further cementing my black-sheep status. It wasn't an executive decision, as far as I knew, but I was one of the only teenagers who didn't get asked to drive other people's children. The stigma placed on me was that I was unsafe, that I was not a responsible person.

I was so scrutinized, I had a hard time enjoying myself on fun outings, such as Brent and Shirley's annual ski trip to Loveland, Colorado. It had taken two years for Shirley to even include me, and I tried my best to get my insecurities under control on the vacation. All the kids and teens would pile into the Phelps-Ropers' huge van for the eight-hour drive to Denver, where we'd ski and snowboard for a week. Brent was so much fun, helping us to improve our skills by moving us from the blue trails to the black diamonds. Even on the slopes, though, I felt like I was being compared to the Phelps kids, and I always came up short. I craved acceptance. I wanted respect and recognition for the things I did do well, but I was so torn down or picked apart for small, inconsequential mistakes that my self-esteem was being completely eroded.

The worst part was, now that everything I did was being watched, my mother was on my case more than ever. She had always been insecure about her own status and about how our family was perceived. The Phelpses talked in a very condescending, highfalutin way: they knew the Bible better, they had more children, and their children did everything for their mothers. My bad status meant she was a bad parent. On the occasion that Shirley criticized me in front of my mother, Mom would respond by saying to me, "Oh, Lauren, you are so embarrassing." I believed Mom was so desperate to elevate her own status that she thought ripping me to shreds in front of others would ultimately be good for her. Plus, I was the oldest, so I represented "the best" of Steve and Luci Drain's parenting.

If we'd been assigned a neighborhood project such as raking leaves, my mother would ask, "How many bags did you get? Did you get as many bags as the other girls?" For a cleaning project, it would be the same thing. "Did you clean up as much as the other kids?" She was a wreck over the thought that I wasn't as valuable to the group as someone else, and she was relentless in comparing me with people she thought were more worthy.

The first time my parents asked me if I thought I deserved to belong to the church, it scared the hell out of me. It was after I'd kissed the boy from the tech school that they questioned the validity of my membership, and I was reminded that I could fall off at any time and be thrown into hell. Such fear did keep me in check. It made me think twice before saying or doing things.

According to the church, when you died, you were in heaven, or you were in hell. There was no delay. Everyone who was dead was in one of those two places immediately upon his death and was there right now. Being a baptized member when you died was imperative for going to heaven. If you died out of membership, you were bound for hell. "Membership" did not extend to being in fellowship with other churches or congregations, just the WBC. The reason other churches fell short was that those institutions of God should have been out visibly and vocally protesting things and situations in His name. The end of the world was upon us, there were so many sins, and these other churches were just sitting on their hands. That meant God hadn't sent them to spread His Word, like He had sent us.

The WBC had a specific vision of what the afterlife was like. Heaven was being with God. You were with all knowledge and became all-knowing, like God. You were aware of all the scripture of the Bible, and all discrepancies and enigmas fell away. On one side of a divide were all God's people, which was heaven. Then, there was a gulf, a fence, a fixed area you couldn't pass, and beyond that gulf down below was hell.

There were billions of people in hell, 99.9 percent of all the people who had ever lived and died. The other 0.1 percent was in heaven. The "saved" could see the reprobates down in hell burning, which was conveyed to us as the most appealing part of being one of the chosen ones, though the way it was presented didn't make it look sadistic. Megan, Bekah, and Jael would tell me we were going to recognize the people who were covered in flames. I, too, bought into the idea that we deserved the pleasure of watching them get their due as they writhed in torment for all eternity, and every second filled with the worst pain imaginable. Just as we in heaven could see them, they could see us relishing God's glory in heaven, making their torment that much worse. Our comments and judgments could also pass through and be heard by the hell dwellers. Those of us in heaven could shout scripture and tell them, "I warned you, but you chose not to obey." We would also finally get to see who had made it to heaven before us. Sometimes, the pastor would search for a sister church of like opinion, not to merge with ours, but so that we could find other chosen ones. On the rare occasion that he found one that was quite similar, he would find something wrong with it, and that would be it. The WBC had been picketing since 1991, and had been all over the United States. If God had wanted our church to find a co-church, He would have made such a union happen by making the churches find out about each other. But it was not God's will. We were the only chosen few.

At one point in time, the pastor thought of the Westbrook New Testament Baptist Church in Indianapolis, Indiana, as a sister church. He and Westbrook Baptist's pastor, Forrest Stanley Judd, were longtime friends. When Shirley was growing up, she had been particularly fond of the pastor's wife, Iva Jean, and was heartsick when Iva passed away in 1986 at the age of sixty. Shirley and a few of her siblings accompanied the pastor to Indianapolis for Iva's funeral, where Gramps performed the eulogy.

Nobody from our congregation had been back to their church since then, but when our picketing took us to Indianapolis, Shirley arranged for us to meet up with some of Westbrook's surviving members. On the drive to Indianapolis, she was wavering between joy at the reunion, sadness at remembering the loss of her friend Iva, and extreme apprehension that something was going to be wrong. She was having an intuition that they were no longer going to share our beliefs. The thirty of us in our group met up with them at a Burger King near our picket site. They were going to join us at a large convention where a homosexuality-endorsing event was taking place. They had their own signs and picketed locally, which was why the pastor thought they were like us.

196

It didn't take long for us to realize that they had changed. Megan, Bekah, and I were standing with the girls from the other church on one of the four corners we were occupying, as Megan led the questioning about their beliefs. We found out that women in their congregation had been cutting their hair, which was disrespectful to God. They gave us plenty of excuses, saying it was too heavy and giving them headaches, but they were changing other things, too.

For example, they now condoned divorce. While talking to Pastor Judd, Shirley learned that he had remarried, which he was allowed to do as a widower. However, other parishioners had divorced and remarried, which was considered adultery in our faith. We started yelling at them, chastising them for changing the rules of their church, and they became really angry. Shirley, who believed it was the pastor's new wife who was steering the congregation in a new direction, was crazy upset. She was convinced that Iva had been the last good person from that congregation. The WBC believed that one good person could keep a church and a country alive, but now this congregation was doomed.

In our own community, though, the pastor really and truly wanted the people to stay in the church. He wasn't a condemning, debasing fire-breather all the time. In fact, he was actually a little compassionate. "You've learned your lesson—let's move on," he'd say. There couldn't possibly be constant humiliation, or nobody would stay. "You're not going to leave me? You're not going to do anything foolish?" the pastor would ask all of us, usually leaving it to the other elders to keep everyone in line and dispense the hard-core humiliation.

I saw a few people get kicked out for various sins. Chris Davis had been kicked out before my family got to Kansas, and I saw him get kicked out for the second time. He was married to

Becky Phelps, the eighth of the pastor's children, who worked as an attorney at Phelps Chartered. Becky once told me that she had been a wild child when she had been my age. She used to go dancing and skating, and actually smoked cigarettes and wore makeup. She said her disobedience had gotten her in a lot of trouble with her father, but as she matured she had come around. Becky and Chris had been married a long time and had four children together.

Chris was in his late forties when the pastor started having serious doubts about him. The pastor's biggest grievances were that Chris was lazy and not a proper head of his household. He was considered a slacker because he rarely went to pickets and never showed up at the construction projects to pitch in. It was not required, but it was expected that guys would help, since they were the sole source of labor for these renovations. Five to ten guys would show up on any given day and put in a few evening hours working on whoever's house was being remodeled. Otherwise the jobs would never get done. Chris was reminded to put in hours, but he never did.

Chris was also overweight, and the pastor said he hadn't been instructing his kids to do physical exercise, and they were becoming overweight, too. He thought that Chris and his kids were simply not making the effort to stay in shape. Besides the laziness and weight issues, Chris's kids were also being unruly and not doing their chores, which meant Chris was not serving as an effective head of the household.

I heard that Chris's supposed laziness and lack of familial authority were enough for the congregation to vote him out, although if he could prove himself worthy they would allow him back in. He was permitted to remain in his house with his wife and children during this probationary period. There was no absolute set rule as to the length of time for a suspended membership. In Chris's case, about a year passed before they voted to allow him back in. Of course, he was married to a Phelps, which helped his case.

I was there when Chris was thrown out for the second and final time. He had been back in the church for about a year, and his children were still misbehaving. I thought Chris was a decent guy, but I agreed with the consensus of everybody who had known him a lot longer than me, that he was lazy and a slacker. This time, Chris was not going to be allowed to stay in his home. Members held a secret meeting to come up with an eviction plan. Shirley was going to be the leader of a big SWAT team–style effort. Church members knew that as soon as word got out that someone had been deemed unworthy, there was no telling how he or she would react, and that he could potentially freak out and get violent.

"He is dangerous; he is the devil," Shirley would say about anyone who was being disfellowshipped; in this case, it was Chris. The church needed to protect the wife and children in case of violence, so members would sneak them out of their houses before delivering the news. The leaders of the operation against Chris thought they should surprise him when he was sleeping to minimize his chance of reacting badly. The okay to proceed always came from the Holy Ghost through Shirley. She'd get an overwhelming feeling and know the time was right.

That very night, the eviction took place. First, Chris's wife and children, already on board with the plan, were quietly removed. Then, with a heavy shake, the disfellowship team woke Chris up, ordering him, "You need to get out, get your stuff out." While he was still packing, they told him he would be divorcing his wife. Technically, it was going to be a separation because marriage was a lifelong covenant. They also told him he needed to give the church monthly financial child support for his four children or risk being sued for the money.

After Chris got kicked out, Becky started telling everyone how unhappy she had been in the marriage, and how peaceful the household was now that he was gone. She knew she'd never marry again, but she also knew she couldn't bear living with slovenly Chris anymore. Sometimes, I wondered if Becky wasn't behind a plot to get rid of Chris because she was tired of him.

Chris, though, was totally distraught. Hoping he could still win back the favor of his church and his family, he picketed some places by himself using a GOD HATES FAGS sign he still had in his possession. However, pickets were church-sanctioned events, and anything related to them—T-shirts, picket signs, printed materials—was owned by the church. Disfellowshipped former members were not supposed to be in possession of any of our materials, so when Shirley learned what Chris was doing, she ordered him to turn in his signs and told him he wasn't al-lowed to picket anymore. Chris then tried other things, such as e-mailing Shirley about money issues he was having, but she told him she couldn't help him. Several months later, some of us ran into him in the city. He looked like he had lost a hundred pounds, probably from all the stress. At one point, there was some discussion about whether he would be allowed to come back, but Shirley never acted on it, and Becky never particu-larly pushed for it, either.

The saddest event was when Bill and Mary Hockenbarger, after having been in the church for almost five decades, found themselves under intense scrutiny. For years, the pastor had been trying to get them to move to the block, saying the world was ending soon. They lived about half an hour away, but the Phelpses wanted everybody close. Shirley and others who had money were still buying up houses, and they had one they thought the Hockenbargers should occupy. Bill and Mary said no; they were happy where they were. Shirley thought it was because they were older, so moving would be too much trouble for them.

She started to send e-mails about them, beginning with lines like "I wonder what is going on with them." E-mails and church gossip started to intensify. "I kind of want to go over to their house and see what is going on, because maybe they have too much to do to move," Shirley would say or write. The Hockenbargers had no idea they were the center of discussion, because they were older, didn't use e-mail, and weren't around the church to hear the gossip. Finally, one day Shirley said, "Let's just go do it. Let's go help them move." Everyone listened to Shirley about things like this. She had a very generous heart and knew the collective action of the community would really make the task manageable, like a barn raising.

One day about thirty of us showed up at their house. As was typical, the workforce was mostly the young people, sprinkled with a few elders like Dad and Shirley, who liked this kind of hands-on work and acted as the overseers. Two of the Hockenbargers' grandchildren, Charles and Katherine, were also with us that afternoon. We descended on the Hockenbarger property in a few vehicles and parked along the street to begin the surprise cleanup, pack-up, and move. Mary and Bill met us at the door.

We were almost in shock when we saw what was ahead of us. We'd known that the Hockenbargers had a hobby of going to garage sales and buying things, but we thought it was a casual pastime, something they did on Sunday afternoons. It turned out that they had so much stuff, we couldn't get through the rooms. It looked like a hoarder's mess, with garbage, clothes, and useless things everywhere. The garage and shed were filled with rusted tools, an old tractor, and a big rusted snowplow.

Shirley ordered a Dumpster to be delivered immediately to get rid of the "idols." She was always talking about "idols," which weren't just images but any worldly possessions you had become attached to, as well as attitudes and behaviors. Anything that was put before God in somebody's life, such as pride, vanity, or even a child, could be labeled an "idol." The church members would find your idols if you did something wrong before God.

As soon as the Dumpster arrived, we followed Shirley's order to throw everything in it. The Holy Ghost was telling Shirley to tell us to clean this house now, and we got started immediately. There was no reason to postpone a decision to think it through. If you were not doing it right away, you were not serving God.

The thirty of us began throwing away everything in this house of idols, from lamps and knickknacks to household appliances that no longer worked. We began tossing things into the Dumpster with abandon, and having all the kids together made the gigantic task fun. Bill Hockenbarger had no choice in the matter. He was stunned and shaken. "Your idols are gone," Shirley preached at him in front of everyone. She was practically taunting him. "Are you upset we are doing this? If you are, then you are going against God."

My father was trying to use a more practical approach, explaining to Bill that getting rid of things that had no function was for the best. He found a set of rusty levels that were totally outmoded. Dad thought he needed to show him how useless these tools were by demonstrating how the metal piece of the level toppled over when he tried to use it. He was trying to reason with him, but he was being really overbearing and controlling. I wasn't sure why watching the way my father was speaking to Bill struck me as really funny, when it was really so sad.

This was Bill's lifetime hobby, collecting all this stuff. He was freaking out and pacing. When we moved toward his old snowplow in the shed, he began screaming. Normally, he was a soft-spoken, gentle, skinny old guy, but the anxiety was killing him. "You are not throwing this away! Get out!" he screamed, throwing himself onto the plow. A few people wrestled him away, picked up the rusted heap of metal, and dragged it into the Dumpster.

We all stopped what we were doing. We looked to the elders for what to do next. Shirley said, "We are done, we are done with them." She looked at Bill and said, "You are over. You are out"—just like that.

"We're leaving them with their idols," Shirley announced to the group. As we walked to the vans, she threw up her hands. "Well," she said, "we had to kick someone out because of their love of trash." As quickly as we had arrived, we left the Hockenbargers with half their possessions in the Dumpster. The consensus was we didn't need them any longer. The church was a complete body. If there was a member missing who was supposed to be there, the church would be off balance until it was complete again. On the other hand, people who weren't supposed to be in our community were like a cancer, and the sooner we got rid of them the better. Leaving there that day, I knew that the disfellowship process was about to begin.

The process of banishing someone was the strangest thing I'd ever witnessed. Some people were just stunned, like the Hockenbargers. Others, like Chris, were unbelievably distraught. I personally had a weird feeling of entitlement before another member was kicked out. There was so much power in telling someone he was unworthy. Sometimes, I couldn't wait until the day came when we would disfellowship someone. But other times, I was so heartbroken over the loss I would bawl my eyes out.

The official meeting to declare the Hockenbargers disfellowshipped took place in two parts: first, the members met to discuss the matter in private, and then the Hockenbargers were invited in to make their case. The private meeting took place in Shirley's basement. Those who were out of town or couldn't make it joined by conference call. We were all invited to share remarks about their transgressions. "They are rebellious and not part of God's people," someone said. Everyone started making fun of Bill and how he liked old tools, an old snowplow, and garbage more than God. Even his son and grandson joined in, with his grandson repeating, "Just get him out, just get him out."

I was crying and very upset, but I didn't have anything to add in their defense or to further the attack on them. The harshness was overwhelming. Mary and Bill had been in the church since 1955, had raised their children and grandchildren there, and had great-grandchildren on the way. Most people were red-faced mad at the Hockenbargers, but Bekah, like me, was crying, too.

Jael's mother, Paulette, tried to console me. "This is the way it is supposed to go down," she said, telling me to get a tougher skin. "You can't avoid God's will."

As the discussion continued, I got the sense that the members were leaving the final decision about the Hockenbargers' fate until after they heard from Mary and Bill.

When the premeeting was over, the Hockenbargers were invited in. I watched them shuffle in slowly and take two chairs placed just for them. Once everyone was settled, Shirley asked

Bill if he had anything to say, but all he did was lament the loss of his snowplow, and said nothing about wanting to stay in the church. Mary didn't have much to add, either. The meeting started to get a little out of control, as the expectation had been that Bill was going to admit to his transgression and atone for it. When Mary and Bill got up to leave, some of the members surrounded them outside the meeting room. Through the taunts, I could hear Bill yelling, "Just give me my snowplow back!" They managed to get to their car and drove off.

I loved the Hockenbargers. I couldn't believe what was happening to them. I thought, *How dare we get rid of the snowplow?* I had seen how much it meant to Bill when we had been at their house trying to throw it away. I knew they could have changed people's minds if they had just offered some words in their own defense. If Bill had shown any regret, they might have given them a second chance. Once you were kicked out, communication with your family members who were still in was forbidden. You were at the bottom of the world. You had no authority and no say. You were done. That was God's will—the way it was going to be.

The Hockenbargers didn't make any attempt to come back. They remained in their home in Topeka, but as far as the church was concerned, they were just gone. The Hockenbarger family had been the church's second largest family group after the Phelpses. As high as the animosity in the disfellowship meeting had been, many other members besides me were hurt by the decision to cast them out, but we made peace with it, knowing it was God's will.

Two years later, Karl Hockenbarger, Bill and Mary's son, was also kicked out. He was fifty-three years old and had been baptized into the church when he was nine. He and his wife, Kay, had seven children, two of whom were married to Phelpses. But Karl had committed two transgressions. The first had to do with disciplining his children. He had both underpunished his son by sparing the rod, and then allegedly overcompensated by hitting him too hard. His other sin had been a lack of grace, which meant not living up to God's standard. In his case, it manifested itself as misbehaving at pickets. He was willing to get into physical fights with people who assaulted our groups on the picket lines, which was forbidden. Matthew 5:39 and Luke 6:29 stated that if someone struck you in the face, you were supposed to turn the other cheek, and doing otherwise would severely compromise the integrity of our message.

Unlike his parents, Karl desperately wanted to stay in fellowship. Being kicked out meant he could no longer talk to his wife or children. In the early days of his exile, he had to look for photos of his family on our godhatesfags.com website, where we posted the albums from our latest pickets. Two of his children, James and Michael, left within a few months of their father. James, who was then in his midtwenties, departed on his own, because he was interested in a relationship with a woman at work. Michael was seventeen when he left. He had always been a troublemaker. In the middle of a Bible study, he'd say something absurd like, "There's no proof Pharaoh died." He was arrogant and always begging for attention. When he started defending Karl, the membership asked him to leave.

Eventually, Kay left, too, to be with her husband, though both Kay and Karl wanted to get back in. I heard that they were terrified of going to hell, the hottest part of which was saved for people who were thrown out of the WBC or had left on their own. There was no chance for their salvation, since they were no longer part of God's elect.

Shirley would go through the motions of sadness when somebody left, either by choice or the church's decision. "They just didn't make it," she'd lament. Then, everyone would get overwhelmed with happiness, whether they were truly happy or not. We would have to offer praise to God for His decision. "It's God's judgment, God's will" was the joyful consensus. The members would dramatically declare they had never loved the person who'd left. They'd bash the person's character with any negative comment they could think of. Libby, Megan, and Jael were particularly mean-spirited. I would always feel relief that I was not the one God had sent away. I could only imagine what would happen to my reputation if I were to get kicked out.

When anyone left, the church members would get so giddy and excited about the cleaning out of the church, the sweeping out of the imposters and weak members. Ever since our arrival, the church had been getting smaller and smaller. But it didn't seem to be cause for concern—according to the pastor, this meant we were getting closer and closer to Judgment Day, the end of the world. On Judgment Day, the Lord Jesus Christ would return in a form that everyone would recognize, a human form, an authoritative form. Every person on earth would be able to see him and know who he was. Instantaneously, everyone would know if he or she was doomed or going to heaven.

The standards for the heaven-bound were simple enough to understand—be a chosen one and repent for your sins. The degree of sinning that could be atoned for was impressive. Shirley had given birth to Sam Phelps out of wedlock, which was not a secret. Anybody in the press who attacked her or the church seemed to bring it up. Shirley tried to minimize it, saying it was due to the foolishness of her youth, but that at least it hadn't excluded her from learning and doing better than other reprobates. She admitted that sex out of wedlock was a sin, but she said the people who mentioned it were engaged in a personal attack, because she had already atoned for it.

Liz Phelps, the pastor's ninth child (and fifth daughter), also had a baby out of wedlock. I heard she blamed her transgression on stress. She had been on a picket where church members had been injured in an attack, and the situation had caused her a moment of weakness. As a result, she had slept with an African-American man and given birth to his baby. "You don't understand—I was stressed out about serving God too much," she'd say. She'd mention her atonement in a totally sanctimonious manner.

I saw such hypocrisy in these kinds of situations. It seemed to me that forgiveness was not being doled out evenly for everyone, that only the Phelpses got to make justifications for their sins. They often blamed transgressions on stress—the stress of the law firm, the stress of being in service to God, the stress of being hated. But they had atoned. It was all about the sins they'd atoned for. God forgave them, but nobody else had the liberty to mess up and atone. I thought it was so bogus, but I tried to submit and understand.

Others seemed to struggle with this, too. Betty Schurle-Phelps, Fred Jr.'s wife, made the mistake of holding a grudge against Shirley on account of her fornication. Betty and Shirley were about the same age and hadn't been friends for years. Betty was a church member before the time Shirley had given birth to Sam out of wedlock, so she held on to that bit of information and tended to use it against Shirley if Shirley was acting too righteously.

All the women of that age group—Shirley, Betty, all of Shirley's sisters, and my mother—were in a meeting together when Betty said something insulting to Shirley. My mom spoke up for the first time ever. We had been in the church for about four years by then, and my mother was finally feeling empowered. "You really need to stop this; you need to get along. You are both women of God," she said with conviction. "The only reason I'm bringing this up is because I'm an outsider, so God sent you someone who has an outside perspective."

Shirley and Betty were both stunned, especially since this came from someone as nonthreatening as Mom. They preached that everyone was supposed to be humbled in one way or another, but they usually didn't think it applied to them. The two women did get along after that, so I was sure it made my mother feel like she was part of something important. It gave her some sense of identity to advise on the subject of humility in such an appropriate, sober manner.

Margie wasn't without her own black marks. Her weakness was described as a preoccupation with having a baby, perhaps fueled by seeing Shirley with all of her kids. She didn't have a husband, which was a bit of an obstacle. She had already chosen a name for her daughter, Hannah, and she had the name sanctified so nobody in the church would ever be able to use it. In time, Margie adopted her son, Jacob, from a pregnant client of hers and had raised him on her own. I found Margie's treatment of me hypocritical, especially in light of her own personal story; she had clearly forgotten what it was like to be a young girl who was attracted to men and wanted a family.

Jonathan Phelps, the pastor's seventh child, had been involved in a scandal in 1984. He was a law school student when he met Paulette Ossiander, a high school graduate who was not a member of the WBC. She joined the church to please the pastor, but she was still considered substandard by the pastor because she wasn't headed to law school, like his children were. The pastor soon found out that the two were sexually involved and threw Paulette out, but allowed Jonathan to stay under extremely tight restrictions, including being monitored by another church member twenty-four hours a day. The next thing anyone knew, Paulette, by then living nearby with her parents, had given birth to a baby girl, Jael. Six months after the birth, Jonathan petitioned the court for joint custody, since Paulette was refusing to let him have anything to do with her or the child.

At their first court appearance, they both fell back in love, and Paulette invited him to move in with her and her family. They stayed out for more than three years, until the pastor accepted Paulette and brought their whole family back into the fold in 1988. He personally married them at the pulpit of the church. Jael, who was then three, was at the service. They made their atonements, asked God for forgiveness, and picked up their journey from there. The pastor was truly blessed in his decision to invite them back. Jonathan and Jael grew into two of his most faithful and fiery supporters.

Jonathan had actually been the fourth of the pastor's children to leave. Nate, Mark, and Katherine had all left in the 1970s. Katherine supposedly left because her father had been very harsh to her after she talked to a boy on the phone. I heard that she tried to run away a few times, but the pastor always found her and brought her back. When she was eighteen, she left for good. Nate and Mark also left after alleging that their father had physically abused them, their mother, and all their siblings. They said he beat them with his bare fists or a wooden mattock handle, and they couldn't take the torture anymore. Nate was talked into coming back, only to make his final farewell three years later. Dortha, the last of the pastor's children to part ways, left the church in 1990, and changed her last name to make sure her disassociation with the Phelps family was complete. According to her, she chose the surname Bird because that was how she felt: free as a bird.

The Phelpses who had left were pretty vocal about their opinion of their father, but I thought the pastor had a different sensibility about the self-initiated exiles of his sons and daughters. They weren't children of God, plain and simple, and therefore they were liars. They didn't believe in obedience and preferred chasing the opposite sex, the common thread being they had all left out of lust. As for the allegations of abuse, they lied about that because they held grudges about their childhood and their father's military-style application of discipline. We were warned that every media person who brought up the pastor's wayward children was trying to mock the church, so I knew I was going to be subjected to that skewed viewpoint. We did believe in corporal punishment, but we didn't engage in scarring or torture such as the estranged Phelps children tended to describe. Any kid under the age of ten who misbehaved could be taken to another room and spanked and yelled at, but there wasn't anything I saw that was over the top. Before the church, I'd been exposed to corporal punishment, too. Since I had never spoken to Kathy, Mark, Nate, or Dortha, I took the pastor's word for it that the media was asking manipulative questions and trying to demonize the church.

However, I did hear some harrowing stories firsthand. One day, I was sitting with some of my friends and three of the pastor's children, Shirley, Becky, and Fred Jr., as they reminisced about their childhood in the church.

"It wasn't always this easy," Shirley said.

"What do you mean?" I asked her.

The three of them started laughing as they recounted incidents from the past. Some weren't that humorous, but the passage of time had softened their impact and their recollections came off lightly. "Gramps used to be a lot harder on our generation. He was more demanding and the chores were more grueling," Shirley said with a chuckle.

Shirley, Becky, and Fred went on with stories that had examples of his really extreme behavior, such as the time he made them water plants for eight hours straight. One of them said Gramps had a wicked temper back then and would get irate and spank them or be rough with Gran over little things, such as not watering the lawn sufficiently or being overweight.

I was speechless. She was such a gentle, soft-spoken person that I couldn't even fathom it. The three said other things, too, but I wasn't comfortable trying to get any details. I knew I wasn't supposed to ask questions, because all the sins of the past were supposed to stay there.

The Phelps children in my generation had nothing bad to say about their grandfather. He had never harmed any of them in any fashion. They described him as gentle and compassionate. His nine children still in the church seemed extremely fond of him as well, and some of his children who had left eventually came back.

Sometimes, the Holy Ghost made it known that a sinner deserved a second chance. After a period of time, the Holy Ghost would tell a church member about the opportunity to let someone back. This always baffled me. Why was the Holy Ghost telling the pastor or Shirley or Tim to check on this person and give them another chance? Why didn't the Holy Ghost speak to me?

Another thing was becoming rather obvious, too. The Holy Ghost gave second chances only to the blood relatives of the Phelpses.

CHAPTER FOURTEEN

Because I will publish the name of the Lord: as-
cribe ye greatness unto our God.

—Deuteronomy 32:3

I graduated after two years at Topeka West High School with
a great GPA. As usual, about thirty members of the church
were going to be picketing the graduation ceremony, which was
being held at the Kansas Expocentre downtown. We always
picketed the Topeka West graduations, because we thought
it was a homosexual-enabling school, for example, allowing a
Gay-Straight Alliance club. The school's team was the Topeka
Chargers and the mascot was a purple horse, so in addition to
our usual signs, we had a special one for the graduation, FAG
CHARGERS, featuring an image of a horse.

Jael and I talked in detail about whether we were going to attend the graduation, picket it, or both. We finally decided we
were going to picket in our caps and gowns and then attend
the ceremony to get our diplomas. We would be the first ones
in the WBC to picket our own graduation. Everybody before
us had waited inside with their classmates while the rest of us
were picketing outside. It was such a hoot, Jael and me wearing our caps and gowns and yelling "Fag Chargers" and "God
hates Topeka West." Most of the people coming by to get in-

side, where the graduation was being held, just ignored us. But a few classmates commented. "Oh Lauren, why do you always have to picket?" one guy said.

When it was time for the ceremony, Jael and I ran inside and took our seats in the auditorium. The rest of our group put away their signs before joining the audience. As my name was called and I crossed the stage, Dad, Mom, Taylor, Shirley, Megan, Bekah, and the rest of our crowd rang cowbells and yelled "Yay, LAUREN DRAIN." Jael's entrance got the same whooping enthusiasm. Everybody seemed proud of us, and we were very satisfied with our accomplishments.

Jael and I had both been accepted into the nursing program at Washburn University, and we registered for the exact same classes and labs. Washburn University was a highly acclaimed public university in Topeka, with two programs particularly favored by the Phelps family—nursing and law. Almost everybody from our church went there. We were discouraged from going to colleges farther away because the pastor thought we might be led astray if we went to some unknown "evil" campus. Some people were allowed to go to Kansas State in Manhattan, Kansas—about sixty miles from Topeka—or Kansas University's satellite campus in Kansas City, if they could present a good argument as to why they needed to go that far. Libby went to KU in Kansas City for a degree in physical therapy, although the pastor had discouraged it. He thought going away was selfish and foolish, and it was better to stay close to your family. He also worried that if your faith wasn't strong enough, you might get torn away by another religion. You would be putting yourself at risk, and you could literally be pulling yourself away from God.

Even though I chose to stay local for school, college life was definitely interesting. Everyone on campus knew who we were—we were the ones picketing our own school. We stood out because of our long hair, ponytails, braids, and lack of makeup, although we dressed like everybody else on campus, in jeans, yoga pants, exercise clothes, Nike running shoes, and anything else comfortable. There had probably been one Phelps or another at Washburn almost every year for the past four decades. Almost every one of the pastor's children were alumni. Some of the next generation were there or had just graduated when Jael and I enrolled. The church had been holding protest signs along the sidewalks of the campus since the early days of picketing, condemning the university's tolerance of homosexuality.

We were the group most actively trying to change the world. There didn't seem to be many others who cared. Jael was one of the more vocal and politically oriented Phelpses on campus. She had designs on public office. She frequently wrote letters to the editor of the college newspaper. Many of the pastor's grandchildren had been active letter writers to the city newspaper since they were sixteen or seventeen years old. By the time I was sixteen, I had been to multiple city council meetings and had spoken to our mayor and our state representatives. I had been to a presidential inauguration. I had picketed revivals of Billy Graham and Joel Osteen, two of the most popular evangelical preachers in the country. My fellow students didn't have the kind of commitment and political experience that Jael and I did.

Washburn had a fantastic study-abroad program. I thought it was something that I might want to do if my parents would ever allow it and I could fit it into my nursing curriculum. I really wanted to go abroad to study Spanish. I explored the requirements, but when I ran it by Dad, I learned that church members were not allowed to leave the country, even to picket. The pastor said our website created great controversy, and as it was accessible around the world because of the Internet, studying abroad could cause us danger. Freedom of speech wasn't protected outside the United States, and going to a different country was the same as picketing that country, he said. In America, we could say what we wanted. In other places, however, expressing our points of view could get us in serious trouble. The devil somewhere wanted to shut us down, and he put us at risk for being arrested, injured, or killed.

The first week of classes, Jael and I were given the assignment to pick a current event and discuss it in front of our sociology class. We were psyched to go first, which made the other students in the class really angry. They didn't like our views, and they hated that we were showing off. They had nothing to say, and we were so passionate, especially when we had an audience. We knew what we thought, and we were always ready to go first. That was our life: knowing current events, telling people what we thought, and raising issues and concerns. We didn't have to do a lot of research because we knew what was going on already. Some kids went so far as to switch out of our classes, finding us really annoying.

I loved being provocative in class. One assignment from my freshman English professor was to write a position paper on any subject of our choosing. I picked imprecatory prayer, which is prayer for bad things to befall people or a nation. They were pretty intense and seemed to always stir controversy. My paper was well-written. I used passages in the Bible to back up my position. Sure enough, my teacher questioned my paper. "Do you really think this is what that means?" he asked me. First off, I told him the Westboro Baptist Church didn't invent imprecatory prayer. Second, I told him that many things were open for interpretation. I broke the passages down for him, confidently giving him a quick study in the Bible. I quoted from Psalm 109, where some disagreeable things were wished upon a sinner, like that his days be few, his children be fatherless, and his wife be a widow. There were parts of the Bible that were not happy, but I couldn't do anything about that, I told him. Those were the words of God. My professor wasn't convinced and returned my paper with a lot of red marks, pointing out what he thought were erroneous interpretations, but he still gave me an A in the end.

Jael and I were very focused in our worldview. For example, we felt passionately that the war in Iraq was not supposed to happen in the first place. There were inconsistencies with how it started, and they were continuing to pile up. Our country was killing our soldiers. We wanted to raise awareness of the issue that our military men and women were dying in vain, leaving their wives without husbands and children without fathers or mothers. No matter if I held a sign about it or not, people were dying every day. I didn't want to sit at home doing nothing. This was a pressing issue people needed to be concerned about. Not only was I bothered by the deaths, I was concerned about the families who were grieving at home while their loved ones were going straight to hell. The soldiers were dying, dying for a bad cause, and dying defending a nation that enabled sin. I thought by picketing the funerals of dead soldiers I was doing a good service, on my own dime, on my time. I believed I was helping others to see these issues, and maybe even prevent them from fighting for a bad cause.

I thought our nation was going south. I had great knowledge of the world around me, and I took great pride in that. Most people my age didn't know what was going on and didn't care. Even in class, most kids didn't know about current events.

They'd talk about an issue on a superficial level, and that was it. I was getting saturated with news every day. Among the church kids my age, we were in constant competition to know the most about what was going on in the world.

It was too hard to watch the news and not do anything to help. And of course, it was a daily obligation to check the news. For me, it was a big deal. I was obsessed with it. Everyone in the church had to share a strong opinion about it one way or another. We had an arrogance about our viewpoint.

The Phelps kids loved to dominate. They had grown up and watched their parents be a certain way. Their parents had loved the spotlight, and the girls my age wanted to be the center of attention, too. Shirley's kids especially aspired to it. They were very vocal in their classrooms and to their teachers. Most of the time, the other students in the classes would get really annoyed. "There go the Phelpses again, saying stuff," they'd mumble. They hated the church because they knew us only from our protests. They automatically hated our side, and I automatically disagreed with them.

A lot of our professors liked the controversy we brought, though. We had one professor who loved that there were going to be four of us from the church in one class. It was in the humanities department, a social economics class with an emphasis on how humans interacted with one another. He was so eager to have us that he began e-mailing us before the class even started, telling us what an interesting semester it was going to be. There was a hot topic in Topeka politics at the time. An openly gay woman, Tiffany Muller, was running for city council, and her candidacy was going to be debated in the classroom. The professor was actually anxious to disprove our opinion about homosexuality, knowing that we debated on an intellectual level. Each class ended up turning into a theological discussion. If anyone was going to bring up our religion, then we were going to defend it. Sometimes, other professors would get annoyed because we would dominate the discussion. But then another student would mention it, and it would be game on.

If issues involving homosexuality were brought up in class, we were all over it. The topic might be: Should homosexuals be allowed to be teachers, pastors, or priests? Should they be allowed to adopt children? Divorce, remarriage, and abortion issues raised equal wrath.

A number of our professors were under the impression that we were just mouthpieces for the opinions of our parents and the pastor, rather than freethinking, highly intelligent individuals. They thought they were going to challenge us to see if we really knew what we were talking about, versus saying things because we had to. Everybody found out pretty quickly that we were very educated, well-spoken, informed, and committed to our convictions. Of course, we were obligated to stay on top of the news.

In high school, we hadn't had much theological discourse. The curriculum was so tight and structured around state requirements and state testing that there hadn't been much room for social debate. College was different. Professors there had the freedom to raise and debate religious issues, which excited both them and us. We would tell Shirley and everybody else at the church how we had stood up to them. Shirley loved it and gave us tremendous support for it. She liked to hear the details and listened enthusiastically as Megan and Bekah described a debate that we had all participated in. She was impressed by our courage to express our convictions. I loved her approval and felt so proud. I wished I could go home and tell my parents about my day and win the same kind of approval, since in my mind I'd earned it.

But unlike Shirley, my parents made sure not to overload me with compliments. They were more suspicious about anything I did. "Well, you know, you shouldn't really bring up some of those things in class," my father would say, making sure Shirley knew that he was keeping my problem with vanity in check. Only when he got verification that the other girls were bringing up the same kinds of issues in class, that we were doing it together, did he finally concede that he approved. Only as long as it was okay with Shirley, and I wasn't upstaging the Phelps girls, then it was okay with him.

Some people on campus or in our classes would spontaneously counterprotest us and say really mean things to us. Jael, Megan, Bekah, and I were still attractive girls, despite how plain we had to keep our appearances. Guys would tease us to try to get a rise out of us, but it ended up being kind of a flirtatious teasing. Girls would usually just plain hate us. So many people hated us. The homosexual students and their supporters were the most aggressive, often saying really mean things right to our faces. Other communities, such as devout Christians, would say nothing at all or be nice to us. They didn't like us, but being Christians, they weren't outright mean.

Now that I was in college, I was hoping to start regaining my personal freedoms. I was still under twenty-four-hour watch as punishment for my behavior at Brian's house a year earlier. At least I had Jael as my primary guardian, although in no way did she go lightly on me on account of being my best friend. One time before school, I brushed on a tiny bit of mascara that I thought was barely visible, and Jael instructed me to remove it. She wasn't scolding me. In fact, I thought she was even trying to protect me. She could have reported me to an elder, but she never did. I loved Jael like a sister. We were so inseparable neither of us had to speak to know what the other was thinking. We shared feelings with each other with complete trust. I couldn't imagine a day when we wouldn't be friends. She knew all the pressures I was feeling at home, and her empathy and lightheartedness made bad days bearable.

My parents were still all over me. When I was home, I had to explain every move I made, from how long I would be on a jog to what my motive was for wearing certain clothes. I was allowed to jog alone as long as I was willing to answer my mother's cell phone calls every couple of miles along my route. I jogged as often as I could, because it released a lot of my feelings of paranoia and anxiety.

Faith Marie, the newest Drain, eased some of the intense focus on me. My baby sister was born almost three years after Boaz, and she was the cutest baby girl I had ever seen. She looked like a mini-me, with her blonde hair and blue eyes. Boaz adored having a baby sister, and he took enormous pride when I gave him the responsibility of helping me change her diapers or spoon-feed her.

Aside from Mom, I was still Faith and Boaz's main caregiver, despite my parents' reservations about me. I tried to schedule my classes around their needs. I'd come home right after my last class of the day and be on duty, which meant my only downtime was on the drive home. Being in charge of a toddler and a newborn was exhausting, but they were honestly the best part of my day. When Boaz started school, I'd take him there and back every day.

If I had class, Boaz and Faith went to day care. I set my college schedule so I would be done with all my classes by 2 or 3 p.m. I went to campus on Mondays, Wednesdays, and Fridays, so I'd dedicate my Tuesdays and Thursdays to them. Sometimes

I'd get annoyed with my parents, who rarely relieved me when they got home in the evenings and would get upset if I asked for a little time to study. Taylor helped some, but she was in school five days a week, so she could lend a hand only after school and on weekends.

Boaz and Faith made a great team. Once they were a little older, Boaz loved dressing up in superhero outfits and running around in the yard, which would prompt Faith to dress up in one of her princess dresses and chase him down. Faith was really smart. I taught her shapes and colors when she was one. She adored Boaz and wanted to copy him: if he was doing a puzzle, she would pick it up and master it. She loved singing and animated movies, especially *Finding Nemo* and *Shrek*, and I bought the two of them practically every film that Disney made. Boaz loved to read, so Faith begged me to teach her to read, too. She never wanted to be left out.

Boaz and Faith were outdoor kids. We'd go to different parks for walks, and once in a while, we'd stop at the toy store for a treat on the way home. I had pretty horrible eating habits at that time, and I might even take them to a Wendy's to complete the afternoon. It was easier to take them on outings than to stay at home with them. When we were at home, I'd have to play with them or they'd get into mischief. They were all over me. When they got sick, I got sick, but I still had to watch them.

Jael and I both babysat at the church day-care center when we had time, which at least allowed me to make a little money when I took care of Faith and Boaz in that setting. I was expected to pay for my own college tuition, and every little bit of income helped. Thankfully I had earned a partial merit scholarship. Paying for school had nothing to do with my punishment. Fiscal responsibility was very important to the church, which meant it was important to my parents. They had opened a

credit card in my name when I was eighteen, which I was supposed to use frequently to establish credit. To my surprise, the
big items purchased on my credit card were stuff for them. Dad
wanted a new $1,000 refrigerator for the kitchen he had just in-
stalled. He also wanted to replace our old couch in the living
room with a fancy red wraparound one. I paid the $300-a-
month installments on the big-ticket items to improve my own
credit with the bank.

I was supposed to pay my tuition in full at the beginning
of each semester, as well as pay for all of my textbooks. Any
debt for things not "necessary for life," even student loans, was
frivolous and evil. Paying taxes, maintaining good credit, and
spending wisely were three values I learned early. On top of tuition, I had to pay tithe to the church and give money to my
parents for household bills. By the second semester of freshman
year, I had finally earned my nurse's aide certification, so I could
earn substantially more money. Even though I was paying for
my own clothes, my mother expected me to get really inexpensive stuff, so she allowed me to shop only at Payless, Walmart,
and Target.

I was already twenty when I was given permission to go
clothes shopping by myself for the first time. I took Taylor with
me to Forever 21, and I came home with three really great shirts
that had cost me a total of $100—a little more than I usually
spent, but fantastic bargains nonetheless. When I shared my receipts with my mother, she was disgusted with me and didn't
allow me to keep a single one, telling me that I needed to stop
fanning the flames of vanity. That was the last time she allowed
me to shop for clothes without her.

Meanwhile, my parents were still bickering over their own
budget. Unnecessary expenditures of any sort really bothered
Mom. Dad would say he wanted to buy a new, expensive cam-

era, but my mother would tell him they needed to first pay down his student loans, which still amounted to more than $100,000. The church didn't bother him about debt he had acquired in his past, but my mother sure did. Instead of listening to her, though, Dad bought enough equipment to set up a whole new editing suite. He would tell her his purchases were items that served the church, so they were worthwhile, good, and "necessary for life." He would reason that Shirley was going to reimburse him for some of it. I always respected my father's request that disputes in the family stay in the family. I wasn't so sure other families didn't have their own share of secret arguments, either. With so many Phelpses already all over me, I didn't think bringing up those kinds of shortcomings in my family was going to improve my status. They were either going to call me a liar or, even worse, throw us all out. My father had moved us to Kansas to save my soul, and I didn't want him to lose everything he had worked so hard for.

CHAPTER FIFTEEN

But the king covered his face, and the king cried
with a loud voice, O my son Absalom, O Absalom, my son, my son!

—2 Samuel 19:4

Megan's high school graduation received the same picketing treatment that Jael's and mine had received a year earlier— thirty of us outside the Kansas Expocentre ringing cowbells and pumping our FAG CHARGERS signs high in the beautiful May sky. Jael and I were particularly excited, because Megan was going to be joining us at Washburn in the fall. She was going to be in the business program, not in nursing, but at least we'd all be on the same campus. Bekah still had one more year at Topeka West before she would be joining us in the nursing program. For now, following the tradition Jael and I had started, Megan was in her cap and gown proudly declaring to the families of her classmates that they were going to hell for disobeying their Lord. Minutes before the pomp and circumstance processional began, we all went inside to cheer Megan on.

The graduation picnic that took place in Shirley's backyard wasn't as festive as it might have been, but Megan's accomplishment deserved to be celebrated, and Shirley wasn't going to cancel it. Megan's eight younger brothers and sisters were helping their mother with the platefuls of cookies that had been brought for the occasion. Sam, Megan's oldest brother, was there as well—but Josh, the second oldest, was noticeably absent. He had defected in the middle of the night.

When Shirley had gotten up that morning, she had found a letter from Josh, explaining his decision. In it, he ranted against the church, saying it was too judgmental and too harsh, and he didn't want to be there anymore. He had met a girl at his part-time job at Sears, and he didn't want to be attacked for it. He finished the letter by saying he wanted to stay in touch, but he knew that wouldn't happen. Shirley had run downstairs to his room, where she saw that he had packed up and taken all of his belongings. He had used the family truck to move them to a friend's house but had managed to return it before anyone woke up.

Shirley thought Josh's timing was a deliberate attempt to sabotage the graduation celebration. Megan was extremely angry that her brother had stolen her thunder, but she was fairly resigned to his departure, and I wondered if she had even seen it coming. "I always knew he wasn't as into the church as I was," she said.

After the picnic was over, the pain of Josh's departure finally sank in. Shirley had never had a child walk away, and she was a mess. I had never seen her so upset and torn apart. She was completely beyond composure, bawling insanely and blaming herself. "Why me? What have I done? Why did he leave me?" she asked desperately. Looking very weak and drawn, she was inconsolable for at least a week. Nobody was assertive enough to say, *Shirley, stop, this is not how we react*, so we simply coddled her, trying to make her feel better.

The Sunday after Josh's departure, the pastor delivered a whole sermon about how "that grandson" was a lizard and a snake, not referring to Josh by name, but chuckling at each clever insult. He said he was glad to be rid of him. Shirley had to sit there and listen for thirty minutes while her father condemned her son to hell.

Bekah cried, as usual. "That was my *brother*," she lamented, before Megan started mocking her for her emotions. "You are crying because you are weak," Megan replied coldly. In a couple of days, Bekah came around. "I know he was evil," she said without conviction. She said she was angry with herself for being upset when he left.

Everyone in the church was entitled to mock Josh now that he was gone. In fact, you were called into question if you didn't mock the departed and agree that he or she hadn't belonged. Even I had to step it up. We were practically duty-bound to celebrate the loss of an unworthy sinner, especially someone who had thumbed his nose at us.

Much to my shock and embarrassment, my father went to Sears when he knew Josh would be working to beg him to come back. He told Josh he would be an enemy of Christ unless he returned. I thought my father must be trying to impress Shirley and the pastor with his power of persuasion. "I had a good relationship with Josh," he told them. "He'll come back if I let him know he'll be forgiven."

Dad's arrogant belief that he carried that much influence was appalling. Even Brent, Josh's own father, hadn't gone after him, instead saying, "Josh was useless," and leaving it at that. Dad always liked being the best, front and center, on top and in the praise. His arrogance annoyed me, but I was powerless to say anything. Josh had heeded the long-standing advice of the pastor—if you wanted to leave, it was best to sneak out in the middle of the night or you'd hear it from him. My father was conceited and foolish, thinking he could change Josh's mind or God's will, and Josh never did come back. This incident made a few things painfully obvious to me. For one, members spent so much time passing judgment on everyone in the world, whether they were inside the church or out. For another, so many of their judgments were filled with hypocrisy. Members who were not in the Phelps family who wanted to stay in the fellowship were thrown out on their ears, and Phelpses—like Josh, who walked away—were chased down and begged to return. We had rules, which we honored obediently, and we had punishments and humiliations for the times we weren't obedient. Yet the rules and punishments weren't meted out equally—instead, they favored those with status or a Phelps pedigree. It was so arbitrary how atonement would be enough of a consequence for certain people, but not others. There were huge holes in the core of the WBC's righteousness. Sometimes, I would wonder why I was in a church where blatant hypocrisies, two-faced double standards, and selective morality were rampant.

A perfect example was the summer the pastor decided we had too many members who were overweight. A lot of news reporters at the pickets had been insinuating that if homosexuality was a sin, so was gluttony. They were referring to the overweight people in our group, which included Paulette and John, Jael's parents; Teresa Davis, a longtime member in Shirley's generation; and Abigail, Liz, and Margie Phelps. After the pastor's announcement, everybody was supposed to combine diet and exercise, and report to Shirley's basement for a weekly weigh-in. The basement had been outfitted with bathroom scales, and the wall had a poster with everyone's starting and target weights. The weigh-ins went on for several weeks with mixed results. Certain members were not slimming down. Liz Phelps was still extremely heavy, and according to the chart, she had barely lost anything. I babysat for her son on occasion, and had noticed her pantry was full of fatty foods and cookies.

Liz's sisters weren't dropping much weight, either. Abby and Margie had been diagnosed in the past with two different kinds of cancer, so slimming down and living a healthy life-style was the medically prudent course for them. Margie tried to be really healthy by making good food choices, but she was struggling. I couldn't see any noticeable changes in Abby, whose progress chart in Shirley's basement seemed to be lack-ing in data. Jael's mother, Paulette, announced that she was pregnant a couple of weeks into the program, so she was ex-empted from the weigh-ins.

Jael was really excited. She loved my little siblings, and hav-ing only brothers herself, she was hoping to welcome a baby sister into their house. As the months went by, and Paulette's abdomen didn't grow, it became evident she was never going to give birth to a child, and Jael stopped mentioning it. Jael's fa-ther, John, failed to shed any pounds during the summer, either.

In the end, nobody lost much weight. There were never any guidelines about weekly goals or how much leeway was in the target weight, nor was there any accountability. The intrachurch e-mails that were supposed to go to everyone with the results of the weekly weigh-ins never materialized. The only person who faced any consequence was Teresa Davis. She didn't lose the weight, and she was kicked out. Other transgressions of hers were brought up at the disfellowship meeting—not paying her tithe and hoarding idols were both mentioned—but the weight-loss is-sue was the most egregious. Abby wasn't censured or kicked out, nor were Margie, Liz, John, or Paulette. But Teresa was Chris Davis and Kay Hockenbarger's sister, so the Davises were cer-tainly done. There seemed to be one set of standards and rules for the Phelps family, and another for the rest of us.

When I first got to Topeka, church members could still be in communication with family outside of it, if they so desired.

Brent's relatives, the Ropers, would come to visit once in a while. A few of the pastor's nonmember friends would also stop by. But things changed when Fred Jr.'s father-in-law died. Fred Jr. and his wife, Betty, had intended to go to the funeral, but they were told that the pastor forbade it. The pastor didn't want us attending the funeral of anyone we didn't think was godly and had gone to hell, even if he was a relative. We were supposed to be happy when people like that died, so we were not supposed to be in mourning. No members died when I was there, but if someone had, we all would have been happy and hoped that he or she was in heaven. If the person had gone to hell, we would have been happy, too, because that would have been God's will. It was after Betty's father's funeral that the pastor decided we would no longer have any relationships with outside families.

Mom was really upset by the new restriction, even though she pretended it was not a big deal. Up until then, she had been occasionally exchanging letters, e-mails, and holiday cards with our family back in Tampa. They knew we didn't celebrate Christmas, and out of respect for our faith, they didn't send us gifts. After the pastor's announcement, Dad sent a really long letter on Mom's behalf to my grandmother in Tampa, explaining why he thought their family was not good for her. His letter was typed, not handwritten like Mom's always were, so they would know it was coming from him. He cited scripture and told them why they were all evil and going to hell. My mother contributed some lines to the letter, but Dad read it over and edited her parts. Grandma wrote us a couple of more times, but eventually she stopped. As for my mother, she would have put our entire family in jeopardy if she hadn't obeyed the order and could have even been kicked out. I felt so bad for her.

The world was getting smaller and smaller now that we

couldn't even communicate with our extended family. The pastor had already banned bringing new people into the church through marriage, and now we couldn't communicate with our own extended families. I was wondering how I would ever find someone to marry. With Josh's departure, the only viable candidate was Margie's son, Jacob. I still couldn't picture myself with him. I didn't even have the ability to question if I liked him. I heard that he told one of the other Phelps boys that he had started thinking about me, and the boy told him, "Don't think about Lauren. She hasn't graduated yet."

Slowly, they were changing the rules. During a phone call I had with Margie, somehow we got on the subject of marriage. I figured this was the perfect opportunity to clarify the procedure for finding someone. "I don't think there should be marriages anymore," she responded. "I don't think it's appropriate. I'll be God-damned if I ever sit in the pew and watch another person get married."

I was shocked. When I asked her why, she said with the end of the world so imminent it wasn't necessary for us to keep marrying and procreating. We could wait for Judgment Day with the membership we had, with, of course, those children born to members already married. She wanted me to know that it was better to rejoice in the fact we would never get married and have families of our own. After all, it was a privilege and a blessing to be able to focus on being obedient to God.

For whatever reason, I took Margie's declaration personally, especially when she said she had known for a while that I wanted to get married. "It is worldly lust to want to marry," she proclaimed during the phone call. "You are so vain and selfish."

Margie tried to argue that the marriage ceremony was an American tradition, and just as the church no longer honored the Fourth of July or other American holidays, we'd stop celebrating marriage, too. I tried to challenge her on this point. "Where in the Bible does it say there shouldn't be marriages?" I asked sheepishly. When she couldn't find any passages, I began to cite verses that wholeheartedly endorsed my position, going so far as to say, "Marry or burn." Margie was totally offended and told me I was being outrageous. However, she always had a way of spinning her own views to make them sound reasonable and shut down the conversation.

Whatever my thoughts had been up until then, I was really angry at Margie for thinking that she could just invent a new rule on a whim. I wanted to obey the rules and to look for guidance when I wasn't sure. But that marriage was no longer a possibility? That was ridiculous. I started asking the other members what they thought of Margie's new "rule." Some of them clearly hadn't heard it yet, but by the way they reacted, they were beginning to put it together. Most of them took her side immediately and said, "How dare you try to preoccupy yourself with marriage and pregnancy?" I should be picketing instead, they told me.

The only one who gave me any hope was Ben, the pastor's oldest grandchild, who married a few months before we arrived in Topeka. Ben called me on the phone to tell me that Margie didn't get to make the rules, despite her very strong influence over the other members. He said that it wasn't up to Margie to declare a ban on marriage. Ben's opinion was that I could marry anyone I wanted, as long as my choice proved to be a good person and joined the church. If it was God's will, God would bring me somebody, and it would all work out. To me, it seemed so unlikely. But at least I didn't have to resign myself to not marrying at all.

I couldn't help but think that Margie's crusade was motivated by an overwhelming desire to ensure I didn't end up with her son. She had never been married herself, so there was just the two of them. I had never felt that she liked me much, nor did she seem to like anyone in my family. Margie and my dad frequently butted heads. Both of them had type-A personalities, so if my dad was speaking, Margie couldn't be talking, and vice versa. Margie was extremely overbearing and overprotective of Jacob. Nobody was ever going to be good enough for him. Banning marriage was a surefire way to keep him close.

Besides Ben, the rest of the church members still thought I was marriage obsessed, and I couldn't seem to please anybody. Any time I thought I had a grasp on the behaviors that defined a good Christian, the rules changed. If I asked for clarifications, I was attacked for that as well. Our focus in life was supposed to be our pickets and protests. I was told by several of the elders that I didn't need to be married to do that. In fact, if you were married, you were going to have kids, and you couldn't be out protesting with tiny infants. Infants tied you down and took you away from what you were meant to do. Besides, no one was good enough to marry Shirley's or Margie's kids. No one could possibly prove to be as Christian as they were. They had been doing this ministry since they had been born.

Shirley ripped into me for objecting to the marriage ban, which made me think that she didn't want the rest of her kids married, either. "How dare you question God and his plan?" she asked me. "The Lord is returning soon and the world will end. Everyone will be judged. The Lord is going to destroy the world, save the people who are good, and send the rest to hell for all eternity." I had no hidden agenda. I was only twenty-one, and I just couldn't accept the idea that I would never be married.

CHAPTER SIXTEEN

> But sanctify the Lord God in your hearts: and be
> ready always to give an answer to every man that
> asketh you a reason of the hope that is in you
> with meekness and fear.
>
> —1 Peter 3:15

Jael and I finished nursing school and graduated together near the top of our class. In keeping with tradition, we picketed our college graduation, and neither of us went to our pinning ceremony. We accepted full-time jobs in the cardiac wing of St. Francis Hospital, where we had both worked part-time for several years. If I wasn't working, I was focusing on everything the church expected of me, studying the Bible without being contentious or splitting hairs. I was successfully staying away from boys and evil, spreading the Word of God, and contributing financially to the church coffers and to my family.

On top of my usual contributions for room and board, I used my $5,000 signing bonus from St. Francis to cover the down payment for Dad's new Ford F-150 at his request. He said the truck he was driving was too old, and he needed a new one for the church to use. Mom and Dad said my paying for these things was a good idea, because they had taken care of me my whole childhood. I wasn't particularly happy about that, but having feelings was lame, anyway. Shirley liked to let us know that God didn't mention feelings all that often in scripture. "He

didn't mention one word about the feelings of the sixteen billion rebels he sent straight to hell in Noah's flood," she wisely
pointed out.

By the time I finished nursing school, I had already been picketing on behalf of the church for five years and still found it
thrilling. More so than ever, picketing was the favorite tactic of
the church, and the pastor was definitely working hard to give us
a presence at the location of any calamity or sinful behavior in
the nation we could get to. As far as he was concerned, doomsday was undeniably imminent. Although no specific date was on
the calendar, the day was getting closer, and the church started
firing up its rhetoric against Jews. They didn't see the message
as anti-Semitic—the pastor was actually welcoming of any Jew
who might be one of the chosen few. I had never had any Jewish
friends, so I wasn't personally offended. I wasn't the one hating
Jews, God was, and it was all in the Bible. It wasn't meant to be
an ethnic slur. The pastor said it was prophesied in Revelation
that in the end, all nations of the world would march on Israel,
and only 144,000 righteous Jews would survive. He said the rest
of the Jews were false prophets and Jesus killers who mistakenly
considered themselves the chosen ones. He even put out an invitation that if any of the 144,000 Jews eligible for heaven read
his message, which he'd posted on godhatesfags.com, they could
emerge and join our ranks. "Join the Church of the Lord Jesus
Christ! We are your friends and brethren, we are eager to meet
you; to oppose the Wicked with you; and to join Christ in the air
with you, when he comes in power and glory to claim his own
and punish the disobedient!"

Atheists, Catholics, Muslims, Irish, Australians, and Swedes
made the list of the specific kinds of people God hated as well.
Although the ignorant might think some of our targets were
ludicrous, God was guiding us to the locations that piqued his

wrath, usually on the grounds of homosexuality or religious practice. Our godhatestheworld.com website had a map of the world on it, where you could click on any country to find out why God hated that country. All the countries had subcategories: "Filthy Manner of Life," "God's Wrath Revealed," "False Religious Systems," "Government," "Poster Children for Sin," which gave more details about our specific objections. We picketed appliance stores that sold Swedish vacuums, because God hated Swedes for their tolerance of homosexuality. We picketed Coretta Scott King's funeral, because she supported gay rights. The late Princess Diana was referred to as a royal whore. Anyone at all who was prominent in society should use his or her position to take a stand against sin. If he didn't, he was abusing his power, like Caesar. The more powerful and prominent someone was, the more likely he or she was to be the subject of one of our pickets.

Every untimely death, from murders perpetrated by madmen to deaths in storms, floods, or accidents, was really an angry sign from an angry God. The pastor believed that God sent warnings before total destruction. There were the minor destructions, sent to wake up the nation to a grand revival. God hadn't destroyed our entire country during his September 11 wake-up call. Things happened for a reason, and our nation didn't wake up; we were doomed. Sometimes, the punishment of a minor calamity woke you up to your spiritual side.

But a year or so after September 11, nobody was protesting the sins that provoked the attacks. We realized that there was no more hope for this country. We had to pray for God to destroy it, because there was no enlightenment here. The pastor told us that the apple of America had gone rotten, and though we were the elect, there still could be hope of enlightening a few. All the other churches were praying for God to bless this nation. He had blessed it, but no one had been listening. In January 2006, Shirley began signing people up to picket the funerals of twelve West Virginia coal miners who had lost their lives in a mine accident in Sago, West Virginia. "Thank God for this tragedy on America," the pastor said in his flyer. The pickets no longer had to have direct links to homosexuality or the military, because God created havoc wherever there was tolerance of homosexuality, which was in every corner of our depraved nation. We went where the news trucks went, basically. God's anger toward America was obvious to us, even though the mining community and the rest of the world might have thought their miners were innocent victims.

Within twenty-four hours of sending out the protest request to the municipal hall of Buckhannon, West Virginia, the church received its highest-ever number of angry phone calls. "You better not come here, we have guns," some of the messages warned. Shirley decided no one under eighteen could go. She said she was going to replay the messages for the police department to hear, so that they could be prepared to protect us properly. Our picket location had to be relocated after West Virginia Wesleyan College refused to let us stand on campus property, but other than that, nothing extraordinarily violent took place. There was just the usual hurling of insults and vulgar names by the counterprotesters. My father was among those who went on the picket. He, Shirley, and the other in-your-face people always signed up for the pickets that stirred the most controversy and grabbed the most media attention.

Mass shootings were another way God was punishing America. When a milkman shot and killed five Amish schoolgirls in their one-room schoolhouse in Nickel Mines, Pennsylvania, before killing himself, we were planning to picket the funerals. However, Shirley made a deal with Mike Gallagher of the nationally syndicated *Mike Gallagher Show:* In exchange for an hour of airtime on his program, we would forgo our demonstration. On the show, Shirley commented that the girls deserved to die because the Amish created their own form of righteousness.

The pastor also agreed with her that the slayings were justified. They demonstrated God's retaliation for sins committed by the blasphemous governor of Pennsylvania, Ed Rendell. The governor had recently signed legislation that made it a crime to picket within five hundred feet of funerals or memorial services in Pennsylvania, and then slandered the WBC on Fox News. In truth, the logic of God taking the lives of the young Amish schoolgirls made sense to me. If God was mad at America, He was going to hurt its people where it hurt the most—by killing their children.

The contrast between how the Amish community looked at the tragedy and how we viewed it was stunning. Both communities were strict adherents to the Word of God in every aspect of their lives. However, the Amish, through God's grace, forgave the shooter and prayed that God would judge him with mercy. We, on the other hand, just knew everybody was going to hell. If it was God's will that I spread His Word at these kinds of events, then even if I personally found it distasteful and exploitative to picket the funerals of small children, I was in no position to say no.

Dad always wanted to sign up for the high-profile, controversial pickets, like one declaring the Sago miners going to hell, and he was happy to take vacation days to travel to them. He didn't want my mother or me to go to the same ones, however, because he thought we were inferior picketers. At least Shirley had the generosity and genuine pride to share the big ones with her children. She said they could represent our message just as well as she could. My father never made me feel that way. He seemed to prefer pointing out my shortcomings or not trusting me with responsibility at all.

Once, Shirley was away for almost a week and had her phone calls forwarded to our house. She frequently got calls from the press, outraged strangers, or people with a fascination about us. That entire week, Dad didn't allow me to answer the phone, thinking I wouldn't be able to handle myself in the event that a phone call came in from somebody wanting to mix it up. Only he knew how to do that.

I was still permitted to answer some of the e-mails we received from people on the outside. Once in a while, they would even turn into more of a correspondence. Because we were a community determined to be visible and provocative, so many people out there knew exactly who we were. On pickets, we'd identify ourselves by name if anyone asked, and would even encourage people to contact us. People knew about the websites because we advertised them a lot, on the T-shirts we wore at every picket, on our church building. We directed any media person who approached us to our website. We'd get phone calls and e-mails from almost every picket, and every kid had a responsibility to answer certain ones. That was how we kept up with our "fan mail," a couple of e-mails a week for each person. I was in charge of corresponding with about seventy people. One of them was a guy about my age named Scott, who e-mailed the church for the first time in July 2007 and showed a lot of interest in our religion. I was the one assigned to respond to his query.

More than likely, the harmless correspondence between us would have gone unnoticed save for the timing. The summer of 2007 had seen a lot more stressors for the church than usual, which gave rise to a lot of paranoia and exacerbated already strained relationships. A lawsuit against the church was heating up, and a few people really seemed to be cracking under the tension.

The lawsuit was bigger in scope and more far-reaching in consequences than most of the suits filed against us. The pastor, the primary defendant named in the case, was convinced the media was out to get us. He thought hidden in the horde of people always seeking to interview or needle us might be an undercover spy, using a deceitful tactic to gain access to us through an unsuspecting insider who would take him in confidence.

The lawsuit causing all the fear had been filed a year earlier in the U.S. District Court in Maryland. The pastor, Shirley, and Becky, as well as the church itself, were the defendants facing five felony charges, including defamation of character and intentional infliction of emotional distress. It had all come about after the picket of the military funeral of Matthew Snyder, a U.S. marine killed in Iraq in a noncombat accident. The church had the proper permits, stayed the required one thousand feet away from the Catholic church hosting the service, remained behind the police barriers, and carried its standard message by way of our signs, SEMPER FI, SEMPER FAGS and GOD HATES DEAD SOLDIERS, among others. We had already picketed dozens of military funerals by this point, and nobody from our church accused Matthew Snyder of being homosexual, saying only that God punished our nation for its tolerance of homosexuality in the military. The pastor's position was no mystery; he'd say that "military funerals are pagan orgies of idolatrous blasphemy where they pray to the dunghill gods of Sodom and play taps to a fallen fool." The Snyder family wanted financial redress in the millions of dollars from the Phelpses and the church for their personal pain and injury. The case was scheduled to go before the court that October.

The pastor usually took on lawsuits with full confidence and cocky arrogance. Because so many of the Phelpses were lawyers, using them hardly cost the church a thing, and as lawyers, Phelps family members involved in any case before the court were entitled to payment from the state for services provided. We never picketed illegally, so we could not be denied or fined on legal grounds. As to our message, we had systematically won any case against us that had to do with freedom of expression. The rulings allowed us to speak our opinion, no matter how distasteful. We won monetary judgments in those cases, as well, so being sued was kind of a win-win.

If the pastor wasn't the defendant, he was the plaintiff. I had the feeling he loved suing people who came at us, anybody who tried to limit our First Amendment rights. I heard that he once had two hundred cases pending in federal court at one time. The pastor had a reputation for taking grievances to litigation, and they didn't have to be related to free speech and freedom of religion. Years before my family arrived in Topeka, he sued Sears in a class-action suit for $50 million when they couldn't locate a television set he had purchased on their layaway plan. Six years and many court appearances and adjournments later, he settled for a payment of $126. Lots of people who filed complaints against the church might find themselves served with a complaint of their own from Phelps Chartered.

As the lead attorney, Margie was taking on the brunt of the casework for the trial of *Snyder v. Phelps*. The matter was straightforward, but who was going to prevail—the Snyders, seeking tort compensation for the disruption of a private funeral, or the Westboro Baptist Church, exercising its rights so clearly protected under the Constitution—was never guaranteed. We thought what we said could not be considered slander because we were speaking "rhetorical hyperbole," not "verifiable fact." However, in the court of public opinion, we were extremely unpopular. The lawsuit, which had festered for more than a year before the trial date, had Margie and the pastor convinced the media were out to get them. One way or another, the devil was always trying to ruin the church. In truth, we were all scared that we might lose our houses or the church, but no one was more up in arms than the pastor. He was so anxious about the lawsuit, his blood pressure was either way up or way down. He'd have Jael or me check it multiple times a day. He was seeing his doctors constantly for feelings of lightheadedness on his bicycle. He would do repetitive things, and fast on blueberries and lettuce for forty days or ride his bike for hours at a stretch.

We would tell him that he was being crazy, but we couldn't get him to relax. He started badgering Marge and keeping her awake all night, asking her why God was forsaking them. She got so anxious that she left him and went to live with Shirley for a month.

The pastor seemed paranoid about people, too. He stopped doing interviews and became an extreme homebody, rarely leaving the house out of fear somebody was going to assault him. If he wanted a Subway sandwich from the nearby shop, he sent someone else to pick it up. Shirley had to set up a mission whereby every day two people would go into his house to feed him, but then they would leave immediately. He began freaking out that Shirley was trying to seize control of the church. She was just writing e-mails and talking to people about ecclesiastical matters, as she'd always done, but now he took it personally, and wrote up material in response. Flyers appeared on all of our doors claiming that Shirley was undermining his authority, with support from Bible verses. Not only was his attack on Shirley highly unlike him, it was also the only mission that took him outside his house or fenced-in compound the entire summer.

When I listened to someone with as much authority as the pastor, I tried to justify to myself why something made sense, even when it didn't. Hearing his desperation was scary, and I was very scared for him. I thought he had lost the grace of God. If he had, then we all had. God would no longer send us on pickets to spread His Word, because He did not love us. All of us fasted and prayed that something so dire would not happen. We lay on the floor praying for God to grant us forgiveness and direction.

We also held a church meeting with the pastor to discuss his behavior. We followed up with him a couple of times, although nothing helped. He still acted oddly, but he did want to be proactive and keep thinking about the future of the congregation. "I am going to start another church in Texas," he told us. "I am so tired of all this." Then, he would come full circle and threaten to stop preaching altogether. It was such an emotional, traumatic time for me. He was the pastor, and I loved him as our leader, the one who was guiding us and leading us to salvation. Having to question if he was doing the right thing was really difficult for me. However, if we didn't deal with it, we wouldn't be going to heaven, either. I talked about it a lot with Jael, trying to find a positive way to handle it. "What do you think about thanking God that we are being sued?" I suggested.

Right in the middle of this chaos, a British journalist and documentarian by the name of Louis Theroux came to film us for three weeks, and Shirley welcomed him warmly into our midst. He was very funny and charming, with a great British accent. He went by the informal pronunciation of his first name, "Louie." Although we found him really ignorant of the Bible and religion in general, we really liked him, so we didn't mind when he'd ask us loaded questions that he thought would make us slip up. He hoped his documentary, which he had already titled *The Most Hated Family in America*, would reach an international audience.

Although Louis was staying at a hotel in Topeka, he and his crew practically lived with us during waking hours. Louis went to all the pickets and Bible studies and followed us around anywhere we went. He could go to Sunday sermons, interact with us on pickets, eat meals with us, and film anything he wanted. One afternoon, he even went on an outing with us at a local bowling alley. The only thing he couldn't do was shadow the pastor, although on a couple of occasions, he managed to ask him a few questions about scripture. The pastor was dismissive, and referred to Louis's questions as "stupidity in spades."

Shirley and her children loved the whole concept of such grand media exposure, as though Louis's interest in the Phelpses meant that they were precious. Everyone became so caught up in Louis and the cameras that they started competing with one another for the fame the film would generate. It was like a Phelps family reality TV show. Libby was practically obsessed with Louis, and Megan treated him like he was her pet project, inviting him with her everywhere to give him interviews. Shirley and Megan even bought Louis and his crew expensive gifts at the end of their stay. I didn't understand it at all. I liked Louis being there, but my fellow church members' competition for male attention was, for lack of a better word, shocking.

The pastor, on the other hand, was extremely anxious about the whole thing. He did not want to get exposed to the world during his moment of weakness. His behavior appeared to be irrational, and his confidence shaken. He stayed away from Louis as much as he could.

We knew Louis was a journalist and respected that, even though we thought he intended to offer a more objective opinion about us, rather than the gonzo-style comic piece that he ended up creating. But we were fine with the result, in any case. He was going to hell either way, and sadly for him, he was now going to a hotter part. He was not nearly as insidious as the journalist Margie thought was out there in cyberspace. She went so far as to say the spy was from a Boston newspaper, and she fed the pastor's paranoia by telling him that she thought I could possibly be an unsuspecting part of a media trap set up by my new Internet friend Scott. She wanted to see every correspondence between us. Even though she never saw anything that supported her mole theory, she told me I could ruin the church by talking to imposters.

Everything started to spin out of control when Taylor started to notice that I was on my computer a lot. "Are you playing a game?" she'd ask. "Let me see." I'd tell her to go away, but she kept snooping and saw that I was on a chat site she'd never seen before.

"I'm telling Mom and Dad," she threatened.

"What is there to tell?" I replied, convinced that she was just bluffing. Taylor and I were pretty close, so I didn't think she would try to get me in trouble. I had never communicated socially online with anyone I didn't know before, and I thought I was going about it the right way.

Scott, who lived in Connecticut, had seen some of our song parody videos on the websites. Dad had been taking advantage of YouTube's huge following and had started putting some of the shorts on that website, probably hoping his controversial little numbers would go viral. Scott had seen my "Big Fibbin," a parody of Jay-Z's "Big Pimpin'" written by Megan and rapped by five of us: Megan, Libby, Jael, Bekah, and me. Scott had liked it enough to get in touch with us. He said he appreciated our message, and wanted to know more.

At first, we only exchanged e-mails, but eventually we started talking in a chat room. He asked me lots of questions about the church, our religion, and our beliefs. He said he wanted to join the church one day, and asked me if I thought the pastor would let him come visit. These kinds of exchanges went on for several weeks until he started flirting with me, telling me I was beautiful and sexy. I started flirting back. I was lonely, it was fun for me, and I thought it safer to flirt with someone who was fifteen hundred miles away than doing it in person. I never thought I would actually meet Scott, and if I did, it would only be because he had come to Topeka to join the church. I thought the situation was really harmless.

Taylor figured out I was chatting with a guy online using YouTube channels and Yahoo Instant Messenger. I would hide my screen when she came around, and she told Mom and Dad. She had been baptized one year after I had, and she took her commitment to the church very seriously. Dad checked my computer when I wasn't around and found a cache of e-mails. That afternoon when they both came storming into our room, I knew something serious was up. Dad did all the yelling, while Mom stood silently by.

"Listen, Lauren," my father warned me. "You need to stop talking to this guy."

He had found a picture that Scott had e-mailed me, a shot of his face snapped from his cell phone. "You want to *marry* this douche bag? This loser with a *beard?*" he raged. "Let me e-mail him and rip him a new one."

Dad did e-mail him once, and Scott replied with something like "Oh, hi, Mr. Drain. I had written a couple of questions to the church about a video I saw on YouTube, and I didn't get any responses until Lauren e-mailed me, but she told me I needed to have your permission to talk to me."

My father didn't like the response at all. "I don't trust this guy," Dad said after he read it to me. "He reminds me of me when I was a kid. He reminds me of a guy who just wants to get in your pants." He told me Scott was not coming into the church, and said if I ever talked to him again he would be really upset. I had stayed away from every guy I had come across in college to make sure no one could call me a whore. I wanted to do everything the right way, but in all honesty, I did want to meet someone who already knew that I was a member of the WBC and accepted my convictions. When I had been in college, I had other boys ask me out who hated my religion and what it preached. They were interested in me only, not the church. Chatting with Scott online was playful and fun. I didn't have a long-term plan in mind, but I was Internet-flirting with someone I thought could share my beliefs.

All of us flirted because we liked a little positive reinforcement once in a while, despite or maybe because of the fact that we were never going to be with anyone. For whatever reason, I always seemed to be held to a higher standard than the other girls. I was twenty-one years old and had never had a boyfriend, or even kissed a guy except for Brian. I tried to defend myself by explaining to Shirley that I thought corresponding with Scott was safe, because I wasn't the only one doing it. I had found out that Scott was also in contact with Libby. He had seen YouTube messages from Libby and me, and he began talking to both of us privately. I didn't want to tell on Libby, but I had no recourse. After all, Scott was supposedly a danger to our church and a covert media spy.

When I told Shirley about Libby, she didn't believe me. None of the elders did. Libby somehow had more credibility than me, although I didn't know why. She was afforded a lot of independence. She was allowed to go by herself to the University of Kansas's satellite campus in Kansas City, an hour and a half away, for her physical therapy degree, where she'd spend hours hanging out with people who weren't in the church. She joined the volleyball team there, which took her away from pickets. When she finished her degree, she worked at a physical therapy place in Kansas City and went out with people after work. She did lots of things that were questionable, like carry boys' phone numbers in her cell phone. Megan and Jael thought it was pretty risky for her to do those things, but nobody ever called her out. I was infuriated that everyone was coming down on me, but nobody was checking Libby's computer to see if I was telling the truth. Finally, Megan believed me enough to grill her, and Libby admitted that she had been corresponding with Scott, too. Shirley told her to stop, and supposedly she did, although I had my doubts. I promised to stop, too, but Dad wanted to showcase how hard he was willing to be.

One evening, I came home from babysitting at the day-care center when he announced that he, Mom, and I were going over to Shirley's to "talk." I didn't bother to change out of my shorts and T-shirt, assuming the "talk" would be just the four of us. When we arrived, I found about twenty people from the block assembled in Shirley's office, including Shirley's sisters, Margie, Abby, and Becky, and most of her kids. Dad directed me to a chair that had been placed for me in the corner, across from Shirley's desk. No one else had a seat. My parents stood on my left-hand side—my father next to me, and Mom on the other side of him—but it soon became clear they weren't there to defend me.

My father was the one who had called the meeting for the sole purpose of chastising me in front of everyone. "I am losing hope in my daughter," he addressed the group. "I don't want to put up with her anymore."

I was in total shock. At this moment, I realized my father had lost all human emotions for me. He was not talking to me; he was talking about me like I was some type of exhibit on display. "This is the disobedient daughter who never listens. She won't stop talking to boys. I thought I would bring it to everyone's attention," he bellowed.

I had gone through so much with everyone in the church. I had seen how they intimidated people, including my father. When they had chastised him, I had felt so bad for him. When Shirley, Margie, and Sam had told me not to be so close with him, I never could pull myself away. But clearly, he did not hold the same level of allegiance to me. Sitting and listening to him speak about me in the third person made it clear that the church was now more important to him than his own daughter.

My mom didn't say much. I could barely see her, but she would interject a few words here and there. "We have been talking to her about this, but she does not seem to listen," she said in a soft voice. I knew she wouldn't stick up for me. Sometimes I felt sorry for her, but at this moment, I thought she was pathetic. I understood that she wasn't allowed to have independent thoughts. I could sense her struggle with what was happening at the meeting and how my father was attacking me. I also knew that sacrificing me was her way of elevating the family's status, but I still wanted her to say something in my defense.

The meeting lasted almost an hour. One at a time, the other people in the room got to ask me questions and say a few things to me. One person called me a whore. Another said I was always causing problems for the church. "Poor Luci and Steve, they have to put up with a daughter like you," someone yelled out.

When the floor was turned over to Abby Phelps, she held

nothing back. "She is just a stupid bitch," she sniped. "I don't know why we are even talking to her."

"I saw this coming," her sister Margie added. "I have been warning everybody about this."

Bekah didn't say anything. She looked worried and on the verge of tears. Megan wasn't mean, like so many of the others in the room. She asked me, "Is there a chance you will stop?"

I told her I would, but my father cut me off with a dismissive comment. "There is no hope," he told Megan. "I am done with her!"

Shirley was the gentlest of all. I could tell she was upset about the situation. She was almost in tears when it was her turn to ask me questions. "Is there any hope for you?" she wanted to know.

"Yes," I said, holding back my own tears. I was very apologetic in all my answers. I loved Shirley. She was more motherly than my own mom, and she didn't like to lose members, especially those she was close with. She turned the agenda from an attack on me to a plan that would keep Scott from contacting me.

"Can we make sure this guy can never contact her again?" she asked the group.

Dad told Shirley he had changed my e-mail.

"Have you ever talked to him on the cell phone?" she asked me.

I told her that I hadn't.

"Does he have your cell phone number?" she continued.

Again, I told her no.

"Okay, so he should have no way of contacting you, correct?"

"That is correct," I told her honestly. "I have cut off all forms of communication. Dad changed my e-mail, and I told Scott to leave me alone. I don't want to lose my family and my life. A random guy is not worth it."

"If that is the case, very good," Shirley said, giving me confidence. My father was still saying he was done with me, and he let everyone know he didn't think the plan was going to work. He would have been just as happy to cut me loose right then and there, but luckily Shirley believed in me.

Sam brought the meeting to a close. He was usually pretty focused on procedure, so he recapped what had been accomplished and how we would go forward. "What are we going to do after this? Are we going to let her continue to be a member?" he asked. "Was this meeting just a warning?" Nobody really answered. But the consensus was that the meeting was my ultimate warning.

After the meeting, I e-mailed Scott one last time and told him to stay away from me, and that if he didn't stop contacting me, I would face dire consequences. Two weeks went by with no communication with him, and I was feeling really good. I didn't have anyone mad at me, and I wasn't thinking about him anymore.

One afternoon at work, my cell phone rang. All the nurses in our unit carried individual cell phones given to us by the hospital. We were in a forty-bed unit so our patients could call us directly when they needed us right away. I answered my phone, shocked to hear Scott's voice on the other end. "How did you get my number?" I asked him. I had never actually spoken to him on the phone, so this was the first time I was hearing his voice.

"I called the hospital and asked them to transfer me to your line," he told me. "I can't believe you are actually going to stop talking to me. I miss you."

I was really flattered that Scott had gone to all that trouble to track me down. I didn't even know he knew where I worked. The call was awkward, not only because I wasn't allowed to have personal calls on duty, but I was forbidden from talking to him. I looked around to make sure Jael wasn't in the vicinity.

"What's going on?" I said. "I told you I couldn't talk to you anymore."

He said he just wanted to hear my voice, but I hung up when my supervisor rounded the corner. He called me at work a couple of more times later that week, begging me to find a way to stay in touch. It took a week or so, but he finally convinced me to communicate with him again. "We have to be very careful," I warned him. The plan was I would e-mail him only when I knew that nobody would catch me. Soon, he wanted to start chatting again, and I gave in. My dad searched my laptop and found out what I was doing online. He was angry, and told me for the second time to stop communicating with Scott. That was the last I heard from anyone in the church regarding our online exchanges.

In October 2007, a jury hearing *Snyder v. Phelps* at the U.S. District Court in Baltimore ruled against the church. It also awarded more than $10 million to the Snyder family—$2.9 million in compensatory damages, $6 million in punitive damages, and $2 million for emotional distress. Although the ruling was certainly disheartening, Margie said their appeal would be filed immediately. She said it would be based on the judge's fatal error to allow a jury to decide the scope of the First Amendment. Juries were unilaterally instructed to assess fact, not law. The American Civil Liberties Union was squarely behind the church on this one, saying the WBC's protected right to free speech trumped any objectionable message.

Our daily pickets continued in Topeka, with occasional pickets out of town for important events. In early December 2007, the church staged a high-profile picket in Omaha, Nebraska, the location of a mall shooting with many casualties. God's wrath had shown itself in the actions of a lone gunman who methodically shot and killed eight people, critically injured five more, and then killed himself in the upper level of the Von Maur department store at the Westroads Mall, Omaha's most popular shopping center. I did not attend the picket, but the picket pamphlet brought out our standard, highly provocative rhetoric: "Hey, Omaha Ogres! Your Public Crocodile Tears Change Nothing! Like The Rest of Doomed America, Your Highly Honed Public Mourning Does Nothing But Enrage The Lord Your God!"

While the families of the murdered mall victims were mourning their relatives in Omaha, my fate was being determined through intuition and in underground discussions in Topeka that I knew nothing about. The very same group of people who were my friends, my family, my mentors, and my spiritual support were in the process of banishing me. I had been present for many meetings with banishment on the agenda, so I thought I knew the procedure. For every person I had seen get kicked out of the church, every member had to be present, to witness, and to raise his hand if he didn't agree. I still don't know if such a meeting took place to discuss me. All I know is that I wasn't there.

CHAPTER SEVENTEEN

Thy prophets have seen vain and foolish things
for thee: and they have not discovered thine in-
iquity, to turn away thy captivity; but have seen
for thee false burdens and causes of banishment.

—Lamentations 2:14

December 14, 2007, started out no differently from any other
winter Friday in Topeka. I got up before dawn, had a quick
breakfast, and went to work. The hospital was getting quieter as
we got closer to Christmas, since patients and doctors preferred
waiting until January to schedule elective surgeries. Most of the
floor was taken by emergency cases only, and patients in various
stages of recovery.

Jael was working the same twelve-hour shift as me, but she'd
been acting very oddly since the shift had begun. Our coworkers noticed it, too. They knew how inseparable we were
and how we synchronized our schedules so that we could work
together. Being consummate professionals, Jael and I never
brought up our religion at the workplace, so if any of them was
offended by our affiliation with the WBC, nobody said anything
about it to us. They called us the "Phelps girls," even though
they knew I had a different last name.

That morning, Jael was in such a state, I thought that something had happened to one of her patients or that she had been
in a fight with a cousin. It didn't cross my mind that it had to

do with me. Halfway through the day, she dashed off and ran into the nurses' lounge looking visibly upset. A couple of my co-workers suggested that I check on her, so I found her sitting at a table in the lounge. I sat down across from her, but she didn't say anything. When she finally looked up at me, she had tears streaming down her face. She gave me the kind of hurt, distant glare you would give somebody who had broken your heart. But she refused to say a word. I knew it must be a church matter, be-cause we only got emotional when it had to do with the church. Judging from her demeanor, I also knew it had to be big.

When she finally broke her silence, she said, "I'm just so disappointed." She kept crying but wouldn't say anything else. Although I wanted to comfort her, I was also beginning to feel really paranoid that my best friend was bidding me good-bye forever.

She refused to say anything. She just repeated that she was disappointed, while crying into her hands. After about ten min-utes, I left the lounge feeling confused and scared. Instinctively, I picked up my cell phone to call my parents, thinking they might know something about what was going on with Jael, but I noticed first that I had a voice mail from her, which I played on the spot. In the message, her voice was shaking as she said some of the meanest and dirtiest things I could imagine her say-ing about me. I heard my best friend say that I had shamed her and she didn't even know me. She asked me to stay away from her and everyone else in the church, as well. She told me that no one wanted anything to do with me. My blood began to boil and I flushed from head to toe as I listened to her ranting dia-tribe. At one point, the coldness of her tone turned fiery. "You have shit on people and their good names," she railed.

When the message was over, I closed my phone, stunned and devastated. I doubled over in the hospital hallway, unable to move or think. I loved her more than anything. How could she say these things? I had to keep working, though, so I picked myself up and did everything I could to avoid her for the rest of my shift. Our coworkers could see the tension between us and must have noticed we were dodging each other. Because I didn't know what was happening, though, I couldn't enlighten any of them, and Jael certainly wasn't going to, either. The shift was becoming interminable.

Finally, at 7 p.m., it was time for me to head home. I gathered my things and went to the elevators, which, like in most hospitals, were notoriously slow. I was in no mood for a confrontation with anybody, I only wanted to go home and see if I could learn anything there. I pushed the elevator call button, and just as the doors opened, I saw Jael a long way down the hallway making a dash for the same elevator. I got into the car and simultaneously pushed the Ground Floor and Close Doors buttons, making sure she would be left behind. I was damned if I was going to let her have the last word. The terrible things she had said in my voice mail were enough for me.

The fifteen-minute drive home from the hospital was torturous. I didn't know exactly what I had done, or what to expect when I got there. I'd heard all of Jael's nasty comments and seen her angry behavior, so I figured I was in some sort of trouble at home, but I had no idea what I could have done that was so horribly wrong. I inventoried some of my indiscretions from my recent past and came up with one quick swipe of mascara and the three moderately extravagant shirts. It didn't go through my mind that it might be related to Scott. I hadn't told anyone that I had started talking to him on the phone, and that he was even thinking about coming to Kansas to visit us and possibly considering joining. Even then, I didn't think this was a behavior that would warrant anything like a banishment. On my drive home, I decided that if Scott was in fact the issue, I would admit my mistake and apologize. I would tell everybody I was going to work on being a better person. I figured at the very least, I would get a talking-to from my parents, and then I would just have to stay under the radar for a few weeks.

I can still feel the physical sensations of that evening, the chill in the air as I parked my car on the street in front of my house and proceeded to walk quickly up the path to the front door, shivering. I can feel the warmth of the house and the smell of my mother's dinner waiting for me on the stove.

When I pushed open the front door, I could tell something was wrong beyond anything I had imagined. My parents, Taylor, Boaz, and Faith were standing around waiting for me, and I could tell they had been anticipating my arrival for some time. They each said "hello" without any sense of warmth, although I thought my paranoia might have been getting the better of me. I could see a plate of food my mother had left for me at the kitchen table, but I wanted to change and shower first. I kicked off my shoes and headed for my bedroom when Mom told me to sit down and have my dinner now. This didn't seem like a time to argue.

I sat in my usual chair, and Mom pushed the plate with my food toward me. Everybody else had already eaten. Taylor, who characteristically isolated herself in the bedroom in the evenings, hovered around gawking at me as I ate. My mother stayed in the kitchen, too, but she was anxiously pacing around without actually doing anything. My father was coming in and out without talking to any of us. I felt like I was eating my last meal before an execution. The tension was too much for me, so I pushed away the plate and looked up at my family.

My father stepped forward, as if sensing I couldn't take the suspense any longer. He made no introduction, no preamble. In a strong clear voice, filled with the conviction and certainty of his words, he stated, "You have been kicked out of the church." I was shocked and horrified, unable to think of anything that would make his statement untrue. I couldn't figure out how or why it was possible that I'd been banished.

At this very moment, I was being simultaneously disowned by my family forever. That part went without saying. Without the slightest hint of emotion, my father commanded me to pack my things. At exactly 10 p.m. on that cold winter night, he told me that I had to leave, that he'd booked a hotel room for me for two nights in order to give me time to find my own place. I looked at my mother, desperate for her to snap out of it and intervene. She was still pacing back and forth across the kitchen tiles, her eyes welling up with tears, but she didn't say anything and didn't stop my father. All I wanted to do was die, right then and there.

I next looked to Taylor, expecting her to react, to protest, to at least show a little sadness. But all she did was offer to help me pack. In fact, she looked a little gleeful at the idea that she could expedite the packing process and get me out of the house even more quickly, as though I was some anonymous competitor in a race to the death, and I had just fallen off the cliff. Boaz and Faith climbed around in the living room, staying away from the kitchen except to peek in once in a while.

I was completely numb as I packed. Taylor followed me down to my basement bedroom, as my parents had instructed her to do. Dad told me to hurry, as it was getting late, and he wasn't sure how long the hotel's reception desk was manned. Taylor helped me put my things in a suitcase and a couple of smaller bags, deathly quiet the whole time. I was silent, too, not wanting to cry. I thought maybe there was still hope. Maybe if I followed every instruction right now and kept quiet, this would just turn out to be a warning, the church trying to show me what could happen. I thought if I went without fighting, without showing emotion, maybe the bad dream would go away. I didn't want to lose my family.

I didn't know how to begin to pack. I told myself I wasn't going to need to take that much, since I would be back. I'd talk my parents out of it somehow—they'd have to come around. It wasn't as if I had committed a sin like murder or fornication, not even close. Maybe in a week, maybe in a month, they'd allow me back. This couldn't be it forever.

I packed pictures of my family and church members, a few Bibles, picket songbooks, and some clothes. I looked up at the wall to the poster Jael had made me for my birthday a few years before. It was a collage of photos of a bunch of the church members holding white signboards that read WE LOVE YOU and HAPPY BIRTHDAY and had Bible verses. Jael and I had always made each other extra-nice personalized birthday gifts. I took the poster down off the wall and rolled it up. I wanted it with me.

I finished packing everything I thought was important that could fit into my suitcase. And then, it was time to go. I tried to convert my shock and sadness into an emotion that would make me feel stronger. I took a long look at my two precious babies, Boaz Abel, who was now five, and Faith Marie, only three, standing sheepishly in the kitchen. I had helped raise them. I remembered all the afternoons I had spent looking after them, making their snacks, reading to them before putting them down for naps. I wanted to hug them as if it were the last time I would ever see them, even though I didn't believe it would be. However, I had seen what happened when other people were disfellowshipped, and my parents were behaving like this was really the end. In fact, they even refused to let me touch them. At that point, the loss was just too much to bear, and I left the house without a fight.

My mother didn't come outside, so Taylor and my dad helped carry my bags to the car. The fifteen-minute drive to the hotel was surreal. The two of them were chatting away in the front seat about a lot of little things, laughing and carrying on. I was in the backseat, feeling like a criminal in the back of a cop car who was being taken to a remote place and dumped.

When we arrived at the hotel, my father and I went to the reception desk, while Taylor waited in the car. By now, I was feeling disgusted with myself for my transgression, even though I wasn't absolutely certain what it was. My father had not even hinted at a reason. I was just ashamed of whatever could merit this kind of punishment and humiliation. I thought the receptionist must know how vile I was, and that I had been rejected by the people who were supposed to love me the most—my family.

I was surprised when my father made up a story about why I was staying a couple of nights. He told the clerk a long, overly detailed story about how a flood in our basement had damaged my bedroom to the point where it was temporarily uninhabitable. I could not figure out why he went to such trouble to create the story, but maybe it was to show me just how little regard he had left for me, or maybe he didn't want the clerk to disapprove of him for disowning his own child.

Dad, Taylor, and I got my things from the trunk and went up to my room. They dropped what they were carrying on the floor and left without saying anything. That was it. I shut the door after them and sat down on the queen-size bed. Now, I was completely, undeniably alone. The first thing I noticed was how cold I was. I was exhausted from my twelve-hour shift and the traumatic showdown at home, but I still couldn't sleep. I called my mother when I knew Dad and Taylor would be en route.

"I really don't know what to say" was all she had to offer. She told me to stop calling and to pray instead. I was too unnerved to stay in the room, so I walked to a CVS nearby and bought poster boards and markers to make myself a time line of my sins and some charts of "dos and don'ts" going forward. My plan was to hang the posters all over the walls of the hotel room to re-mind myself what my shortcomings were. I created a few before I passed out on the floor with an uncapped red magic marker in my hand.

The next day, I called my father to see if he had had a change of heart. "Is this it, Dad?" I asked. "When can I come home? I am sorry, and I love you." I tried to present him with a few op-tions. "Can't you just ground me?" I asked him. "Can't you just say I can't take care of the kids for a while?"

I wasn't sure why he took my call at all, but maybe he just wanted to be sure I unequivocally understood my fate. He was absolutely ice-cold. "Why are you calling?" he asked me, like I was an annoying telemarketer. "What's the point? I have noth-ing to say to you." He was serious. The church had decided, and there were no options left for me. His tone made me understand for the first time that I was dead to him. It was as if I had never existed.

Over the next two days, I slept a few hours here and there, but for the most part I was on my knees crying or reading the Bi-ble. I had the weekend off, so at least I didn't have to pull myself together to work a long shift. Since I had never been invited to speak before the membership, I went to the library to use a computer and write a four-page letter of apology. I begged for forgiveness for anything I might have done to anyone. I cited stories from the Bible of other people who had done wrong and were ultimately forgiven, and I ended the note with a sincere request to attend church with my family on Sunday. When I e-mailed it to the list, it bounced back as undeliverable—the church had already blocked me. I sent it to my father instead, asking that he share it with them as soon as possible.

I got back to the hotel to find that Dad had dropped off my black Toyota Camry in the parking lot and a note with my car keys at the front desk. His note instructed me not to call them, come over, or see them, even in a life-or-death situation. Later that evening, I got a terse call from him giving me permission to attend Sunday service as long as I went in the door for non-members in the front.

Sunday morning was very cold and icy. I drove to SW 12th Street and waited on the slippery sidewalk outside the gate for at least twenty minutes before Rachel Phelps, the pastor's daughter, finally came and let me in. She asked me if I was okay, but I didn't know what she meant by *okay*. I didn't join my family when I entered the sanctuary, sitting instead in a random chair that had been left for me in the back left-hand corner of the room. I left my jacket on with my hood up, feeling terribly self-conscious and embarrassed when everyone started snickering at me. My family was in the back right pew, where they always sat. Shirley came over to them and hugged each one of them, asking in turn, "Are you okay?" "Are you okay?" But nobody came over to me. I sat through the sermon without really hearing a word. When it was over, only Marge, the pastor's wife, came back to see me. She hugged me and asked me if I would like to talk to Gramps. I was happy, but unsure. "Am I allowed?" I asked. When she gave me permission, I approached him near the pulpit.

"I am so sorry," I said to him.

"Well, Lauren," he replied. "You just have to get right with God." With those ten words, he turned and walked away. No one else talked to me, so I left the same way I had come in.

I tried to put my situation into perspective, but I was overwhelmed when I thought about it. Two months earlier, the pastor had had a judgment against him for a sum of more than $10 million. A week earlier, we were thanking God for nine violent, untimely deaths in a mall in Omaha. Today, I was ripped from God's grace and my family's love because I had talked to a boy. In the grand scale of the universe, I couldn't even fathom that my transgression would be on it.

Later that day, my mother called to tell me I was never to come to the church again. I asked her, "How will I know when I'm right with God if nobody sees me?" She didn't have a direct answer, but she said I could listen to the sermons online if that helped. I couldn't figure it out. I had been so respectful in the church that morning. I hadn't complained or disturbed anyone. All I had done was sit quietly and show my obedience, but I was still denied. The only place left for me was the hot fires of hell.

The more I thought about it, there was no way I would have been kicked out for talking to someone on the Internet. The transgression, the punishment, and the urgency to get rid of me without the usual disfellowship meeting really didn't fit the crime. I was beginning to realize that Margie had made up her spy story to get the pastor on board with banishing me. She likely knew that Scott didn't work for a media outlet, but she made him into a devil who was conspiring to take the church down. Once the pastor bought into it, everybody got behind the decision to kick me out. I had seen the church create other conspiracies to get people kicked out, but this was the craziest of all.

I knew in my heart my banishment was the result of this plot dreamed up by Margie and probably supported by my father. In fact, my father often made a fool of himself tracking down defecting Phelpses, like Josh, begging them to come back. He wasn't chasing *me* down; he was chasing me out. Ultimately, though, the whys of the situation didn't really matter; one day everything was fine, and the next day it wasn't. My parents had disowned me in every way.

CHAPTER EIGHTEEN

When my father and my mother forsake me, then
the Lord will take me up. Teach me thy way, O
Lord, and lead me in a plain path, because of
mine enemies. Deliver me not over unto the will
of mine enemies: for false witnesses are risen up
against me, and such as breathe out cruelty.

—Psalm 27:10–12

My last morning in the hotel, I knew I had to take action because there was nobody coming to my rescue. The night my
father dropped me off, he had given me the number for an
apartment complex where Josh Phelps had stayed when he had
first gotten out. It was on the bad side of town, but when the
manager told me there were furnished units available for $500
a month, payable on a month-to-month basis, I drove straight
there. That Monday, I moved my few suitcases and bags con-
taining everything I owned into my new home in about ten
minutes.

It wasn't much of an apartment, but I needed one with furniture, since I didn't have any and didn't really know how to go
about buying it. The place was like a small motel suite, about
five hundred square feet. There was a half kitchen on one side;
a regular sofa, a chair, and a television in the living room; a
sparsely furnished bedroom; and a small bathroom with a tub. I
bought only a microwave and a few dishes, pots, and linens, not

wanting to accumulate much stuff. Even though I was twenty-one and a legal adult, I had been controlled for so long that I had no idea how to live independently and without support. Something as simple as grocery shopping for myself was overwhelming. After the years I'd been told exactly what items to buy, what route to take to the store, and how long the round-trip journey should take me, I found myself missing the comfort of rigid rules and systems.

One day, my mother called me out of the blue and asked me to come over so she could give me the title to my car and my birth certificate, remove my name from her credit cards and her name from mine, separate our bank accounts, and cut off my cell phone, which was still tied to hers.

When I got to the house my brother ran to me, threw his arms around me, and said, "Sissy, where have you been? I've missed you." My baby sister was already mocking me. "You don't live here anymore," she told me, and turned to my mother. "Isn't that true?" My mother looked at me coldly. "Lauren, don't confuse the children," she said without any emotion at all.

Not long after my banishment, I reached out to Scott, the only person who I knew would still talk to me. A couple of weeks later, he offered to fly to Topeka to give me moral support. It was a surprise, but I was so nervous, alone, and desperate that I welcomed his company. This was going to be the first time I had ever met him in person. I drove to the airport and hid in the crowd by the gate, not wanting him to see me first. I knew what he looked like in his picture, but that didn't mean he didn't look scary or creepy in the flesh. If he looked suspect, I could leave him there, because I didn't want to end up dead. I recognized him right away when he stepped into the arrival area. He was tall and well-built, with blond hair and a beard. He looked pretty harmless, so I approached him to say hi. It felt really awkward. We smiled at each other, but didn't touch. After a bit of small talk about his flight, we sat down to wait for his luggage. I felt really weird driving this guy straight to my house. He wasn't aggressive, and in no time we were comfortable and enjoying each other's company.

Unfortunately, my mother found out about the visit, although I didn't know it. She had checked my bank statement in the process of separating our accounts and saw that I had used my credit card to purchase a round-trip plane ticket from Connecticut to Topeka.

While Scott was here, I got a call from my parents asking me to come pick up my stuff. I was really paranoid about going by myself, not knowing how it was going to go down, so I reluctantly allowed Scott to come with me, but only after he promised to stay in the car. I also chose a time to come when I knew my father would be at work, preferring to do business with my mother.

I thought it was odd that she and Taylor had been dragging everything that they thought was mine onto the driveway, eliminating my need to enter the house. I tried to think they were just being helpful. A dresser, a couple of lamps, two more duffel bags, a plastic wastebasket filled with toiletries—shampoo, brushes and combs, headbands, and other things—a hamper, a little three-shelf bookcase, my bike, and my desk chair sat in about two inches of slush, with more by the front door ready to come outside. Just then, to my horror, my father arrived in his truck, traveling so fast I thought he was going to run over all my things. He slammed the truck to a stop, went into the house, and then came back out foaming in fury.

Immediately, he started calling me every curse word in existence and told me what hell had in store for me. By what he was screaming, I realized my mother must have seen Scott in the car and called my father about it. "I can't believe you'd pick this piece of shit over me," he raged. As his anger escalated and he began hurling my things from the front door to the lawn, Scott rolled down the car window and started cursing at my father and told him not to say such horrible things to me. "She doesn't deserve a dad like you," he said. Unfortunately, his attempt to defend me only escalated the situation, and I was furious that he was getting involved. Dad was screaming, "*You can have her!*" Mom and Taylor were opening and closing the front door as they dumped my stuff outside, and I was yelling at Scott and Dad to shut up, feeling sick to my stomach at the madness. Pretty soon, every Phelps on the block was in their yard or at the road watching, with their arms crossed and their faces sneering at me in disgust. I could see Margie, Becky, Shirley, and a few of her eleven kids, and Tim with some of his nine, although I didn't see Jael or Megan in the assembly. I managed to throw everything into my trunk and backseat and got out of there in about eight minutes flat, numb and exhausted. The only thing I remember about the trip back to the apartment was that Scott drove.

After that horror show, I felt totally exhausted and overwhelmed. I hadn't wanted it to go like that, with my family hating me more than ever. Now that I had all my paperwork, I found the bill with a plane ticket charged on it that my mother had discovered, and I realized she had known that someone from Connecticut was in Kansas before I had arrived at the house.

"It's over," she said when I called her to apologize. "You can never come back. I can see how lost you are. You flew someone out here? I don't love you anymore." I thought God must have been behind her finding the one bill that had something damaging enough to make her stop loving me.

Scott stayed with me in Topeka for two weeks before going back to Connecticut, and then we stayed in touch via Instant Messenger. After he left, I began going through my paperwork, but I had no idea how to handle my personal affairs. I didn't even know what I was supposed to do with my car title, nor had I ever been to the DMV to do anything besides get my State of Kansas driver's license. My mother shut off my cell service before I had a chance to get a new number. A couple of days later, I forgot what day of the week it was, failed to show up at work, and got in huge trouble when no one could contact me to find out what was going on. I knew that if I didn't get my life together, I would end up homeless.

I might have been delusional, but even though the whole church knew I had brought a boy with me to my parents' house, I truly thought my banishment would last for only a month or so. One time, when I had a day off from work, I visited my little brother at his school. I watched him at recess, afraid to approach him, because I thought my parents would press charges if I tried.

I called Mom several times, even though I wasn't supposed to. The conversations were short, and each ended without any hope of forgiveness or reconciliation. In January 2008, she called to let me know that she and my father were claiming me as a dependent on their income taxes, so I had better write that I was a dependent when I filed mine. That was as personal as our communication got. I was still in shock and denial about how my life had changed at the flip of a switch. My new freedom felt nothing like an emancipation: I had lost my identity, my parents, my beloved sister Taylor, my sweet babies Boaz and Faith, my friends, God, and my salvation. Every source of happiness I had had was gone.

For six months, all I did was go to work, go home to my

tiny apartment, eat TV dinners, go to bed, and go to work again. I got a flea-covered cat named Fozzy free of charge from the animal shelter near my apartment, to keep me company. I had numerous panic attacks, thinking I was dying and God was sending me to hell sooner rather than later. One afternoon, I was driving home from the supermarket when I felt such a pain in my chest that I thought God was actually killing me in that moment. Barely able to breathe, I pulled my car over to the shoulder and sat there for the longest time, consumed with panic. My time had come, and God was sending me to hell. I was so terrified, I called my mother from my cell phone, not even worrying that it was against the rules. "Is this an emergency?" she asked me when she picked up, and I started crying. I told her I was possibly in the midst of a heart attack, and she talked me down, suggesting that it might be a panic attack. "Mom, what do I do? What do I do?" I begged her. She replied that when I was settled enough to drive, I should go home and pray.

Every day, I was anxious and exhausted. Sometimes, I'd try to go out with a few of my friends from work, but I couldn't relax and would leave shortly after I got there. I didn't like being lonely, sitting home for months on end eating microwave dinners and feeling depressed. I couldn't even entertain the idea of going to a therapist, despite the suggestion from my sympathetic boss that I was anxious and depressed. I thought therapy was for weaklings, a subhuman and demeaning process for dealing with pain. There was no way a therapist could understand me or my religion. No person who hadn't been a member of the church was capable of empathizing with my profound sense of betrayal. I had spent the past seven years in faithful obedience and had picketed every chance I could, and they had thrown me to the dogs.

I worked twelve hours a day, changing colostomy bags and volunteering for any other tasks that would keep me busy at the hospital. My coworkers knew the basics of what was going on, but I had no one there I used as a confidante. I had no home phone number, but I didn't have anyone calling, either. I hid my depression as best I could by either being home sleeping or working overtime.

I was careful to keep a close watch on my schedule so as to overlap with Jael as little as possible. Jael was dreadful to me. If I ran into her at work, she'd say anything she could to taunt me and make me understand how unwanted I was. She'd make sure to mention some exciting picket the church had been on or reference a lovely encounter with my babies Boaz and Faith. I had been by her side for seven years straight: high school, college, nursing school, church, pickets, and work. Now, she was so arrogant and cruel, I hardly recognized my former best friend. She complained to our manager that I was hard to work with, and she requested that I be transferred to a different floor. Instead, our boss replied, "Jael, if you cannot handle working with Lauren, then you are free to leave or transfer, but she does an excellent job here." After that, we stayed on the same unit.

Once, in the hallway of the hospital, Jael called my parents from her cell phone within earshot of me. "Hi, Luci," I heard her say. "I hope I can come over for dinner and see Faith and Bo soon." I reacted by calling my mother as soon as Jael gave me her "so there" look of satisfaction. I pleaded to come home for one night just for dinner, and Mom said yes. Timing my call to make sure Jael overheard turned out to be a rash mistake. Jael immediately called my father, who called me. "Don't you dare come over here," he warned me. "You are trying to get us in trouble with the church by coming over. How dare you put Jael in this awkward position!"

On top of that, Taylor worked at the Dairy Queen right across the street from my apartment complex. For the first couple of months, I thought about dropping in on her there, but I was too anxious about it to actually do it. After all, she was working, and I might mess up her composure by making her feel awkward and divided. I knew the church rules—by talking to someone evil, you became evil—so I kept her best interests in mind and stayed away. A couple of times, though, I ate at the Dairy Queen when I knew she wouldn't be working. Shirley called me up about that and left a message on my voice mail. "You are not allowed to do Dairy Queen. That's the kids' place of employment—stay away." My self-esteem was so low that I obeyed. I hoped Taylor would visit me one day, but I was too nervous to call her and put her in the middle. We had been so close. Five minutes was all I wanted. But I would have hated myself more than I already did if I got her in trouble.

One time, I saw my father in the St. Francis cafeteria and realized that my mother was in the hospital as a patient. I figured it was probably something related to her recurring back problems. My father would never have come to my workplace unless there was a medical reason. I did a double take when I saw him. He looked me straight in the eye, then turned around and walked away. He wasn't even courteous enough to acknowledge me. I was a nurse, a person, and his daughter. He looked at me with an expression that let me know that I was not even human in his eyes. It was the scariest feeling I ever had. I suddenly thought that I had no importance, that I was nothing but a ghost. I was not a source of comfort to him whatsoever. That I was his daughter and a Christian—none of that mattered.

There was no way I could have gone to see my mother in her hospital room. For one thing, I would be violating HIPAA privacy laws if I did, and I could be disciplined or fired. Unless someone summoned me and called me in, I couldn't make the decision to visit because I was technically not family anymore. Besides that, since I was no longer a member of the WBC, I wasn't allowed to visit one of God's people. To call on one of our own who was laid up in the hospital was an act of charity and godliness, and I no longer had the right to visit my own mother. I wasn't about to do anything that violated the law or the church, so I stayed away.

However upsetting it was, this encounter in the hospital was actually a major breakthrough for me. It made me realize just how cut off I was. Someone in my family could be dead, and I would never know. At that moment, I realized that I had to carry forward with that in mind.

I ran into other people from the congregation as well. Once, I ran into Liz Phelps and her baby in the Walmart closest to the block. She looked at me like I was demonic and passed me without saying a word. I took to shopping at the Walmart in the more dangerous part of town after that to avoid those kinds of encounters. I didn't care if it was risky; I really didn't care if I lived or died. I ran into Abigail Phelps a couple of times at the gym. I didn't even know we both went to the same YMCA until I heard someone laughing and looked up. It was Abigail, laughing disdainfully and pointing at me. "Oh, my God, it's the whore," she said.

Despite these little emotional setbacks, my spirituality was still a huge priority for me. Without the church, the void where my faith had been was almost unbearable. What did I believe? Had I completely lost my intelligence for seven years? I was so scared of having been lied to or perverted or having lost all my knowledge that I had to hold on to the possibility that the church would invite me back. I didn't want to mess too much with what I had been taught. Making interpretations and judgments on my own was overwhelming.

My life was in a downward spiral. I was in total confusion and turmoil, and I had a god who wanted me dead. I sensed that God was lying in wait ready to kill me. The only reason He hadn't yet was that He liked watching my terror. I had always trusted that the people around me loved and cared enough about me to tell me the truth. Their judgments about me had given me my moral direction, and their picketing had structured my life, too. I hadn't rejoiced in being cast out in any way. It had no freedom in it, only terror. Now that my people were gone, I still believed in the same angry God I had described to anyone who had seen me with a sign and shaken a fist at me. But now, those warnings were against myself. "Prepare to Meet thy God" underscored my every move.

It was so scary, but it was real. I had to second-guess every move I made. I'd been telling people for seven years that these horrible things were going to happen to them, and they hadn't believed me. My predicament was that I *did* believe that the pain, death, and eternal, hottest part of hell were indeed my immediate destiny. Now that I wasn't a chosen one, I couldn't really think for a minute I was going anywhere else.

Scott and I continued our relationship. I really liked his support and had fleeting feelings I was falling in love with him. I had no one else to talk to, so I could vent and release with him. He came to Topeka in early spring for another three or four weeks, even deferring a semester in college to stay with me. He said he would move to Kansas if I wanted him to, but I was in no position to be so committed. I was working on navigating the world on my own.

My mother usually didn't take my calls, but I kept trying.

Whenever she did pick up, I'd beg her to give me a time frame for a second chance. Chris Davis had been invited back after a year. "Is it six months? Is it a year?" I pleaded. She told me the pastor wasn't saying anything, and she didn't add any encouragement that things might turn in my favor. Only once did she briefly ask me about my life. "Are you still with that boy?" I said I was. "That's what I thought. I knew you wouldn't stop," she said before hanging up the phone.

On March 14, 2008, I called my father to wish him a happy birthday. He picked up while he was driving and put me on speakerphone. I could hear other people in the car. He was so rude I couldn't even figure out why he'd bothered to answer when he saw my number on his caller ID. I guess he just needed to sink his teeth into me one more time. "I don't know why you're calling me," he said. "I enjoyed my time with you, but we are done now. I don't really know what else we have to say." He was devoid of any emotion. I was crying, and all he said was, "Well, good-bye." I thought God was reminding me just how much I wasn't missed.

Slowly, I began to trust that there were nice people in the world. I had a few coworkers who were really kind to me, and I also met people at my gym who shared my love of outdoor sports. Still, I really struggled with opening up and warming to people, despite the fact that I no longer thought they were all evil, vile, and unworthy. I was not particularly social. For some reason, I held on to the fear that one of these essentially good-hearted strangers was a fraud and a hypocrite who only wanted to take me down. But I tried to stop judging people's motives, and I trusted that I was no better than anybody else. I might have known more Bible verses, but who was I to say that made me better? I was still too scared to look at things from a radically different perspective, though, because I didn't want God hating me for that, too.

I had spent six months on my own in Topeka, almost to the day, when I made the decision to move to Connecticut. There was nothing in Kansas for me anymore, and I was tired of running into places and people that stirred up my pain. On some sidewalk somewhere in Topeka on any given day, there was a row of picketers who said God condemned fags, fag enablers, Jews, priests, mothers who ate their babies, Louis Theroux, Santa Claus, and me. I was finally sick of believing them. I had flown to Hartford to visit Scott, who was now my boyfriend, and while I was there, I interviewed for a cardiac nursing position at a hospital in his area. When I was hired, I packed up my apartment in Topeka, selling a few little things like my microwave. I made the fifteen-hundred-mile, twenty-four-hour drive with Fozzy beside me, stopping for the night at a motel somewhere along I-80 in Ohio. Scott's family had invited us to move in with them in New Britain, which made the move that much easier.

I needed to study the Bible with someone to find other interpretations to the scriptures, and now that I was relocating physically, I was ready to move spiritually. I saw that there were huge holes in what the church had been teaching me. I had believed every angle of the church's standpoint until they had started shutting me down. When I learned there were other interpretations equally valid as theirs based on the very same words, I was terrified that my last seven years had been all a waste, all a scam. I wanted to know there was hope.

There was something about a god who hated almost everybody in the world with a vengeance that made abandoning faith altogether an attractive alternative. Nate Phelps, the pastor's first son to leave, became an outspoken, self-proclaimed atheist. I don't know if it was easy for him to give up his god, but I still believed in God and cherished my spirituality, even though I no longer went to church. I still loved reading the Bible, and I started studying with my boyfriend's mother, a woman extremely well versed in scripture.

Changing my beliefs was not easy and took a long time. It was like asking someone who had a PhD in math to change his position on numbers not divisible by zero. I already had verses and passages from the Bible memorized, so I knew my scripture by heart. My problem was with interpretation, discrepancies, and nuances. My study sessions with my boyfriend's mother were scriptural investigations that went well beyond the rigid dogma of the WBC, and I discovered that the Bible was fluid and alive. She never shut me down or reprimanded me for asking questions.

After about two years with Scott, I made a break from him. It wasn't a great relationship for me, but I was so used to being controlled from my seven years in the church, I wasn't really able to see what was happening between us until I couldn't stand it another day. I had saved enough money to buy a place of my own, a nice condo within an easy commute of my job. I let my ex keep Fozzy, as they had gotten to be quite good friends.

I liked living alone. My supportive friendships were based on trust, not fear. I was getting self-confidence for the first time in my life, which created a new sense of purpose. I kept faith a daily part of my life. I was already at a really high level of Bible study, and I had been looking up challenging words to find their Greek and Hebrew roots. I would look up each word and then look up the Greek and Hebrew translations. I was still pissed at the approach the WBC took to scripture. You don't just read a verse, not in any version, and revise it a million times until you make it mean what you want it to. In the Westboro Baptist

Church, we used the King James Bible, which is a great English translation of the original languages, authorized by King James I in England in 1604. But it was in English; that was it.

I started watching a television pastor out of Arkansas on public programming by the name of Arnold Murray. His lessons were for people who were sort of beginner/intermediate Bible readers. He did detailed studies on particular verses, which I found fascinating. Most of all, I loved his Q & A time slot at the end of each program.

In the church, I had been shut down and made to feel contentious for so long that listening to this guy answer callers' questions with passion and enthusiasm was like a miracle. Reading the Bible *at* someone was not a process in which the recipient learned anything, but it happened every week at the WBC's services. Half the time, the person reading was reciting the same story over and over. There was little input or room for doubt. Arnold Murray accepted in-depth questions as well as more juvenile ones. He wasn't arrogant enough to pretend he had all the answers. Things he didn't know, he'd look up, right then and there. "I am here to instruct and not to judge," he'd say. He admitted he had stances on certain things, but those were his opinions and not necessarily the absolute truth. I wholeheartedly believed him and loved his teaching style. I liked that more than anything.

One day, my aunt Stacy found me on Facebook. After a few online conversations, she gave me her telephone number, and we started to speak on the phone. She told me that my grandmother was very anxious to talk to me and asked me to give her a call. When I reached her, she was happy and upset at the same time. She was always so emotional. She was under the impression that the church held people against their wills, and she thought my mother might be a prisoner. She was not in great health. Her kidneys were failing, and she thought she would have to go to the dialysis center near her home on a regular basis.

She told me she thought my mother had been calling her recently, based on a number of hang-up calls to her house from the Topeka area code. "I hope she's not feeling trapped," she said. I couldn't help but feel a little sad for my mother. My father had severed her relationship with my grandmother by taking her to Kansas to save me, and then threw me out, severing her relationship with me, too.

Sometimes, I agreed with my grandmother that my mother might be struggling and feeling helpless. There was virtually no one for her to turn to. She couldn't go to people inside or outside of the church with complaints or problems, because either way she would be kicked out. When I was still living at home, I'd sometimes heard my parents arguing about church doctrine. My father always told me that he and my mother were "clarifying," which I think he said because he didn't want Shirley to get wind of their disagreements and scrutinize Mom.

After my grandmother told me about the calls, I wanted Mom to know I was there if she needed me. I loved her madly, despite everything we had been through. I didn't have a guy in my life, I had a steady job, and I had my condo with a spare bedroom if she ever needed to come live with me. I decided to reach out to her. I hadn't talked to her in two years, but I wanted to see if there was anything I could read into what she said that would let me know she was okay.

"Lauren, why are you calling me?" were the first words out of her mouth. I immediately felt like I'd made a huge mistake.

"Hi, Mom," I said. "I just wanted to talk to you. I miss you. I love you." She didn't hang up, so I continued. I told her what I was up to and about my job. I shared with her I had a room for her if she was considering leaving.

"I just wanted to find out if you are okay," I said.

"Why do you want to know how I am doing?" she asked. I told her I had just talked to Grandma, who was worried.

"You are lying right now," she said. "You are not supposed to be talking to them." I didn't point out to her the absurdity of the statement. The church no longer had me bound by their rules, although obedience was still second nature to me, and hearing my mother scold me made me feel loved. Plus, part of me still feared going to hell. It was so ingrained in me that either you were part of God's elect people or you were destined for eternal incineration in the lake of fire that sometimes I had fleeting thoughts of trying to get back into the good graces of the church. I didn't want marks against me if I ever changed my mind.

My mother told me there was no reason for me to contact my grandparents or my aunt. They were ungodly and would never be capable of having good advice for me. She went on and on about it for what seemed like several minutes. It was so nice to hear her voice that I didn't pay that much attention to the bombastic statements about whom to avoid. Finally, she let me speak without interruption, and I had the chance to tell her the gist of Grandma's phone call.

"Grandma and Stacy still love you," I told her. "They care about you. They miss you." I told her about my grandmother's concern and the hang-ups from the Topeka area code. I asked her if it had been her calling.

She was totally offended. "Do you think I want to break up with your father?" she asked indignantly. "I don't understand the purpose of this phone call." We concluded with a hasty good-bye.

We haven't spoken since.

Unfortunately, we hung up before I had a chance to tell her about my life. I would have liked her to know that I am happy, that not every day is perfect, but sinners are not at every turn begging me toward evil, and God's blessings are widely available. I meet all kinds of people and have friends of every persuasion, all really good people, very worthy, and very kind. I make a decent, honest living doing work I really love. I have time and opportunity for travel and adventures all over our great country. Most of all, I would have liked to tell my mother how grateful I am to have been part of the Drain family, and I love them all. If it is God's will, we will see each other again someday. I hope it happens. Sadly, they have made the decision for me to not be part of their lives. But my well-being is not dependent on their approval. Banished I was, but happy I'll be, because I have it right with God.

EPILOGUE

Any system of faith requires making various judgments and holding sometimes unpopular beliefs. I have no problem with minority religions; it's only when taken to the extreme that they become dangerous. When I was in the WBC, I was often driven by misguided self-righteousness, and I spent a lot of time moralizing and censuring other people. I am still very spiritual, and I have strong beliefs and convictions, too, but I like to think I am now approachable, reasonable, and fair. So many members of the Westboro Baptist Church think they *are* God or his only prophets. They feel their judgment is God's judgment. They use scripture by heart, and they use it so well, they find passages to justify their right to judge so righteously. They think God's glorious kingdom is a place to continue judging, mocking, and condemning others. . . . I'll let God be the judge of me and them. The God I love and know wants people to have perfect love that casts out fear and judgment.

The trouble is, the church has a tendency to switch things around and view them backward. They tell others to thank God for everything, including calamities, but when bad things happen to them, they can't handle it. Their fervor and their zeal can be attractive, until you change your perspective and realize it is all about control.

The church thinks the Bible is talking to them and about them exclusively, and they assign prophetic meaning to current events. I believe in the Bible, too, but everything has a context, and the Bible is a historical document. Not every prophecy has the same meaning in every age. In reading something, I have to ask: Is it applicable now, or was it only applicable then? When passages are taken out of context and twisted, the result is a powerful, manipulative, and dangerous weapon indeed.

When I look now at church members on the picket line, I still see the qualities that attracted me in the first place— passion, bravery, a high value placed on knowledge, dedication, and hard work. But my misgivings are stronger. I think they are too judgmental and sanctimonious. I don't think anyone should display such arrogance and righteousness, as they do. They have human errors and human faults like the rest of us. They have crazy hierarchies and paranoid conspiracy theories in their church, too. The extreme taunting, teasing, laughing—it seems crazy, fiendish, and extreme. I don't like that the church thinks it is above everything and everybody else. I also don't see the need to vilify people who have legitimate theological questions.

When I look at videos of myself as a church member, I seem mean. I think I might have been taking out my own inner unhappiness on others, projecting all this bottled-up emotion onto the subjects of our pickets. In saying this, I am not trying to avoid taking full responsibility for my actions. What I've done still disturbs me and makes me feel sad and embarrassed. That pathetic, helpless person is not who I am now. When I happen to see footage of my former family and friends now, they look like little drones with dead eyes. The situation they are in, where there is no room to question things, is extreme and cruel.

I was inundated day in and day out with what the church was thinking. I didn't ask myself if I was doing the right thing. I wanted to get to heaven, and picketing was validating me. I went to thousands of pickets. To me, this was proving I was a Christian, a prophetess. I wasn't thinking about anyone else or what kind of impact I might have on someone. I was too busy thinking about what I was doing spiritually and how I was helping someone. I really thought everyone just misunderstood us.

I did have human emotion. If someone came up to talk to me, I would talk to him. I would read about horrible events in the news, very upsetting things like the rape of a child. I thought protesting was a way to bring people's attention to God's wrath. I never thought I had lost compassion for humanity—just the opposite.

I used to fear going to hell every single day, and that my family could fall apart. The Lord could come tomorrow, and if I was not showing my faith strongly enough, I would be doomed. Everybody's story would be told in heaven. It was a very motivating, powerful drive to do and say the things I did. I never had a cruel intention. I never had space to think about people's concerns with how I was judging things and the negative impact of my protesting. At military funerals, I wasn't thinking of who I might be harming and how I might be dishonoring them in their time of grieving. I thought I was just enlightening them that serving in the U.S. military inevitably ended in this kind of punishment. Now I realize how much I was disrespecting each fallen soldier and his or her family and friends, and I apologize deeply for this. I no longer feel this way. I value the military and the selfless service of all of our soldiers.

I apologize equally to the families of AIDS victims and homosexuals whom I disrespected. I will never be a political activist for gay rights, but I like gay people and have lots of gay friends, too. I don't judge them, and I don't believe anyone else has the right to judge them, either. I also won't be a political activist for abortion, but I am perfectly okay with everyone living his or her own life and making his or her own choices.

Without question, the WBC's rhetoric is vitriolic, provocative, and shamefully insensitive. However, I always bear in mind that their right to free speech infinitely trumps their message. Shutting down their rights would be a blow to the constitutional rights of every single American. The *Snyder v. Phelps* lawsuit, in which the dead soldier's family had initially won a judgment of $10 million in U.S. District Court, went all the way to the Supreme Court. On October 13, 2010, Margie herself presented the oral argument for the defense in front of the nine justices, while many Phelps family members picketed outside. The court justices sided with Margie in a historic 8–1 ruling, affirming her position that a law-abiding picket in a public place, even if tasteless and insensitive, was a protected freedom. That was not only a monumental victory for the church, but for all of us who like saying what we think without fear of being sued for it.

I am so glad I am not filled with bitterness and resentment right now. I could have made really dumb choices, first out of anger, then out of shame. When my parents put me out without any regret, I felt so angry and hurt that I could easily have tried to hurt them back. After I had time to reflect on my sanctimonious righteousness, my shame could have gotten the best of me. Instead, I chose to hang on to gratitude. I am happy I chose nursing so young. It's a great, productive field. Even when I look back and see that I was kind of fast-tracked and forced into the profession by my parents, I am still grateful to be in a career that really helps other people.

I no longer believe that I am going to hell. I have a newfound appreciation for God and my right to believe in Him. Not long after completing this book, I traveled to Europe and Turkey on a two-week vacation with my boyfriend, David. The trip was especially rewarding, because when I was younger, I had never thought that I would set foot outside of the United States. The WBC warned us that we would be arrested in foreign countries, where our Constitution had no value. I know I am a work in progress, and even though I am growing more accepting of other cultures, every once in a while, I still get extremely overwhelmed with feelings of shame or fear, remembering how I used to condemn all other religions and ethnic traditions when I was part of the WBC. I had these feelings in the Vatican, and I had them again while visiting the Blue Mosque in Istanbul, Turkey. In both places, I became so upset I started crying. Trying to console me, David asked me what was wrong, but for some reason I couldn't articulate it. It only hit me later that the WBC had instilled so much hate, judgment, and fear in me that I was having a flashback to those feelings.

Thank God, I was able to transcend my emotions and respectfully appreciate those other religions and cultures for what they are, and realize that their existence doesn't threaten my own Christian beliefs. I am grateful to be able to overcome things, even if it's a small step at a time. I really enjoyed traveling, visiting new countries, trying local food, and spending time with great friends. It was an amazing trip, and I'm looking forward to taking many more with David, my best friend and now fiancé.

The church's message that God hates everyone no longer rings true. To me, that is a narcissistic distortion of the highest order. But I do hold out hope for the WBC, as well. God will make His decision about each of them when their time to meet Him comes. Who am I to think that I have the power to say there is no hope for them? I only know that God is not the angry God of their fears. I believe He wants people to love Him out of their own hearts.

I miss my family with all my heart. I miss Taylor, and I wish she knew how strong my sisterly bond with her still is. I feel enormous sadness when I think there will come a time when Faith doesn't know who I am, or Boaz condemns me as if he were a little clone of my father, but there is nothing I can do about that. I love the God I now have. My relationship with Him is not based on fear. It is similar to a human relationship, described so well in Song of Solomon 8:6: "Set me as a seal upon thine heart, as a seal upon thine arm: for love is strong as death."

God will answer you in the end. You don't have to live on the block in Topeka, Kansas, or be a member of the Westboro Baptist Church. I will never go back. I have no desire to be treated like a wicked sinner and endure their hatred. It isn't worth it, and I don't believe I am evil. I don't believe that God rejoices in tragedies, calamities, disease, pain, and grief. In my faith, He has better things to do.

ACKNOWLEDGMENTS

I would like to acknowledge just some of the people who encouraged me, worked with me, or inspired me to tell my story. This has been a whirlwind of a journey for me, from my first days on my own, devastated by the loss of my family and suffering a broken heart, to building up my self-confidence and happiness through my newfound friends and family. These acknowledgments are not in order of importance, but rather chronological.

In May 2010, when I was first approached by Kelsey Myers, editorial producer of ABC News 20/20, to appear on a special, "Raised to Hate," I was not so sure I was ready to publicly expose my time in the church. I would like to thank Kelsey for being so supportive and believing that my story was important. He had the foresight to see that sharing my experiences could be an extremely therapeutic and empowering process for me. Thanks to all the people at ABC News who made this possible, including Chris Cuomo, for his sincerity and genuineness in interviewing me, and for exposing the dangers of raising your kids to hate.

Kelsey Myers also put me in touch with Elisabeth Dyssegaard, editor-in-chief of Hyperion, who introduced me to the amazing Lisa Grubka, my literary agent. Lisa understood that writing my story would not be easy for me, and she did an incredible job of bringing me out of my shell and connecting me with people I could work well with, including Jen Schulkind, who helped me with the proposal. Lisa guided me, explained what was coming next, and provided continual emotional support at every step of the crazy publishing process. I would also like to thank everyone at Foundry Literary and Media who supported the book.

Despite my instant confidence in Lisa Grubka, she continued to surprise me and impress me with her belief in my story. She sold my proposal to Emily Griffin at Grand Central Publishing, who was instantly just as enthusiastic. Emily was extremely professional and had an incredibly sweet nature, which made this process all the more comforting. I would also like to thank Amanda Englander, Liz Connor, Sonya Cheuse, Carolyn Kurek, and everyone else at Grand Central who made the book possible.

As part of her continuous support, Lisa G. found me my coauthor Lisa Pulitzer, to whom I am forever grateful. Lisa P. knew that telling my story was going to be incredibly emotional and at times confusing for me. She did an amazing job of drawing out my experiences and feelings and putting them to paper so eloquently. Working with her didn't feel like work at all, as she has become a trusted friend and like a family member. I would also like to thank Lisa P.'s quirky, fun-loving writing associate, Martha Smith. The two of them, with their Lucy and Ethel–like dynamic, made our work fly by, and turned any sadness I had into happiness. These two made every step of the way enjoyable, as they helped me realize I wasn't an outcast anymore.

ACKNOWLEDGMENTS

All along this incredible journey, I had the love and support of my now-fiancé, David Kagan. From our third date, where I had asked him half-jokingly if he had Googled me yet, until two years later when we became engaged, he has loved me for who I am, never judging me for who I used to be. When he first heard the idea of me writing a book about my past, he said, "Let's go to New York," without caring that one day people would know everything about the girl he was dating. He encouraged me to open up, despite my hesitation and fear of being judged. He has guided me through moments of shame, fear, and sadness and helped me develop ways to cope, see things differently, and make new friends, all of which have led me to my newfound happiness.

I am ever-grateful to the extended family members who reached out to me during my time of weakness, including my dear aunt Stacy, my trusted childhood cousin Amber Parker, and my sweet Grandma Stout. Although I had lost touch with them for almost eight years, I had been close to them in my formative years, and their love and support has rekindled my sense of family and hope. I carried around a lot of pain and guilt until they reached out and filled that void with love, forgiveness, and understanding.

I would also like to thank all the friends who have supported and continue to support me sincerely. There are times I needed somewhere to live, a shoulder to cry on, protection from those who would harm me, motherly advice, or just a good time. To my friends—you know who you are, and you are fantastic! Just to name a few: Angela H., John and Mel C., Dima and Jen B., and Maria K.

I have dedicated this book to my siblings, whom I still hold incredibly dear to my heart and who were my inspiration for writing this book. Although I will never again hold

291

up a sign judging another person, I want you each to know that I have not lost faith in God. I believe love of family is one of the most incredible and precious things in life and a gift from God.

I will forever miss and love you, my sweet Faithy Marie, who I know I will never get to know as I deserve to, being your eldest sister. To this day, I can hear your cute little voice in my head saying "I love you, Sissy," as you hugged and kissed me before bed each night, as if it were yesterday. I wish I hadn't missed a single day of you growing up, as it was such a pleasure to watch.

Boaz Abel, you are my only brother and have the sweetest little personality, always wanting to take care of young Faithy and protect her, even when you were as young as a toddler. I remember you always running around the house, dressing up in costumes, begging me to take you to fun places, and sneaking down into my room when I was studying. I will never forget the look on your face when I came back to the house after being kicked out, or that you grabbed me tightly when we both knew we wouldn't see each other again. You are such a sweet boy with tremendous potential, and I hope one day you will see that God's love is not celebrated through hate.

Taylor, you are a grown woman now, but I can honestly say I will always see you as my little sister and closest friend for sixteen years of my life. The sadness I have over our separation is beyond what words can express. The things we have been through together honestly surpass any bond I have achieved thus far in my life. I remember you sitting every day in your cute little crib always smiling at me when Mom and I came to visit you at the hospital. You have always been incredibly smart, and I remember studying in high school and college and realizing your potential was beyond mine. I wish I could have been there for you on every special occasion, birthday, and graduation to show you how proud of you I am.

I hope you do not hold regrets against me and know I will always be here if and when you are ready to pursue the real love of God and discover the love of family. I love and miss each of you.

ABOUT THE AUTHORS

LAUREN DRAIN works as a registered nurse. She lives with her fiancé in Connecticut, where she enjoys outdoor activities including endurance races, hiking, dirt biking, and camping. This is her first book.

LISA PULITZER is a former correspondent for the *New York Times*. She is the author and coauthor of more than a dozen nonfiction books, including the bestselling *Stolen Innocence*.